# Giorgio Agamben's
# *Homo Sacer* Series

# Giorgio Agamben's *Homo Sacer* Series

## A Critical Introduction and Guide

Colby Dickinson

EDINBURGH
University Press

Edinburgh University Press is one of the leading university presses in the UK. We publish academic books and journals in our selected subject areas across the humanities and social sciences, combining cutting-edge scholarship with high editorial and production values to produce academic works of lasting importance. For more information visit our website: edinburghuniversitypress.com

© Colby Dickinson, 2022

Edinburgh University Press Ltd
The Tun – Holyrood Road
12(2f) Jackson's Entry
Edinburgh EH8 8PJ

Typeset in 11.5/15 Adobe Sabon by
IDSUK (DataConnection) Ltd

A CIP record for this book is available from the British Library

ISBN 978 1 4744 8669 9 (hardback)
ISBN 978 1 4744 8672 9 (webready PDF)
ISBN 978 1 4744 8670 5 (paperback)
ISBN 978 1 4744 8671 2 (epub)

The right of Colby Dickinson to be identified as the author of this work has been asserted in accordance with the Copyright, Designs and Patents Act 1988, and the Copyright and Related Rights Regulations 2003 (SI No. 2498).

# Contents

| | |
|---|---|
| Acknowledgements | vii |
| Abbreviations | x |
| | |
| Introduction | 1 |
|    Overview of the Present Study | 5 |
|    Charting a Course for Reading | 12 |
|    A Brief Outline of the *Homo Sacer* Series | 13 |
|    Framing the *Homo Sacer* Series | 14 |
| | |
| 1. Religious and Political Implications of the *Homo Sacer* Project | 35 |
|    The Fiction of Sovereignty | 35 |
|    Oaths, Language and the Divine Name | 42 |
|    On God and Gods from the Point of View of a Modal Ontology | 52 |
|    An Ontology of Demand | 61 |
| | |
| 2. On Aristotle, Actuality and Potentiality | 66 |
|    Aristotle and the Problem of 'Potency' | 66 |
|    Potentiality as a Form of Resistance | 76 |
|    Contemplation of the Inappropriable | 85 |
|    Demand, Memory and the Place of Thought | 90 |

3. Glory and the Significance of Political Theology  95
   Kingdom, Government and Sovereignty  95
   The Desire for Order  101
   Sovereign Glory  105

4. Economy and its Inoperativity  114
   The Bipolar Sovereignty of Identity  114
   Subjects and the Suspension of Identity  117
   New Uses of the Body  122
   Messianic *or* Hypernomian  126

5. The Border between the Human and the Animal  132
   The Fiction of the Human Being  132
   The Problem of Anthropogenesis  140
   Anthropogenesis and Metaphysics  145

6. Paul and the Messianic Division of Division  157
   A Possible Hermeneutic  157
   The Gesture of Pope Benedict XVI  161
   Towards a Negative Dialectic  168
   Dialectics at a Standstill  173
   The Messianic and the Future of Dialectics  176

7. Form-of-Life beyond the Law  180
   The Temporality of Fashion and Art  180
   What is Form-of-Life?  185
   Form-of-Life as End Goal  196
   Mystery and Desire  199

Conclusions  206

Notes  212
Bibliography  227
Index  232

# *Acknowledgements*

The following book began as a series of invited lectures that were delivered on a number of occasions on two continents. The first among these were two keynote lectures presented at a colloquium titled 'Politics, Economics, Theology: The Contributions of Giorgio Agamben's Work' at Universidade do Vale dos Sinos (UNISINOS) in São Leopoldo, Brazil in May of 2017. The gracious invitation extended by the Instituto Humanitas Unisinos (IHU) at UNISINOS was instrumental in making these talks happen, and their hospitality while I was among them was second to none. My thanks are extended to everyone there, and especially to Susana Maria Rocca, Cleusa Maria Andreatta, Marcia Rosane Junges, Rejane Machado da Silva de Bastos, Rodrigo Karmy and Alain Gignac, among others, for the wonderful and fruitful conversations that took place there.

During this same visit to São Leopoldo, I was fortunate enough to make the acquaintance of another Brazilian scholar working on Agamben's thought, Glauco Barsalini, who invited me to speak at his university the following year. I gladly accepted and was again privileged to deliver a larger series of lectures over the course of a week in May of 2018 along with the members of the PPGCR Research Group at PUC-Campinas in Brazil. My time there was an opportunity to further develop my intuitions regarding Agamben's *Homo*

## Acknowledgements

*Sacer* series, and I am very grateful to many individuals at PUC for the invitation to speak with them. My thanks are accordingly, and happily, due to Glauco Barsalini, Douglas Barros, Renato Kirchner, Ana Rosa Cloclet da Silva, Ricardo Evandro Martins, Hélerson da Silva, Breno Martins, Cristina Micaroni Hilkner, Cláudio de Oliveira Ribeiro, Aretha Beatriz Brito da Rocha, Mariana Pfister, Jefferson Zeferino, Marcelo Saraiva and the many other professors, students and various participants of the lecture series. Having since welcomed both Mariana and Glauco to Chicago for research stays, I am overjoyed at the wealth of intellectual contact being developed between our research universities and am hopeful for many future conversations shared together.

During this last trip to Brazil, I also had the honour of being accompanied by two doctoral students from Loyola University Chicago, Marcos Norris and Kim Berkey, both of whom continue to inspire my work in a number of ways. I was very glad for their company, conversation and the outstanding research they presented, not to mention their athletic prowess at various team sports, during our trip together.

After the bulk of this material had been formulated and presented, I was subsequently able to expand a couple of these lectures for another pair of talks given in March of 2019 at both the Centre of Theology, Philosophy and Media Theory at Charles University in Prague, Czech Republic, and at the University of Vienna, Austria. I was immensely grateful for the opportunity to elaborate on some of these themes and am very thankful to Martin Kočí, Katerina Kočí, František Štech, Tim Noble, Virgil Brower, Gábor Ambrus, Adam Kotsko, Marlene Deibl, Bogdana Koljevic Griffith, Natalie Eder, Jason Alvis and Kim Berkey for their roles in making these talks happen and the wonderful dialogues that constituted our time together.

I owe a great deal of added clarity and insight to the book to the constructive critiques of Adam Kotsko, who was so gracious as to provide detailed feedback on the manuscript, and

*Acknowledgements*

Arthur Willemse, who was a most generous reader toward the end of the publication process.

Lastly, I owe a debt of gratitude to my research assistant, Evan Marsolek, for all of his work on the text, including the formatting, editing and referencing of the entire manuscript.

# *Abbreviations*

CC   Agamben, Giorgio, *The Coming Community*, trans. Michael Hardt, Minneapolis: University of Minnesota Press, 1993.

CK   Agamben, Giorgio, *The Church and the Kingdom*, trans. Leland de la Durantaye, Calcutta, India: Seagull Books, 2012.

FT   Agamben, Giorgio, *The Fire and the Tale*, trans. Lorenzo Chiesa, Stanford: Stanford University Press, 2017.

HP   Agamben, Giorgio, *The Highest Poverty: Monastic Rules and Form-of-Life*, trans. Adam Kotsko, Stanford: Stanford University Press, 2013.

HS   Agamben, Giorgio, *Homo Sacer: Sovereign Power and Bare Life*, trans. Daniel Heller-Roazen, Stanford: Stanford University Press, 1998.

IP   Agamben, Giorgio, *The Idea of Prose*, trans. Michael Sullivan and Sam Whitsitt, Albany: State University of New York Press, 1995.

K    Agamben, Giorgio, *Karman: A Brief Treatise on Action, Guilt, and Gesture*, trans. Adam Kotsko, Stanford: Stanford University Press, 2018.

KG   Agamben, Giorgio, *The Kingdom and the Glory: For a Theological Genealogy of Economy and Government (Homo Sacer II, 2)*, trans. Lorenzo Chiesa with Matteo Mandarini, Stanford: Stanford University Press, 2011.

## Abbreviations

LD     Agamben, Giorgio, *Language and Death: The Place of Negativity*, trans. Karen E. Pinkus and Michael Hardt, Minneapolis: University of Minnesota Press, 1991.

MW     Agamben, Giorgio, *Means Without Ends: Notes on Politics*, trans. Vincenzo Binetti and Cesare Casarino, Minneapolis: University of Minnesota Press, 2000.

ME     Agamben, Giorgio, *The Mystery of Evil: Benedict XVI and the End of Days*, trans. Adam Kotsko, Stanford: Stanford University Press, 2017.

N     Agamben, Giorgio, *Nudities*, trans. David Kishik and Stefan Pedatella, Stanford: Stanford University Press, 2011.

NY     Agamben, Giorgio, *Nymphs*, trans. Amanda Minervini, Calcutta, India: Seagull Books, 2013.

OHS     Agamben, Giorgio, *The Omnibus Homo Sacer*, Stanford: Stanford University Press, 2017.

O     Agamben, Giorgio, *The Open: Man and Animal*, trans. Kevin Attell, Stanford: Stanford University Press, 2004.

OD     Agamben, Giorgio, *Opus Dei: An Archaeology of Duty*, trans. Adam Kotsko, Stanford: Stanford University Press, 2013.

PJ     Agamben, Giorgio, *Pilate and Jesus*, trans. Adam Kotsko, Stanford: Stanford University Press, 2015.

P     Agamben, Giorgio, *Potentialities: Collect Essays in Philosophy*, trans. Daniel Heller-Roazen, Stanford: Stanford University Press, 1999.

PR     Agamben, Giorgio, *Profanations*, trans. Jeff Fort, New York: Zone Books, 2007.

RA     Agamben, Giorgio, *Remnants of Auschwitz: The Witness and the Archive*, trans. Daniel Heller-Roazen, New York: Zone Books, 2002.

SL     Agamben, Giorgio, *The Sacrament of Language: An Archaeology of the Oath (Homo Sacer II, 3)*, trans. Adam Kotsko, Stanford: Stanford University Press, 2010.

ST     Agamben, Giorgio, *The Signature of All Things: On Method*, trans. Luca D'Isanto and Kevin Attell, New York: Zone Books, 2009.

*Abbreviations*

S      Agamben, Giorgio, *Stasis: Civil War as a Political Paradigm*, Homo Sacer, II, 2, trans. Nicholas Heron, Edinburgh: Edinburgh University Press, 2015.

SE      Agamben, Giorgio, *State of Exception*, trans. Kevin Attell, Chicago: The University of Chicago Press, 2005.

T      Agamben, Giorgio, *Taste*, trans. Cooper Francis, York, PA: Seagull Books, 2017.

TR      Agamben, Giorgio, *The Time that Remains: A Commentary on the Letter to the Romans*, trans. Patricia Dailey, Stanford: Stanford University Press, 2005.

UG      Agamben, Giorgio and Monica Ferrando, *The Unspeakable Girl: The Myth and Mystery of Kore*, trans. Leland de la Durantaye and Annie Julia Wyman, Calcutta, India: Seagull Books, 2014.

UB      Agamben, Giorgio, *The Use of Bodies: Homo Sacer IV, 2*, trans. Adam Kotsko, Stanford: Stanford University Press, 2016.

WA      Agamben, Giorgio, *What is an Apparatus? and Other Essays*, trans. David Kishik and Stefan Pedatella, Stanford: Stanford University Press, 2009.

WP      Agamben, Giorgio, *What is Philosophy?*, trans. Lorenzo Chiesa, Stanford: Stanford University Press, 2018.

WR      Agamben, Giorgio, *What Is Real?*, trans. Lorenzo Chiesa, Stanford: Stanford University Press, 2018.

*Introduction*

Giorgio Agamben's nine-volume *Homo Sacer* series is one of the most significant philosophical and political works in recent memory. Its ambition is one that crosses over from these particular disciplinary domains into those of economics, literature and poetry, legal studies, history, theology and even anthropology. All of this is done with such finesse that the mind pausing to consider the implications of his research is often left with significant gaps in their understanding. With so much happening within the series, and on so many levels, it is frequently difficult to determine what is at stake in it, let alone critically assess it. In many ways, the most fundamental philosophical questions of the twentieth century are realigned and re-presented under wholly new conditions.[1]

When the *Homo Sacer* series is contemplated within the context of Agamben's previous writings, there is much to unpack, such as why his work had shifted so strongly toward seemingly obscure political subjects and even more obscure theological ones. The early focal points of Agamben's thought such as poetry, aesthetics and canonical philosophical questions seem at times to have been thrust aside in an effort to range widely over a vast terrain of historical inquiries.[2] However, at the same time, and as I intend to illustrate, what appears in the *Homo Sacer* series to be (at first glance) tangential to Agamben's earlier thought actually becomes central, and what appears (again, at first glance) to be a digression into political or theological minutiae becomes demonstrative of the entire project. If there is a single lesson to be learned by looking at the scope of Agamben's oeuvre it is that there are certain themes and concepts he often displays in his writings throughout the decades that have remained consistent. This is something that allows his thought to expand into new areas that were wholly unexpected, perhaps even to the author himself, while it also helps to explain why some of his occasional essays outside of the series serve to further reinforce the main ideas within it. This is a point which explains why I will be utilising some of these shorter works in the present study as well.[3]

One reason for this phenomenon lies in the wager that Agamben makes concerning the fundamental nature of human existence, or human *being* (ontology) vis-à-vis other disciplinary approaches. Martin Heidegger had prioritised the question of Being as the primary task of philosophical inquiry in the last century, moving ontology, or the study of being, to the fore of all investigations into existence. Emmanuel Levinas had challenged this presumption by arguing for the primacy of ethical relations that precede one's being, and so elevated ethics over ontology. In many ways, the most significant insight that Agamben's *Homo Sacer* series has to offer philosophical reflection at present is to claim that every ontological position is always necessarily an ethical, political, theological, economic and cultural one at the same time. Any suggestion made by one field immediately implicates another, and so on, addressing practically all of the many facets that characterise human existence. The trajectory of the *Homo Sacer* series in particular, among Agamben's other writings, bears out this insight with remarkable clarity.

This is at least one way of explaining why the *Homo Sacer* series traverses broadly throughout multiple academic fields, judiciously selecting an extremely wide-ranging archive of subject material. However, as I am here also suggesting, the series is implicitly bound up with his overt suggestions that we cannot separate academic fields of inquiry as sharply as we have been accustomed to doing. The implications of this proposal,

*Introduction*

I would add, go far beyond merely indicating the need for further interdisciplinary study – they threaten to rethink the entire way in which knowledge has been structured in the West and historically passed along through institutions.[4]

At the very least, this potential reconfiguration of our knowledge relations helps us to comprehend why certain genealogical studies within the histories of theology, politics and philosophy that search for the 'origins' and meaning of contemporary conceptual configurations are not merely digressions from a more proper philosophical route, as any reader who simply skims the many studies comprising the second-tier volumes in the series – those concerned with performing such genealogical studies – might otherwise conclude.[5] They are rather substantial efforts in their own right made towards removing the borders and boundaries that many had long thought to exist between the various disciplines. Therefore, Agamben's focus on the marginalised figure of the *homo sacer* has had the consequence of opening up philosophical discourse to its own marginalised questions and challenges. It is as if the *homo sacer* itself were an embodiment of the way in which certain knowledges have been treated within scholarly discourse, being subject to sacrifice and marginalisation rather than be included within the construction of any institutional knowledge. This is the 'logic of the presupposition' that Agamben will lift up as one of the central insights of the series: there is always a presupposition made of our *being* itself that serves to capture our being and divide it the moment it is articulated in an institutionalised form, such as with the operations that take place in language. Whatever apparatus, as he calls it, captures being – and there are many apparatuses that do so, from languages to technologies – it subdivides being at the same time and renders obscure the form of life living underneath the words and categories that serve to imprison our existence.

As I hope to show, this divided nature of the presupposition of our being is fundamental to the aims of the entire series, as our being, like our bodies and like the figure of the *homo sacer*,

3

is captured precisely through the championing of abstract, critical thought, thereby negating the possibility for being to be embodied as a 'whatever' singularity (or what he will call a form-of-life) lived beyond the law's ability to inscribe it within its own structures and identities. This conclusion follows naturally from the final volume of the series, *The Use of Bodies*, where Agamben is repeatedly given over to rethinking the role of embodiment – or what is presupposed within the formulation of our (sovereign) subjectivity – within human history altogether. As follows eventually from such a reconsideration of the body, the marginalisation of the *homo sacer* as an embodiment of excluded knowledge is a figure parallel to the form-of-life. Just as the creative realm of ideas cannot be co-opted into any definitive or exhaustive political model, so too does the form-of-life resist being identified with any common system of classifications. The seeds for political resistance are thereby stored deeply within philosophical reflection, a point that Agamben will defend vigorously, if subtly, throughout the length of the series.

Beyond simply elucidating these claims, another aim of this volume is to provide an introduction to Agamben's *Homo Sacer* series, as well as his philosophy on the whole *as perceived through the series*, by presenting a collection of essays that focus upon some of the major implications that the series itself points toward. This book is therefore not a simple or straightforward introduction to the series; it is instead a creative effort involving close readings of major passages in the series in order to piece together the main lines of thought that his work on the figure of the *homo sacer* brings to the forefront of contemporary scholarship.[6] In the exercise of working through Agamben's thought, this text aims to highlight the possible construction of *another* form of sovereignty, but not the form that typically dominates our world through the presupposition of being, the creation of the *homo sacer* and the state of exception that legitimates the sovereign's rule.[7] There is perhaps rather something like the autonomous sovereignty of the form-of-life, or whatever being as an irreducible singularity, that contests the political forms of sovereignty that we have otherwise come to know so well in our world.

## OVERVIEW OF THE PRESENT STUDY

Though it will be immediately obvious to the reader that my comments on the *Homo Sacer* series in what follows are not entirely restricted to the nine books that comprise it – including at times extended analysis of some of his shorter texts – my intention throughout is explicitly to develop the main lines of inquiry that Agamben has set before us in the series itself. It is my expectation that such an undertaking might give the reader a sense of what Agamben's monumental *Homo Sacer* project implies for our world at present and how it has most profitably reshaped the ways in which thought operates today.

After a brief excursus that introduces the individual books of the *Homo Sacer* series immediately following this introduction, the first chapter concerns one of the central observations of the *Homo Sacer* project: the inherently fictional nature of sovereignty. Though it is crucial to the historical legacies of politics and religion, it is not entirely clear if this fiction is a necessary illusion of some sort, if it can be permanently eliminated from our world, or if there is another way to live in relationship to it. That is, if sovereignty can be done away with, perhaps antinomianism is a defensible position. If it cannot, then antinomianism is itself an illusion, and perhaps a purely nihilistic one in the end. Or, as I will demonstrate, Agamben argues for another position, one appearing at times as antinomian, at times as allowing for a necessary illusion, and, in the end, advocating for an altogether new relationship to sovereign power. This will become manifest in his work as, what I am calling, the possibility of *another* form of sovereignty.

Agamben's fundamental political reconceptualisation of sovereignty involves new perspectives on language, oaths, processes of exclusion, separation and sacrifice, all of which are pursued in detail in this first chapter. It is, for Agamben, the pure arbitrariness or contingency of human life and of a choice that escapes the realm of sovereign decision (parallel to the difference between demand and command) and so is opened toward recognising a form-of-life lived outside the law that humanity must embrace. As such, the discussion of the fiction of sovereignty, understood through traditional arguments and representations of the divine being and its substance in the West, gives way in Agamben's thought to a (Pauline) weak messianic force that searches for a form-of-life lived beyond the inscriptions of sovereign power. As a result, we must reflect upon an ontology of demand and its nature of being interwoven with sovereign power before we are to progress in further unpacking Agamben's critique of Western metaphysics on the whole.

Chapter 2 addresses Agamben's critique of the Aristotelian categories that have dominated Western metaphysics and theology (e.g. potentiality/actuality, contingency/necessity and so on) and which have led him to interrogate the use of dualisms in Western thought in general insofar as they are used to legitimate traditional political and ethical relations. The dualism of potentiality/actuality is referred to repeatedly in the *Homo Sacer* series, including as the metaphysical basis for the foundations of power – constituted and constituting, governance and sovereignty. One's power, one's *true sovereignty*, comes not from acting, or performing the appearance of having to act, but from refraining from action, from the weakness or impotency 'that turns back on itself' and becomes a 'pure act' in another sense altogether from that which defines traditional forms of sovereign and divine power. As a form of resistance, this alternative power is captured in the figures of Bartleby the Scrivener and of Christ – figures Agamben pursues in depth on occasion. This is precisely where we can locate the *other* form of sovereignty accessed through contemplation as the 'use-of-oneself' that is also a 'zone of non-consciousness', allowing for contemplation to be defined as a habit that occupies the form-of-life. It is at this point that the Franciscan emphasis placed upon both poverty and use becomes

*Introduction*

relevant in determining another mastery of the self that is not predicated upon the Aristotelian dualism of potentiality/actuality, but is grounded only in itself and its weakness.

In Chapter 3, a series of questions frame an extended look at how the arguments surrounding *The Kingdom and the Glory* play themselves out: If God can be said to create the world, through a sovereign gesture of creation *ex nihilo*, then to let it govern itself such that humanity might mistake itself as the divine sovereign, then what are the political implications of particular theological formulations concerning God? And what remains of a possible divinity beyond such concerns? What of a humanity that does not seek to imitate the sovereign deity? Theological discussions on the afterlife, and an eternity of the glorification of God's glory, are really a political theological laboratory for humanity's configuration of itself in relation to sovereign and governmental power. The only thing that such theological conjectures on angelic hierarchies and eternal liturgies reveal is the empty centre that humanity ceaselessly tries to conceal. In other words, such activities only serve the purpose of sustaining a worldly legitimation of reciprocal glory, what tries to suture together the Kingdom and the Government as a single political-theological mechanism. God, as we are led to understand things, is really the concept that conceals an abyss of potentiality and inoperativity that must be ceaselessly hidden.

It is in this place of an experience of failure, which is paradoxically our only hope of success, that we encounter glory, though in a radically different form from sovereign glory. This is what Agamben will later describe as a means of (entirely immanent) grace beyond the (falsely) sacralised forms of theological grace: in other words, the form-of-life lived beyond its inscription in any representational matrix. There is in such gestures, I will argue, a sort of *kenotic* nihilism reconceived as a form of negative dialectics that undoes the divide between sovereign power and governmentality, and which introduces us to our own poverty as forms-of-life, though it is also that which must be recognised as the only way to move beyond the impasse that such political, representational dualisms present us with.

The fourth chapter examines questions of a possible humanity and divinity beyond their historical-theological signatures, turning first to the construction of a political-theological order meant to ceaselessly unite as an economy that which is forever kept separate: the Kingdom and the Government. The historical attempts to conceal and yet maintain such a tension is instructive in that the order (*ordo*) it articulates is one that defines the role of rationality itself. It is from this place that we begin to see how philosophical and theological models of reasoning have neglected the economic ones, such as have been historically articulated in trinitarian theologies, that underpin very this-worldly relations. The entire dualistic representational fabric of politics and theology, as much as of language, is given its particular *raison d'être* through such political-theological configurations of economy which hinge upon an exclusionary inclusion (or inclusionary exclusion) that depends upon its sacrificial machinery. This distinction is in fact the very basis for the entire *Homo Sacer* project that Agamben has undertaken. As such, taking a look at his genealogy of Western notions of economy is essential for comprehending the larger role it plays in particular instances of glory, but also in the construction of the human being and its society in relation to both God and the world of animals. Drawing from Elliot Wolfson's concept of *hypernomianism*, I end the chapter by asking a question of Agamben: are we navigating a certain messianism or some form of hypernomianism?

Chapter 5 is devoted to demonstrating the resonance between his work *The Open* and the *Homo Sacer* series as a whole. Here I take a look at how Agamben enters a discussion regarding the border between animality and humanity through an examination of Martin Heidegger's thoughts on 'the open', or that space that is taken up as the centre of anthropogenetic activity. The open, as the rightful site of our poverty of being, helps us to rethink possibility as a fundamental ontological category. We

*Introduction*

can note that Agamben's solution to the Heideggerian problem of the 'anthropogenetic event' is that we must not add anything to our animality (e.g. the typical definition of the human as above and beyond the animal, as sovereign over animality, or as the 'super-animal' then). Indeed, humanity must not attempt to create any new form at all in order to access our 'emancipation from the metaphysical definition of the human being'. The obvious parallel here is to his suggestions elsewhere that the new form of politics is not some imaginary or utopian ideal, but is another way of reading the human form that is already before us. The key to this emancipation can only be located within the act of suspension or inoperativity, though not necessarily the suspension of one's animality, which is the typical manner by which the human being is constructed as sovereign over the animal world. There is thus 'no content' or substance to the human being as such, as will be noted too in Agamben's development of a modal ontology, though this time it is established in the context of the division between the animal and the human.

As such, we see once again the fiction of a sovereign form operating without any substance behind its claims. The fiction of the human being is the fiction of sovereignty – they are in fact the same fiction. The anthropological machinery, with its empty centre as a state of exception that Agamben wants to suspend, has been extremely effective in creating such fictions in a political sense. This time it is the human being as sovereign who fabricates itself over the animal world by suspending its own animality. The human being includes its animality by excluding it from itself (or 'banning' it) in order to establish itself as dominant. The problem of anthropogenesis, according to Agamben, is that we have traditionally constructed the human being as sovereign and as master through a process of 'othering', or the creation of bare life that can be marginalised, manipulated and controlled. It is the entrance of the Aristotelean dualistic categories (as addressed in Chapter 2) that produces endless scissions across our bodies and through our every identity. Every identity, especially the human being, is characterised by this fundamental division or separation that is regulated by an anthropological machinery (e.g. as we see in the way sacrifice has functioned religiously as generator of the sacred self). Marking the boundary between the human and the animal is what allows humanity to conceive of the self-determining boundary between the human and the divine, as if merely repeating the immanent division of the human-animal became the foundation of another, transcendent division. He seeks to access the void at the centre of human being that can only be seen through suspending our normal representations of ourselves. Hence, the significance of contemplation and of inoperativity in this series as a whole.

The presence of dualisms, as well as the possibility of a negative dialectic active in Agamben's work, is analysed in Chapter 6 and follows his commentary on Paul's letter to the Romans in order to more fully elucidate the 'division of division itself' as one of the major concepts at work in his characterisations of a form-of-life lived beyond the law. Additionally, an exploration of Agamben's work on the abdication of Pope Benedict XVI provides us with a case study of these theories. There is a spiritual power at work within the messianic vocation that undoes the sovereign power aligned with every structure, institution, identity, law and language. This is *another* form of power that Agamben isolates as the weak messianic force we are called to entertain as a corrective power to established norms. At the same time, Agamben's reflections on Pauline thought are central to his solution to the anthropological machinery and its incessant division of human life, even the divisions that characterise the existence of the Church as an institution. He will follow Paul in calling for a messianic 'division of division itself' that takes every dualism and further divides it in half, and so neutralising its destructive force.

For example, as he will famously state in Romans, every identity (e.g. one's Jewish or Gentile identity) is divided from within into flesh and spirit, a further division that renders the first division inoperative – though it also does not replace the primary division with a new one. Yet there is no escaping from

*Introduction*

the identities established in language and in the economies of the world. It is a permanently negative enterprise that only divides whatever social identity – already founded upon a previous division – already exists. Again, as with his study on Franciscan conceptualisations of use, there is not another identity we are searching for, but only a new use of an already existing one.

Lest we become complacent with the force of the messianic, we are reminded as well that such a movement beyond all laws, identities, institutions and norms pushes each form-of-life toward the bankruptcy of all representations. It is a deep dive into the presentation of a world that can only appear as beyond salvation, because it lies beyond what may appear as a utopian world always yet 'to come'. In many ways, then, to grasp the Pauline and Benjaminian sense of the messianic will mean to live beyond every ontotheological formulation and every metaphysical presumption, hence to live as if *without* the divine in order, paradoxically, to dwell in the space of the messiah.

Finally, Chapter 7 takes a look at the most significant concept of the series: form-of-life. To rethink politics, religion, economics and society today, perhaps even to think a form of the multitude beyond the liberal-democratic tensions we are mired in globally, we will have to consider the possibility of a form-of-life lived beyond the law. This is Agamben's central concept, toward which the entire *Homo Sacer* series is aimed. As he will consistently argue, a form-of-life comes about through a messianic generic power that undoes every sovereign form, meaning that the only form of glory which would be available in an authentic way – what I suggest is *another* form of glory – would be an anonymous one, not one of celebrity. A form-of-life overcomes the divisions that characterise humanity, its languages and representations, each of which are beholden to historical theological, political and juridical forms.

As Agamben will discuss historically, if the monk's particular efforts to live a form of life in general 'creates the rules' by which they live, and which cannot be captured by a juridical or legal proscription, then a 'third thing' can only emerge through a form-of-life that is lived beyond all law and property. This gives Agamben's 'Franciscan ontology' its particular emphasis through the development of the concept of use, which was blunted in its radical refusal to own anything by its symbiotic relations with the hierarchy of the Church and the papacy. As the Franciscans will repeatedly demonstrate, to genuinely observe an 'intimacy without relations' we must become attuned to the bodies that we all are, and the personal lives that are concealed within every philosophical expression.

The singularity of what takes place in a form-of-life is due to its implicit willingness not to claim to possess any normative posture or identity. It is perpetually given over to recreating itself – a permanent conversion of sorts that avoids becoming an autonomous sovereign form in that it refuses (normative) relations in order to touch or be 'in contact' with another form-of-life. It is beyond *all* identities or descriptions, though it is not simply, for this reason, able to rest contentedly in itself. If we recall, the messianic revocation of all vocations is nearly impossible, or at least incredibly difficult, to dwell within.

## CHARTING A COURSE FOR READING

As with any form of introduction or guide, determining a starting point can prove most difficult; especially when one is trying to hold together the myriad threads Agamben is utilising while he weaves his thoughts throughout the *Homo Sacer* project.

For those who are unfamiliar with the work of Agamben and are accessing this material to aid in their explorations, I recommend the formal ordering of the chapters. Chapters 1 and 2, in many ways, create a metaphysical and conceptual stage with some of the most primary terms Agamben uses. Furthermore, these two chapters highlight the distinct shift Agamben makes that ultimately becomes indicative of the overall project. These formulations by Agamben return again and again (e.g. the Aristotelian conversations in Chapter 2 return in a slightly different context in Chapter 5).

*Introduction*

These first two chapters can also provide an anchor of sorts, as I am preparing the stage for those more expansive conversations that Agamben opens up. While Chapter 1 briefly touches on theology, these two chapters primarily engage in a more traditional formulation of the political and of philosophy itself, with the noted twist Agamben makes. As mentioned from the outset, these disciplinary distinctions are not as neatly partitioned as we have been led to believe; or so Agamben argues. From here, the following chapters chart a course that highlights the ways in which other disciplines are always implicated. As such, it is my hope that I have also shed light on why sometimes obscure concepts from various other disciplines have become so foundational for Agamben.

For those who are already familiar with Agamben, you may find a rigid journey through the text too confining. While structured in chapters, the subheadings may prove useful to your purposes in engaging this work. As Agamben has become more accessible to the English-speaking world, each scholar contributes to understanding his expansive oeuvre in unique ways. This is, in many ways, the beauty of the far-reaching implications of the *Homo Sacer* project and the ways scholars, from seemingly disparate fields, engage Agamben.

## A BRIEF OUTLINE OF THE HOMO SACER *SERIES*

Before launching into the first chapter, I want to take a moment to provide the reader with an overview of the *Homo Sacer* series in the hopes of making it easier to comprehend the various twists and turns of my own commentary as it follows. First, I will present a tour of the main arguments put forth in the *Homo Sacer* series as a whole by *briefly* summarising each individual volume. I will also outline two additional and related books by Agamben – *The Time that Remains* and *The Open*, both written during the time frame of the *Homo Sacer* series – that I consider crucial interlocutors of Agamben's thought as they pertain to the series. The choice to read these additional texts is made more evident by the way in which these two stand-alone works explicitly factor into the conclusions reached in the culminating summary given at the end of *The Use of Bodies*.

The *Homo Sacer* project comprises a series of nine books, all of which have only more recently been published in a single volume format in the English-speaking world: *The Omnibus Homo Sacer*.[8] The order of the series, which was only firmly established after several volumes were written, is as follows:

I    *Homo Sacer: Sovereign Power and Bare Life*
II.1  *State of Exception*
II.2  *Stasis: Civil War as Political Paradigm*
II.3  *The Sacrament of Language: An Archaeology of the Oath*
II.4  *The Kingdom and the Glory: For a Theological Genealogy of Economy and Government*
II.5  *Opus Dei: An Archaeology of Duty*
III   *Remnants of Auschwitz: The Witness and the Archive*
IV.1 *The Highest Poverty: Monastic Rules and Form-of-Life*
IV.2 *The Use of Bodies*

## FRAMING THE HOMO SACER *SERIES*

At the risk of these summaries becoming too bloated with the myriad threads Agamben weaves together in them, I think it is important to highlight a central premise which guides the entire series. While many themes certainly repeat themselves throughout, the *presupposition of being* he mentions in *The Use of Bodies* that captures our being and subsequently divides it in order to dominate human existence is, I would argue, what provides a crucial key to understanding what is going on in the series as a whole. Though he utilises synonymous language elsewhere to describe the same process, the capture of being through the various apparatuses that permeate our world – most notably, language itself – ceaselessly divides being into varied dualistic frameworks (such as between the potential and the actual, or

*Introduction*

*bios* and *zoē*) in order to control and dominate being. The figure of the sovereign, for example, who rules through the declaration and delineation of a state of exception, creates a dichotomy between sovereign power and 'bare life' (from whence the *homo sacer* is produced) in order to legitimate its rule. Overcoming this essential division of being becomes *the* recurring leitmotif running throughout the series, and it is to that overarching goal that this project is focused. This subject, in particular, is what introduces the first volume of the series, *Homo Sacer*, and it is what recurs with increasing significance throughout the volumes that follow.

I  *Homo Sacer: Il potere sovrano e la nuda vita*, Torino: Einaudi, 1995.
   *Homo Sacer: Sovereign Power and Bare Life*, trans. Daniel Heller-Roazen, Stanford: Stanford University Press, 1998.

The first volume of the series introduces a strategic formulation of biopolitics in the modern period – and here Agamben is deeply indebted to the works of Michel Foucault[9] – that rethinks the exclusion of natural life (*zoē*) from the communal life of the polis (*bios*) in ancient Greek thought. Agamben's assessment of this central division of our being, along with the role played by the economy of the home (*oikos*), lead to the main claim he makes concerning state power and the production of the *homo sacer*.

In short, the *homo sacer* was a figure of Roman law who simultaneously existed both inside and outside of society, wherein their life could not be accepted by the gods (i.e. sacrificed) nor was their life able to be protected from threat of violence of others (e.g. homicide). This biopolitical tool introduces a context wherein one's rights have been utterly stripped, yet a shred of distinction remains that links one to already established societal prohibitions. The creation of this figure results in the existence of 'bare life', which, for Agamben, is the 'nucleus of sovereign power' and what produces the biopolitical body. The figure of the *homo sacer* is in fact the excluded life upon which the sovereign depends in order to establish any political relations at all, thereby also creating a division more original to politics than the German political theorist Carl Schmitt's friend/enemy distinction.[10]

The sovereign, for their part, is at once both inside and outside the law, a state of existence that allows them to declare exceptions (suspensions) to the rule of law. This reality generates a situation that will enable manifestations of the camp, as itself an exceptional site Agamben takes up in this context, to become the political norm of modernity. The camp, as a biopolitical tool to sequester the unwanted of any given body politic (and as has become notorious through historical instances of concentration and refugee camps), is a concept that demonstrates how bare life involves the removal of one's form of life from it, leaving one bereft of the possibility for its existence to be lived beyond its inscription within the coordinates of sovereign power and the incessant divisions of human existence. Through this production of bare life, biopolitics can sometimes slide into its shadow-side: thanatopolitics, whose focus is the elimination of life, not its production and preservation.

For Agamben, there is a need to comprehend a variety of related concepts to the division of human existence that have gone unobserved in relation to each other for far too long. He therefore begins in this volume to discuss multiple and significant distinctions, such as:

- that between an *exception* as an 'inclusive exclusion' and the *example*, or paradigm, as an 'exclusive inclusion', wherein Agamben is careful to lift up the latter and to critically deconstruct the operations of the former;
- the tension between constitut*ing* power and constitut*ed* power as it exists parallel to Aristotle's philosophical distinction between potentiality and actuality, which Agamben claims lies at the centre of metaphysical-political thought and even served to 'bequeath the paradigm of sovereignty to Western philosophy';

- the figure of the *homo sacer* who is outside both human and divine law and indeed approaches a zone 'prior to the distinction between sacred and profane, religious and juridical';
- and the way in which our bodies are at the centre of Western politics due to the modern transference of the sacred into all of our bodies, meaning that the 'capacity to be killed' is the 'new political body of the West'.

Since humanity keeps failing in its attempts to define 'the people' as a new, undivided political body, and so ends up re-creating some of the worst violences possible through recurring exclusionary acts – from civil war and class conflicts to messianic kingdoms and classless societies – Agamben seeks alternative forms of political resistance. In this particular vein, he turns toward the end of the volume to Melville's figure of Bartleby, the Scrivener, whose response that he 'prefers not to' becomes a type of resistance, the form of life wherein a law without content is indistinguishable from life itself. There is an overt resonance here with a certain messianic nihilism in Walter Benjamin's work that, as Agamben describes it, 'nullifies even the Nothing and lets no form of law remain in force beyond its own content'. The messianic, in this last instance, acts as the limit experience of law and of religious experience itself, or that which enables the fulfilment of the law to coincide with its transgression. Messianism is therefore developed as a theory of the state of exception from another angle altogether. Benjamin, for his part, had referred to it as a *real* state of exception that suspends even the sovereign's emergency powers, and Agamben develops Benjamin's notion as a kind of solution to sovereign violence.

## II.1 *Stato di eccezione*, Torino: Bollati Boringhieri, 2003.
### *State of Exception*, trans. Kevin Attell, Chicago: The University of Chicago Press, 2005.

The state of exception is a pivotal political, philosophical and metaphysical concept for Agamben as it exists in a zone of indistinction between law and lawlessness, 'like civil war, insurrection, and resistance'. Agamben is given over to investigating this 'no man's land between public law and political fact, and between the juridical order and life' because it indicates a threshold of law, in political, though certainly also fictitious, terms. Though the modern state of exception was born out of the 'democratic-revolutionary tradition and not the absolutist one', he will portray it as 'an attempt to include the exception itself within the juridical order by creating a zone of indistinction in which fact and law coincide'. By declaring the state of exception through a sovereign decision that will always appear as a necessity – because necessity is finally that which creates its own law – we discover too that such a state is a 'fictitious lacuna' that 'safeguards' the existence of the norm.

Agamben will also contemplate the possibility of whether the right to resistance might be included in the constitution itself, which is to suggest some form of *anomie*, or lawlessness, is inscribed within law and order. This leads him to examine the nature of revolutionary ('pure' or 'divine') violence in both Schmitt and Benjamin, showing how the latter's efforts to install a theory of sovereign indecision (as the *real* state of exception) might make possible a messianic force that 'shatters the correspondence between sovereignty and transcendence, between the monarch and God'. The 'fictive nexus' between law and violence is consequently severed by a pure violence that upends metaphysical constructs and connects modern political thought to Pauline theology wherein messianic fulfilment deactivates the law, or renders it inoperative, without doing away with it altogether. There is, furthermore, a critique of the Schmittian inheritance as Agamben assesses how Schmitt had confused the dictator with the state of exception. While not entirely dismissing this connection, Agamben, once again, digs deeper into the political and philosophical foundations of the West to articulate the contours of the state of exception beyond their frequent associations with sovereign dictatorships.

In a major theoretical exploration, Agamben suggests that the West maintains an ongoing tension between the normative/juridical (*potestas*) and the anomic/metajuridical (*auctoritas*) wherein *auctoritas* can only assert itself in the suspension of *potestas* and so fragilise law itself. Instead of the state of exception being only an emergency measure taken by the state during times of crises, it has become the fundamental governing norm of political life. The extra-legal has become part of the modern world's definition of the legal. When the juridical and the metajuridical, the legal and the extra-legal, are invested in the same person, and blurred together, as happens during certain dictatorial contexts, they transform into a 'killing machine'.

The state of exception is, in the end, ultimately an empty space where 'a human action with no relation to law [*auctoritas*] stands before a norm with no relation to life [*potestas*]'. Though Agamben makes clear that we currently live in such a tension that is headed toward 'global civil war', there may yet be a way for something like a pure law, pure language, pure violence, or pure means without ends to illuminate a new use of human praxis, allowing too for new uses of law beyond what we have previously seen. Much of what takes place theoretically in the series is significantly foreshadowed in this slim but highly provocative text.

> II.2 *Stasis: La Guerra civile come paradigma politico.* **Torino: Bollati Boringhieri, 2015.**
> ***Stasis: Civil War as a Political Paradigm*, trans. Nicholas Heron, Edinburgh: Edinburgh University Press, 2015.**

Written as a seemingly last-minute addition to the genealogical studies lodged within the second tier, the genesis of its contributing materials actually dates from two seminars in October of 2001, given in the immediate aftermath of September 11. This volume's focus is placed squarely upon a theory of civil war wherein civil war (*stasis*) functions as a state of exception sketched out as a threshold between the family (*oikos*) and the *polis*, as well as the corresponding relationship between *zoē* and *bios*, a division introduced in the first volume of the series. Already, the reader is able to see here how Agamben is trying to weave the various threads of his discourse together. He turns, as such, to a tension he will elucidate more fully in *The Use of Bodies* between the sovereign (as *populus rex*) and the multitude that constitutes the political body – a point he drives home in this context through a detailed discussion of Thomas Hobbes's *Leviathan*.

The 'people', he concludes, is a body always divided against itself, a body always present that can never actually *be* present and so must always only be represented. The modern roots of politics are as such revealed by Agamben to be entirely bound up with a theological-eschatological tension between the 'lawless (*anomias*) one' and the 'one who restrains (*katechon*)', which he also perceives to be at the heart of the Church (as he also discusses in his essay *The Mystery of Evil*) and at the centre of all theories of the state in relation to the concept of civil war (*stasis* being a 'war within the family'). It is only by considering the theological origins of modern political concepts, such as found in the 'people', that humanity might be able to rethink political relations anew. It is here too that we can also begin to see more clearly Agamben's understanding of theological concepts and histories as they will slowly begin to form an integral part of the rhetorical structure of the overall project.

II.3 *Il sacramento del linguaggio. Archeologia del giuramento*, Roma: Laterza, 2008.
**The Sacrament of Language: An Archaeology of the Oath**, trans. Adam Kotsko, Stanford: Stanford University Press, 2010.

*The Sacrament of Language* conducts an archaeology of the oath as an investigation into the origins and use of the oath in the West. Agamben embarks on this particular trajectory of research in order to illuminate the modern crisis in language

*Introduction*

and authority – noting the decline or outright rejection of the oath – and thus possibly as well to lead humanity toward new forms of political association.

The oath, here the central concept of his scrutiny, is a rhetorical device that allows language to appear as truthful at all, and as part of its actualisation. The oath in fact helps deal with a fundamental weakness in language by trying to establish a bond through the use of language itself. By attempting to establish such a bond in language that is yet seemingly beyond the fallibility of language, the oath becomes one of the first principles of metaphysics historically given to (and by) humanity. Hence, as Agamben will illustrate, the quest to discover a 'more archaic stage' of human language is not actually a search for a historical stage – it is a force working within history, not the quest for a *homo religiosus* who has never actually existed. In reality, the search he undertakes is not just to locate the origins of the oath, but to reveal a limit concept as the stage of an indistinction between the sacred and the profane, or what allows us to access a space *before* religion and law, even if we cannot locate some mythical point of origin for their coexistence.

It is through this examination of the 'sacrament of language' that Agamben will be able to call into question the 'very nature of man' in terms of its origin in both language and politics. For if God's name in monotheism 'names language itself' and Christianity, for its part, introduced a 'divinization of the logos', then the oath becomes visible as a particular 'consecration of the living human being', and as a sacrament of power made possible through the sacrament of language. To experience language is henceforth to experience faith, wherein the 'certainty of faith is the certainty of the name (of God)' (SL 53/ OHS 341). From this perspective, we can reassess any ontological arguments for God's existence as really stating 'that if speech exists, then God exists'. Ontotheology is little more than a performance of language and metaphysics coincides with the experience of language itself.

Most profoundly, the decline in the legitimacy of the oath in the West is what modernity has labelled the 'death of God', which is really the death of the *name* of God. Living without the force of the oath in the modern era likewise means changing the usual political associations based upon oaths, revealing to us at the same time the truth that we live in an age of blasphemy and God's name can subsequently only be uttered 'in vain'. Philosophy, by this count, begins its operations by putting 'in question the primacy of names' in order to critique the oath and implement specific forms of resistance. As always, these remarks should be understood within the growing overall discourse on biopolitical apparatuses – in this instance, with a more detailed focus on language. After all, for Agamben, language itself becomes the site where human beings are themselves put at stake.

### II.4 *Il Regno e la Gloria. Per una genealogia teologica dell'economia e del governo*, Milano: Neri Pozza, 2007. *The Kingdom and the Glory: For a Theological Genealogy of Economy and Government*, trans. Lorenzo Chiesa with Matteo Mandarini, Stanford: Stanford University Press, 2011.

Taking a cue from Carl Schmitt that all political concepts are theological concepts at their foundation, Agamben's *The Kingdom and the Glory* is an extended genealogical study of historical accounts of theological discussions on the Trinitarian uses of *oikonomia* (economy, or the 'management of the household') as 'a privileged laboratory' for observing the governmental machine at work in our world. This work was unsurprisingly the first major part of the series to significantly catch the attention of theologians, because it was a series of historical theological arguments throughout the centuries that actually evolved the modern political concepts Agamben is here looking to isolate and critique.

What is explicitly uncovered by Agamben is an apparatus, or bipolar machine, in the form of a split Kingdom and Government, as in the related tension between glory (*gloria*) and *oikonomia*, which is itself parallel to that between *auctoritas* and *potestas* as analysed in *State of Exception*. Agamben's claim is quite simple: Western Christian liturgies and rituals offer a more unique insight into political operations than analyses of sovereign power, as the nature of acclamations, doxologies and the Eucharistic sacrifice not only link liturgy and *oikonomia*, but reveal the juridical nature of liturgies in the context of Christian celebrations. Making the claim that he intends to return politics to its central inoperativity as the 'properly human and political praxis', he undertakes an examination of the image of the empty throne in Christian symbolism. Agamben conducts this examination alongside the history of another revealing tension between a political theology (based on paradigms of transcendence) and an economic theology (grounded on an immanent frame for governance), with traditional political philosophies being based on the former and the tactics of biopolitics based on the latter.

The historical reversal by early Christian theologians of the Pauline 'economy of the mystery' into 'the mystery of the economy' – a move that emphasised the role of economy over that of divine mystery – had allowed economy to become what orders 'the divine being into a trinity and, at the same time, preserves and "harmonizes" it into a unity'. This slow shift in emphasis initiated a focus on economic ordering over the ambiguity of divine being, ushering in new religious and political forms that were, in turn, substantiated by theological justifications. In this context, the Trinity was said not to deal solely with divine being or ontology, but rather with action and praxis, things that are truly *without* substance and yet which have a determinate impact on our world. This substanceless impact is the main reason why I will sometimes refer to such configurations the 'necessary illusions' of our world. This shift in thought is what will enable Agamben to claim that 'There is no substance of power, but only an "economy," only a "government"'. These fictions are instrumental in organising political life and the form of the human being itself, though these metaphysical presumptions have been veiled historically by theological claims.

*Oikonomia*, in this context, becomes the central concept of Western politics and theology as it joins together the paradigm of government and the state of exception in order 'to avoid a fracture of monotheism that would have reintroduced a plurality of divine figures, and polytheism with them' (KG 53/OHS 419). Divine being is not split because it is actually divided on the level of *oikonomia* and so not regarding its being, as one might notice from an ontological point of view. This is what he calls the 'secret dualism' introduced by Gnosticism that Christianity cannot leave behind, and which goes beyond merely reformulating Aristotle's notion of an unmoved mover. The immovable mover, representative of the transcendent *arche* exists in permanent tension with the immanent order as *physis* – as Aristotle too had once linked sovereignty and nature as being inseparable from one another. Agamben's subsequent claim is that this paradigm is precisely how kingdom and government are likewise aligned as foundational to Western metaphysics, establishing a firm connection between ontology and politics.

The paradox of glory is made manifest within the circular logic of glorifying God because God is deserving of glory. Humanity is thus created *by* God in order to give glory *to* God. Glory in fact takes the place of the inoperativity of power which is unthinkable and unsayable in its vacuity, allowing glory to fill the empty space symbolised theologically through the recurring image of the empty throne. The Sabbath, as the historical marker of inoperativity, is what is revealed as being 'most proper to God' and what marks an understanding of the Kingdom in Christianity, allowing Agamben to demonstrate, toward the end of this study in particular, how messianic inoperativity in Paul's thought allows for a reformulation of inoperativity *as* messianic life. As he will stress in the conclusion of this study of these tensions between kingdom and governance, modernity did not abandon God for secularism, but placed these theological ideas of the *oikonomia* firmly at its core, through the governmental paradigm that still goes unrecognised today for what it is.

**II.5** ***Opus Dei. Archeologia dell'ufficio.*** **Torino: Bollati Boringhieri, 2012.**
***Opus Dei: An Archaeology of Duty*, trans. Adam Kotsko, Stanford: Stanford University Press, 2013.**

Stepping back for a moment from making his final conclusions to the series so that he might add another contribution to the genealogical studies of the second tier, and in order to more fully explicate some of the assertions made in *The Kingdom and the Glory*, Agamben offers this short archaeology of duty as an exploration of the link between liturgy and office in the Western theological tradition. Here, the 'ministry of the mystery' merges with the mystery of liturgy as the 'mystery of effectiveness' through which ontology, ethics, politics and economy are capable of being thought at all. The office – a term often used to describe the 'divine office' as a liturgy of prayers – becomes 'more efficacious than the law', 'more real than being' and 'more effective than any ordinary human action' through its fictive declaration of being as possible only *through* praxis, thus also equating office with ontology and duty with ethics. In other words, what a person is and what a person does becomes nearly indistinguishable. Agamben goes on to explore the mystery of effectiveness 'insofar as in it being is resolved into praxis and praxis is substantiated into being. The mystery of the liturgy coincides totally with the mystery of operativity' (OD 55/ OHS 694–5, de-emphasised from the original). As such, liturgical mystery exists because of 'an economy of divine being', *oikonomia*, that is an operativity of the divine being: 'this and nothing else is the mystery'.

Liturgical mystery is 'the mystery of this praxis and this operativity', something that gives Agamben room to re-address the nature of substantiality and effectiveness as they have been historically identified together, producing effectiveness as a 'new ontological dimension', as he will call it. Essentially, we see in this particular volume how such mysteries are responsible for one's being duty-bound to one's office in life no matter what the office is, allowing the category of duty to evolve and produce subjects in accordance with a particular anthropology wherein the office of the human is distinguished from that of the animal – merging his remarks here with those made in his book *The Open*. It is the office of the human that ultimately renders life governable for human beings. Hence, the 'institution of life' is presented as sociality itself and so the office of humanity 'thus constitutes the human condition'. What Agamben is trying to do in this work in particular is to think beyond the links forged between duty, office, effectiveness and the will, so that an 'ontology beyond operativity and command' might be formulated that is also 'liberated from the concepts of duty and will', which have dominated for centuries through their theological entrance into Western thought. This is one of the major philosophical priorities of the series and so this 'digression' into liturgy and office is far from insignificant to the overarching goals of this project.

III *Quel che resta di Auschwitz. L'archivio e il testimone*, Torino: Bollati Boringhieri, 1998.
**Remnants of Auschwitz: The Witness and the Archive**, trans. Daniel Heller-Roazen, New York: Zone Books, 2002.

Prefiguring discussions of the remnant in *The Time that Remains*, Agamben here conducts his most thorough investigation of a limit-case for understanding the figure of the *homo sacer* – the *Muselmann* of the Nazi concentration camps. It is easy to see how many of the themes from the first volume of the series are here enfleshed, as it were, through profound and disturbing historical examples. Through an insightful and sweeping commentary on the nature of trying to give witness to what cannot be presented in language – something that the concentration camps recall to mind with horrific clarity – we observe a wide range of topics under discussion, including: the formation of subjectivity through bearing witness to the processes of desubjectification (a point he returns to on numerous occasions in other texts), the introduction of a modal ontology based upon the polarities of potentiality/actuality and incapacity/capacity for subjectivity, testimony converging with the force of the messianic through the concept of the remnant and how this last thought allows us to consider anew the highly significant testimonies of those who suffered in the camps. Within the context of the overall project, we also revisit the figure of the *homo sacer*, who has been rendered nude, and so stripped of all human rights.

It is intriguing to note as well how Agamben analyses the figure of the *Muselmann* as a unique case of anthropological insight, determining that 'The human being is the one who can survive the human being' (RA 133/OHS 850, de-emphasised from the original). His reflections on the limits of language in establishing the human being are therefore reflected by his later comments in *The Open* regarding the possibility (and even failure, hence the shame) of the human to uniquely distinguish itself from the animal world as what defines the human in the first place. It is from this point of view that we begin to see how the concentration camps of the Second World War provide invaluable, albeit horrific, insight on the nature of the human being insofar as they illuminate how 'Testimony takes place in the non-place of articulation'. This is a point that has been debated for decades regarding the possible testimony of those victims to Nazi destruction who could not testify for themselves (and, for example, as Jean-François Lyotard had analysed in-depth in his masterwork *The Differend*).[11]

IV.1 *Altissima povertà: Regole monastiche e forma di vita.* Milano: Neri Pozza, 2011.
**The Highest Poverty: Monastic Rules and Form-of-Life,** trans. Adam Kotsko, Stanford: Stanford University Press, 2013.

This first part to the concluding subsection of the series takes an extended look at how monasticism in the West attempts to create a 'form-of-life', or a life inseparable from its form, through the relationship between rule and life as it is lived in community. The form-of-life, as Agamben will show, has been the 'third thing' sought after, especially in the Franciscan movement, though such movements have typically failed to embody such a life in reality. Liturgy was an attempt made by priests – one that ultimately failed – to bridge the gap between life and law. Monasticism therefore presents us with an almost (but not quite) complete merger between liturgy and life in order to try to think a form-of-life, not as property, but as a 'common use'. As Agamben will note in the preface to this work in particular, he is trying to establish 'how to think a form-of-life, a human life entirely removed from the group of the law and a use of bodies and of the world that would never be substantiated into an appropriation'. Though monasticism too will fail to elicit the form-of-life it seeks after through its indebtedness to forms of liturgy that prevent its realisation, it becomes a case study in how, as he will conclude, the form-of-life 'must unceasingly be torn away from the separation in which liturgy keeps it'.

What had become the case in liturgy and theology in the West was that monasticism's efforts to merge life and time through 'manual labor and prayer' presented 'constant meditation as a fundamental duty' and as a sort of quasi-totalitarian state of existence. The monk's life becomes, as such, an 'uninterrupted Office' wherein their praxis establishes their vocation and leads to a 'total liturgicization of life and a vivification of liturgy that is just as entire'. Such was the monastic liturgical life that eventually overtook cathedral life and which was countered by Franciscan efforts which sought not a new doctrine or exegesis, but only to 'reclaim a life and not a rule'. The Franciscan order had only wanted to identify with life, to live the Gospel and not simply to interpret it.

*The Highest Poverty* is therefore centred on Francis of Assisi's attempts to live a *forma vitae* as a life that cannot be separated from its form. Francis' lack of concern with a rule for his order 'in the proper sense' was a way to emphasise how this form of life was not 'reducible to a normative code'. Francis tried to name something that was neither life nor law, and the tension that resulted was due to an attempt to name something that cannot actually be named. Hence Francis' search for a 'third thing' between doctrine and law, as also between rule and dogma, illustrates too how normative rules cannot capture the essence of this third thing. Despite the fact that such a tension reveals a 'juridical paradox' or 'juridical void' within this empty space between the tensions, it is the state of necessity 'that is the apparatus through which they seek to neutralize law and at the same time to assure themselves an extreme relationship with it (in the form of *ius naturale*)'.

The Franciscans who eventually followed in his steps thus tried to develop an 'ontology of use' 'in which being and becoming, existence and time seem to coincide', in order to bring use and time together and emphasise how life is defined by poverty, not by office. Though Agamben will only briefly attempt to supplement the eventual failures of the Franciscans to either develop such an ontology of use or to live out this form-of-life with his own reference to Pauline thought (which he takes up directly in his commentary on Romans in *The Time that Remains*), he yet manages to demonstrate more fully how the radicality of their order's founder avoided rendering faith into a habit or custom, as the monks did, through a reliance upon use over possession.

IV.2 *L'uso dei corpi*. Milano: Neri Pozza, 2014.
   **The Use of Bodies**, trans. Adam Kotsko, Stanford: Stanford University Press, 2016.

As the concluding statement of the entire *Homo Sacer* series, Agamben points toward a number of fascinating areas within his own research that had previously been less emphasised, including the role of the body in Western thought, the nature of an instrumental logic in relation to our bodily being (involving two fascinating discussions of slavery and technology) and the role of one's private, autobiographical life in philosophical conversation – with this last area giving rise to rare glimpses into Agamben's own history, as well as the personal lives of other philosophers such as Martin Heidegger, Guy Debord, Michel Foucault and Emmanuel Levinas, to name only the most prominently mentioned. Since, as he makes clear, his series has been aimed at rendering the anthropological machinery of our world inoperative, there is no major positive or constructive project detailed in this final volume; rather he aims to establish a *destituent* potential as the principal philosophical concept our world is in need of today.

By starting with an examination of the slave as the 'repressed' of Western culture and the exclusion of the slave/body that brings political life into existence, Agamben provides a trenchant critique of the notion of possession alongside its alternative, the 'originary ontological relation' that 'has the form of a use'. It is *use*, as he had defined this term in *The Highest Poverty*, which 'implies' 'an ontology irreducible to the Aristotelian duality of potential and act' that governs Western culture. It is use and not possession as well, he notes, that recalls the Pauline messianic formulation that does not call a new substance into being, but only a new *use* of being – the Pauline 'as not' that stresses use over ownership and is applicable to one in any material condition. These suggestive connections lead in this context toward a focus on contemplation as a 'use-of-oneself' and as what makes possible an experience of the world as 'absolutely inappropriable', hence as that which gives way to forms of thought focused on poverty, inoperativity and new uses of things.

Contemplation, as a form of destituent potential that emphasises the use of a thing over its possession, renders the split between *bios* and *zoē* inoperative, which also marks a powerful return to the very beginning of the series. There ensues an expansive look at how one might define a form-of-life as it is hidden within the present and not lived outside of it – much as he conjectured regarding the Pauline definition of *kairos* in *The Time that Remains*. Living beyond all inscribed forms of life means living too beyond the identities that have been placed upon humanity, allowing for the 'division of division itself' to yield new forms-of-life lived beyond the law. Any association between such forms gives rise, not to traditional political or communal forms, but to a multitude that lives out an 'intimacy without relations' made possible through the suspension, or rendering inoperative, of the anthropological machinery that had defined the human being for centuries. In essence, Agamben is promoting what is commonly referred to as a *constructivist* approach to identity over against an *essentialist* notion of identity, though he himself does not utilise this language of distinction. It is from this standpoint of how we might comprehend new possibilities for the human being that we glimpse once again Agamben's emphasis upon use, contemplation, inoperativity, the poverty of being (as with Heidegger's discussion of 'the open') and potentiality as the fundamental ontological category.

*Il tempo che resta. Un commento alla Lettera ai Romani*, Torino: Bollati Boringhieri, 2000.
*The Time that Remains: A Commentary on the Letter to the Romans*, trans. Patricia Dailey, Stanford: Stanford University Press, 2005.

Though technically not a part of the *Homo Sacer* series, *The Time that Remains* sees Agamben train his eye upon Paul's letter to the Romans as the fundamental messianic text of the West. Here, the contracted nature of time itself is what allows the force of the messianic to appear within history. Hence, Agamben will claim that messianic time is not that which is simply added to normal time in order to divide it from within. It is actually Sabbath time, or an experience of time that interrupts secular time in the 'here and now'. *Kairos* is already present within *chronos* and vice versa, leaving *kairos* to divide *chronos* from within and thereby giving rise to the most significant Pauline concept Agamben will himself employ: the division of division itself that subdivides every identity from within and allows for one identity to cross over into the territory of another 'as if' all identities were hollowed out, again rearticulating a constructivist view of identity and subject formation. It is an act that separates the surname from its bearer. The division of division introduces a remnant from within the divided whole that does not coincide with itself – offering us a 'zone of undecidability'. As such, the messianic vocation is presented as the revocation of all vocations.

Not only does Agamben here present Paul as a philosopher of the highest order – one he explicitly links to the thought of Walter Benjamin – but he also considers him as a somewhat antinomian thinker wherein faith stands opposed to law in order to render all law inoperative. Indeed, the messianic becomes a moment of crisis in the separation between law and religion, leaving grace to be defined as an excess in relation to law. It is at this point that grace is further portrayed in terms that foreshadow the conclusion to the series in *The Use of Bodies*, as it is grace that ultimately opens life up toward a form of life lived beyond the law. The form of life (without hyphens between the words in this context), however, is deemed difficult to achieve within a Church that tries to strike a balance between grace and law (and as we have already seen as the central struggle of the Franciscans in *The Highest Poverty*). Faith is thus split within Christianity itself, and believing in Jesus Messiah means making a choice to be beyond subject and predicate (as is the case in matters of love, which Agamben will later state elsewhere). From this point of view, there is no (doctrinal) content to faith, but only the messianic suspension of all identities – a task that the Church has denied throughout its long history.

As the contours of the argument are presented, the rationale falls in sync with the larger arguments that we have seen in the *Homo Sacer* series. This is not terribly surprising, as this investigation into Pauline literature occurred during the middle of the writing of *Homo Sacer* project itself. It is the division of division, as he will call it, that proves itself integral to understanding the larger implications of Agamben's philosophical moves. For these reasons, I consider *The Time that Remains* to be an unofficial part of the *Homo Sacer* series.

***L'aperto. L'uomo e l'animale,*** Torino: Bollati Boringhieri, 2002.
***The Open: Man and Animal,*** trans. Kevin Attell, Stanford: Stanford University Press, 2004.

*The Open*, as with *The Time that Remains*, is not formally included in the *Homo Sacer* series. It is, however, central to the argument being advanced in the series and so, in my opinion, worth considering alongside the volumes that comprise the series. In short order, the suspension of the identity of the subject that had featured prominently in *The Time that Remains* is brought into an anthropological context in order to illuminate the failures of humanity to articulate precisely what distinguishes humanity from the rest of the animal kingdom. For centuries, the taxonomies and classificatory systems of biologists and anthropologists have struggled with the difficulty of defining the human being, often settling solely on a self-reflexive definition involving the human being as the only animal capable of recognising, and representing, itself as a human being – something done *in* language and which the other animals appear incapable of doing.

Following the thought of Heidegger more closely here than in any other of his texts up to this point – though still in conversation with Benjamin who has been influential in this project as well as Alexandre Kojève – Agamben develops a notion of 'the open' as the space wherein the human subject is developed through the exclusion of its own animality (and thereby reflecting the split between *zoē* and *bios* under discussion in the first volume of the series). This distinction is one that has been fabricated by the presupposition of being that captures being and subsequently divides it in order to dominate human existence (which, as we have seen, undergirds Agamben's entire project). Thus, such a text is indispensable in unpacking the implications of the *Homo Sacer* series as a whole.

Through ignoring the animal's poverty of world, the human being creates itself in the void, or poverty, that otherwise remains empty. This is a conceptualisation that foreshadows as well discussions of the empty throne in *The Kingdom and the Glory*. Learning to let the anthropological machinery idle, as a suspension of its operations, allows us to think of new uses for humanity beyond the ways in which it has thus far attempted to possess a definition and identity for itself beyond the poverty that more truly accounts for humanity's situation in the world. Going beyond the typical characterisations of humanity means, for Agamben, instituting the Pauline logic of a division of division, or what he here calls a 'suspension of the suspension, Shabbat of both animal and man'.

# 1

# *Religious and Political Implications of the* Homo Sacer *Project*

## THE FICTION OF SOVEREIGNTY

One of the central observations of the *Homo Sacer* series concerns the inherently fictional nature of sovereignty. Though sovereign power is certainly prominent in its articulation and is crucial to the historical legacies of both politics and religion, it is not entirely clear to most if (1) this fiction is a necessary illusion of some sort, if (2) it could or should be permanently eliminated from our world in order to escape all forms of oppression (the *antinomian* question of whether Agamben is trying to establish an argument for an existence opposed to normative order or law) *or* if (3) there is another way to live in relationship to sovereignty's seemingly ineradicable power.[1] When you consider that the marginalised figure of the *homo sacer* – the ancient Roman person who may be killed but not sacrificed – is established only through its relation to sovereign power, as the first volume in the series makes clear, you likewise begin to contemplate ways to bring about an end to the creation of more *homines sacri* in our world.

In many ways, critical receptions of Agamben's *Homo Sacer* series, and exactly what it is that he suggests we do with regards to sovereignty, are somewhat divided on this matter. Therefore, some scholars are left to conjecture that it cannot be removed and others to suggest that Agamben harbours an ultimately antinomian sentiment within his work.² In other words, if sovereignty cannot be done away with, perhaps any lingering hints of antinomianism are themselves utopian illusions and maybe purely nihilistic ones in the end. *Or*, if sovereignty can be done away with, perhaps antinomianism is a defensible philosophical position vis-à-vis the existence of all law. *Or*, taking up the stance that one should neither capitulate to sovereignty nor eradicate it, perhaps Agamben argues for another position. This almost elusive position, one that is certainly hard to articulate in concrete positive, political terms, appears at times as allowing for a necessary illusion, at other times as antinomian, and ultimately as advocating for an altogether new relationship to sovereign power. This will become manifest in the *Homo Sacer* series as the possibility of what I am calling *another* form of sovereignty that I want to address directly as a latent outcome of his elaborations on the form-of-life lived beyond the law.

Though this suggestion is often only hinted toward indirectly in his writings, what is clear is that, historically in the West, a certain conceptualisation of the will has served as *the* foundation for sovereign power. Furthermore, this conceptualisation of the will is also what seeks to suture together the various fractures that characterise the human being (itself brought about through the presupposition and capture of being). This would include the state of exception that legitimates the human being as sovereign over the other animals, and even over other humans who are rendered *homines sacri* through their exclusion from society. It is in this sense that Agamben can refer to the state of exception as a 'fictitious lacuna' that 'safeguards' the existence of the norm (SE 31/OHS 191). It is also in this place that Agamben links sovereign power to a logic of 'the presupposition', where the fundamental metaphysical divisions (e.g. the Aristotelean split between existence and essence, potential and act) rely upon an exclusion (presupposition) of one's being in order to articulate it in language and the symbolic networks that comprise sovereign power in our world (UB 119–20/OHS 1134–5).

There are a few salient points I want to develop in relation to this notion of sovereignty as a fiction that might be helpful to further observe as they are referred to throughout his project.

First, Agamben's discussion of the fiction of sovereignty suggests that we are frequently dependent upon an ontological sense of being and of our substantiality that does not exist in material terms ('in reality'). This will go some way toward explaining why Agamben asserts there is no actual or essential substance to sovereignty, or to the ontologies that have been utilised to defend said substance throughout the course of time. There is no ontotheological legitimation of the divine, of our sovereign selves (as subjects) or even of the human being as such. Put simply: human beings do not ask about who they are, but rather about what they want. This is why the will comes to define this delicate masquerade of an action undertaken in order to cover over the void that most properly defines our being. Put another way: we are only what we compel ourselves to do, *through* the actions that we take. As such, humanity confuses the will for the self and simultaneously demonstrates how the fiction of sovereignty has no substance but is only conceived through its being enacted. This is the activity that will define the self-referential identity of the sovereign: the sovereign is the one who *acts* as sovereign, or as Carl Schmitt had put it, who *decides* – a theoretical point that has been heavily influential upon Agamben's thought throughout the years.[3]

We see such a dynamic illustrated in Agamben's short volume *Stasis* where the unity espoused by a 'multitude of citizens in a single person is something like a perspectival illusion' (S 33/OHS 273). This 'perspectival illusion', a point he develops in conversation with the political thought of Thomas Hobbes, is what will allow him to conclude that 'political representation is only an optical representation (but no less effective on account of this)' (S 33/OHS 273). What we are left with is a situation where the multitude, or 'the people', appears as 'absolutely present' at the same time that they are also 'never present', leading us to formulate political representation as the only possible solution to this paradoxical and illusory situation that is yet constitutive of politics (S 40/OHS 280). Describing this context also provides an explanation of why the potential for civil war characterises every political body, since it is this division that permanently marks it (S 49/OHS 287).

Second, it is due to the fiction of sovereignty that our focus must be placed on returning politics to its central notion of inoperativity, or the void at the heart of its existence, as the 'properly human and political praxis' (KG xiii/OHS 371). This void is what becomes illustrated by the political symbol of the empty throne, which preserves the space for power without anyone being present in it. There is even a sacrality that permeates its existence and which is inextricably linked to the excluded figure of the *homo sacer*. Agamben's analyses, especially as taken up in his genealogical study *The Kingdom and the Glory*, are aimed at trying to profane this potent symbol of sovereign glory in order to 'make room, beyond it' for an eternal life that is not one lauded by theologians. Historical liturgies and rituals do however offer more insight on its existence than direct analyses of sovereign power, as they articulate the emptiness at the centre of power that was bound up with theological discussions on the nature of divine being (KG xii–xiii/OHS 370). It is therefore necessary, as we see over and again in the series, for Agamben to take his time in conducting various genealogical studies of these theological discussions (e.g. glory, economy, liturgy, oaths and so forth) that have surrounded and signalled the operations of sovereign power in general throughout the centuries, and as we saw briefly in the introduction.[4]

And, third, traditional forms of sovereignty become accessible through the implementation of particular political theologies based on notions of *transcendent* governance – a point that Agamben derived from the work of Michel Foucault. Conversely, economic theologies, or particular forms of governmentality which oversee everyday relations, are based on an *immanent* governance of our world (KG 1/OHS 373). Historical configurations of political philosophy are mainly based on the former while biopolitics, as it was developed by Foucault, is mainly based on the latter, though they are so thoroughly intermingled that they can often appear as indistinguishable. Governmentality, however, promotes an ever-changing reality that is always evolving as it is engaged in the management of everyday life, hence there is a tendency to present this side of life as a reality without illusions (and as also having no end). Governance seems, in this case of biopolitics, to not just play the foil to sovereignty's transcendence, but to have all the substance. Unlike sovereignty, which only exists insofar as we act it out (a point I will return to below), governance has always existed and does not come 'from nothing' (*ex nihilo*, as many theologians would have it), but derives solely from nature. From this point of view, one can see why modern rejections of transcendence have accompanied pantheistic sentiments regarding nature, for if sovereignty is a fiction, governance is not as easy to dismiss as a purely necessary illusion. Rather, by definition, governance relies upon its *not* being illusory – that is, on its attempts to trace to its end the material realities that *do* exist and can be explored, perhaps not exhaustively, but always seeking to be as exhaustive as possible. This is why such forces are always bureaucratic in nature.

Though Agamben does not develop this particular example in any detail, we see this tension appear in the history of the debates that existed between the Jansenists and the Jesuits. The Jansenists argued for a sovereign deity who predetermines every event in our world, and who is even willing to intervene in natural events in order to exert God's sovereign self. On the other hand, the Jesuits were frequently accused of casuistry, or of making moral decisions on a case-by-case basis after one's conscience is first formed, giving space to a God who is said to exist 'in all things'. It is no surprise that such reasoning is the basis for modern law codes, as this is indicative of the ways in which an entirely immanent liberalism determines how everything falls under the jurisdiction of law. There is nothing outside of the law in this sense, no miraculous interventions, and this is as frustrating to those seeking to exert sovereign authority as it is exhausting to those who come up against its bureaucratic and legalistic ethos.[5] As Agamben, again following Schmitt closely, will express matters, the secular-liberal paradigm allows for no exceptions (within law) and so no miracles are possible, whereas the sovereign religious paradigm insists upon the miraculous as essential to founding any political-theological order.

These introductory remarks on the fiction of sovereignty are meant to illustrate the bipolar nature of the political and anthropological machinery – in other words, those apparatuses that manufacture the 'human being' through the presupposition of being. These are the apparatuses that Agamben places under intense scrutiny in this series, as they have been utilised in the West, in order to link together sovereignty and governance, the capacity to reign and the ability to rule. As he outlines in *The Kingdom and the Glory* in particular, Trinitarian *oikonomia* became 'a privileged laboratory' for observing this fractured and fracturing machinery divided between Kingdom and Government, or glory and *oikonomia*.[6] This construction, moreover, parallels the divisions between *auctoritas* and *potestas*, or actuality and potentiality, as analysed in his earlier volume *State of Exception* (KG xi–xii/OHS 369). Each of these dualistic tensions are the result of our being having been captured and divided so that sovereignty itself might appear in our world.

The logic of presupposition that Agamben develops in *The Use of Bodies* in fact dictates that our being is divided into a dualistic tension (as between transcendence/immanence, sovereignty/governmentality) that cannot be effaced. Rather it is a tension that is necessary in order to form a matrix of intelligibility, what we commonly call the realm of representations, especially linguistic representations. Agamben discerns how such dualistic divisions are embedded in politics 'as usual' and they are the very reason why such fictions cannot simply be dismissed from human operations, but are considered as necessary illusions. Symbolic networks of meaning rely upon pre-established representations in order to maintain, but also to evolve, a structure (e.g. language, culture, religion) wherein a given duality is joined with other dualities in order to legitimate a given cosmology composed of interlinking dualisms that subsequently appear as the nature of things. Immanence/transcendence, contingency/necessity, potentiality/actuality, spirituality/materiality and so forth, become the polarities upon which our representations are based and widely shared. The connections between concepts aligned on a given side of dualistic tensions are solidified in order to legitimate a particular political nexus of relations (e.g. a sovereign deity acts out of necessity, whereas the world and its materiality are contingently immanent). A particular order or cosmology is justified and adopted as 'natural' in such ways, though the existence of such tensions also dictates that we never rest easy with the divisions. Subsequently, we frequently (re)align our political contestations upon their antagonistic deployment.

Agamben creatively makes the argument that paradigm shifts in thought occur when a particular duality involving a decisive scission or division is reversed so that the alignment is forcibly adjusted in one instance, while allowing the other dualisms to remain connected as they had been previously. Yet, despite the fact that we believe a paradigm to have shifted, giving rise ultimately to new forms of thought and new configurations within the various modes of existence (e.g. politics, religion, economics, culture and so on), the truth is that:

1. nothing has really changed, as the pre-existing dualisms will inevitably reconfigure themselves according to prior configurations though in new circumstances – i.e. every configuration will be infinitely explored, implemented, retracted and then repeated again, and
2. what has really been revealed is the fact that the dualisms are really not fixed and might be manipulated in a variety of ways for particular political ends.

In other words, we continue to repeat the same fractures throughout history and seem bound to do so endlessly as the cost of utilising representation or language at all. These fractures are constitutive of the human being's situatedness in this world because the apparatuses that presuppose our being (i.e. language, or really anything that attempts to shape or control our humanity) are what continue to define humanity, even as they reduce its innate fullness to a series of labels and conditions.

This is where the significance of Agamben's efforts in *The Use of Bodies*, to establish a modal ontology in the vein of Spinoza, becomes extremely relevant.[7] As Agamben's ontology follows Spinoza, it becomes a rejection of traditional onto-theological notions of substance, while also providing a way toward new political and ethical configurations based on the respect for forms-of-life that seek after an 'intimacy without relations' (with 'relations' being any prescribed normative or shaping behaviour imposed on human beings). However, there can be no mistaken impressions that Agamben's critical analyses have not brought about a complete rethinking of the roles of politics and theology if contemplated from this philosophical point of view, for they most certainly have. This is something that will distinguish his political-theological conclusions from those of Carl Schmitt, whom he has cited frequently and that I also want to demonstrate more directly through a look at his analyses given throughout the *Homo Sacer* series of the various contestations of the divine being – the fundamental symbol of the fiction of sovereignty – throughout history.

## OATHS, LANGUAGE AND THE DIVINE NAME

One of the most direct challenges to divine being is highlighted in his analysis of the name of God in relation to the taking of oaths – an ancient practice of swearing a promise that often depended upon the invocation of a divine being. As discussed in *The Sacrament of Language*, the gods are subject to oaths, which are themselves 'the most worthy thing' (SL 19/OHS 314). This suggestion establishes oaths as more ancient than the gods in a sense that is not entirely chronological, though it does perhaps point toward an originary location prior to the establishment of deities and religious propositions. In his words, 'According to this testimony, the oath is the most ancient thing, no less ancient than the gods, who are in fact subject to it in some way' (SL 19/OHS 314). What Agamben reveals is that the oaths of humans have been established and maintained as they try 'to conform human language to this divine model' (SL 21/OHS 316). In this sense, the oath is one of the first principles of metaphysics, among the 'first principles' of philosophy, as he puts it (SL 18–19/OHS 314–15). It is through his genealogical study of the oath, then, that we see him put some distance between his thoughts on metaphysics and the purely logical speculations of Aristotle.

The words of God are in fact oaths (SL 20–2/OHS 315, 317). This is a point that will converge with his later development of an ontology of command that has dominated Western theological articulations of the divine being and which eventually culminates in Kant's establishment of an ethics upon a notion of duty. At this point, the oath serves to legitimate divine being in a way that likewise calls the divine being's sovereignty into question: 'On the one hand, in the oath human language communicates with that of God; on the other hand, if God is the being whose words are oaths, it is completely impossible to decide if he is reliable because of the oath or if the oath is reliable because of God' (SL 22/OHS 317). Oaths and God are inseparable, as the nature of the oath reflects the nature of the divine: things are established in both contexts through the act of calling something into being, and thereby bringing about the substance of the being itself. This is the foundational principle of any substantial ontotheological claim regarding the divine inasmuch as it is the definition of the oath at the same time.

It is in this manner that Agamben reminds us of the metaphysical implications of oaths. The oath is marked historically as a form of *sacratio*, as it was used in ceremonies that rendered a man (*homo*) as *sacer*, or consecrated to the gods, but excluded him from the community and liable to be killed (SL 29–30/OHS 323).

This was of course the main issue taken up in the first volume of the series, *Homo Sacer*. This deep political structure of the oath, and so of the command that undergirds an ontological form, is revealed as the substratum of politics in the West, much as Agamben had discussed it earlier in the project. As such, the oath is implicated in the establishment of the most fundamental political conceptualisations: exclusion, separation and sacrifice.

The oath functions as a form of self-consecration, allowing the subject to bring itself into being *as* self. This is only possible as a tautological circumscription that characterises sovereign power as the only power that can found itself (traditionally, theologically, *ex nihilo*). The oath serves as an affirmation or invocation of God as both a witness and a curse, forming a 'single institution' that links faith, oath and sacrament, with sacrament being a general sense of sacrality associated with any oath-taking rites (SL 31–2/OHS 324). The oath, witness and God 'coincide in the utterance of the formula' that invokes the deity (SL 33/OHS 326). This juxtaposition brings about a convergence which highlights the potentiality, or 'signifying power of language', within every speech act and as what links the *logos* to the foundations of religion, especially as Christianity elevates this connection to its central tenet.

If all the names of the gods in polytheism are actually events or actions, as the event of language itself, then every act of naming becomes an oath, leaving the name of the God within monotheism as a 'seal of this force of *logos*' wherein names are purely semiotic, like an interjection (SL 46–7/OHS 335–6). Monotheism is deeply implicated in the presupposition of being that language introduces into our world. Agamben – in perhaps the most significant claim he will make about monotheism's relationship to language and to the origins of the sacred in our world – will further describe this state of things:

> One can thus understand the essential primacy of the name of God in monotheistic religions, its identification with and almost substitution for the God it names. If, in polytheism, the name *assigned to* the god named this or that event in language, this or

that specific naming, this or that *Sondergott* ['special god'], in monotheism *God's* name names language itself. The potentially infinite dissemination of singular, divine events of naming gives way to the divinization of the *logos* as such, to the name of God as archi-event of language that takes place in names. Language is the word of God, and the word of God is, in the words of Philo, an oath: it is God insofar as he reveals himself in the *logos* as the 'faithful one' (*pistos*) par excellence. God is the oath-taker in the language of which man is only the speaker, but in the oath on the name of God the language of men communicates with divine language. (SL 49–50/OHS 338)

Faith is entirely bound up with the existence of the oath. It is the ability to testify to one's relationship to language which cannot actually be said *in* language. Within this illumination of relations, the mystery of language becomes the *sacrament* of language itself insofar as human beings search to name their God through their relationship *to* language. Here we can begin to understand the mystery and importance surrounding the Hebrew peoples' naming of God through the Tetragrammaton (YHWH) and the accompanying Cabbala's investment in locating within God's name the 'origin of all language' (SL 50–1/OHS 339), as well as why Agamben finds it helpful on numerous occasions to draw assistance from the writings of both Walter Benjamin and Gershom Scholem on various Jewish topics such as these.

Ontological implications subsequently abound within the history of theology as a particular experience of language becomes the experience of faith itself (SL 52/OHS 340). This is what we encounter, for example, with Anselm of Canterbury's providing a proof of God's existence as the highest thing that can be thought. In Agamben's words, 'the name of God expresses the status of the *logos* in the dimension of the *fides* oath, in which nomination immediately actualizes the existence of what it names' (SL 52–3/OHS 340). As he will further clarify:

> We can therefore specify further the meaning and function of the name of God in the oath. Every oath swears on the name par excellence, that is on the name of God, because the oath is the experience

> of language that treats all of language as a proper name. Pure existence – the existence of the name – is not the result of a recognition, nor of a logical deduction: it is something that cannot be signified but only sworn, that is, affirmed as a name. The certainty of faith is the certainty of the name (of God). (SL 53/OHS 341)

In this formulation, we can also trace the movements of sovereignty and those commands which are fundamentally at their core, as Agamben will later develop, part of an ontology of command. The sovereign action is to name things as if it were an oath that were being taken or adhered to. It is to let every word fall as an act of naming and to produce a judgement upon whatever one speaks to. Consequently, the movement of sovereignty and its command 'cannot be signified, but only sworn'. In his words, 'To speak is, above all, to swear, to believe in the name' (SL 54/OHS 341).

What this all boils down to is that the ontological argument 'says that if speech exists, then God exists' rendering ontotheology as a linguistic performance and leaving Agamben to conceive of metaphysics as that which coincides with the experience of language (SL 56/OHS 343). In line with the analysis I have been pursuing so far, this is the performance of sovereignty that gives rise to the sovereign in the first place – again, a tautological construct in which the sovereign gives itself its position *as sovereign* through an act devoid of any real substance. What we are witnessing is a parallel formation to the existence of language itself, which, in its own existence as mere words, is certainly also devoid of substance. We live, however, as if all of our speech and writing somehow allow language to achieve a substance of its own, making it perhaps the most significant apparatus within human existence. However, our linguistic existence is also an experience that cannot actually be said *in* language, or *with* words. In this manner, Agamben will claim, it is actually the decline in the legitimacy of the oath, or that which reveals the fragility of language as a human apparatus, that we in the West have taken to calling the 'death of God', or what is really the death of the *name* of God.[8]

## Religious and Political Implications

In a stunningly lucid passage that brings together the death of God with the name of God and its decline, Agamben expresses a significant revision of the history of metaphysics:

> Considered in this perspective, the ontological (or onto-theological) argument simply says that if speech exists, then God exists, and God is the expression of this metaphysical 'performance.' In it, sense and denotation, essence and existence coincide, the existence of God and his essence are one sole and identical thing. That which results performatively from the pure existence of language exists purely and simply (*on haplōs*). (Paraphrasing a thesis of Wittgenstein, one could say that the existence of language is the performative expression of the existence of the world.) Ontotheology is, therefore, a performance of language and is in solidarity with a certain experience of language (that which is at issue in the oath), in the sense that its validity and its decline coincide with the strength and decline of this experience. In this sense metaphysics, the science of pure being, is itself historical and coincides with the experience of the event of language to which man devotes himself in the oath. If the oath is declining, if the name of God is withdrawing from language – and this is what has happened beginning from the event that has been called the 'death of God' or, as one should put it more exactly, 'of the name of God' – then metaphysics also reaches completion. (SL 56/OHS 343)

Since the use of the oath is linked with the profession of faith, what we are witness to is a 'split in the experience of language' that gives birth to both law and religion (SL 58–9/OHS 34–5). This is where the 'sacrament of power' is forged, in the close bond between language and the human being. For Agamben, power becomes vested in its many human guises, most frequently in some formulation of sovereignty that conditions all subsequent human relations. Sovereign power, in this sense, depends upon the same sacramental origins that language does, as both give rise to the human species as that which identifies itself through its 'origins' in language. The power of the sovereign is inherently grounded on the same premises as the instantiation of language, giving both language and power a sacramental quality that defies any attempts to locate its 'origins' and so displace them.

This site is where language, through its very existence, puts human life in question wherein the 'oath is situated at their intersection, understood as the anthropogenic operator' (SL 69/OHS 353). This is also where the human being uses the *logos* to constitute themselves – hence displaying a power that could only be considered *as* sovereign – as the 'living being who has language'. As such, only humans can 'promise themselves' to the *logos* and through this promise only a bond, or sense of belonging together as human beings, is produced. As Agamben will phrase things, the human being is the one who makes language their own and who possesses the 'I' (SL 71/OHS 355).

Since we live in the modern secular age of the 'death of God', we acutely experience how living without the oath means changing our usual political associations, which are no longer based on the word being established as a bond between persons (SL 70/OHS 354). Hence, Agamben will argue, we live in an age of blasphemy that is entirely dependent upon the secularised laws that govern our world (i.e. governmentality), bereft of the legitimations for sovereignty that we had been reliant upon previously. God's name can only be uttered 'in vain', as the decline in the power of God's name indicates a concomitant decline in those justifications for sovereign power. Accompanying this decline is the descent of the power of language itself, once bound to the name of God, a decline indicating too that perhaps the prestige of language needs to be questioned in a way it had previously never been.

*Or*, I want to ask, are we to also sense here Agamben's longing to restore, or re-legitimate, the fiction of sovereignty? Readers can understandably be divided on just this issue, as it is not always clear if Agamben wishes to renounce language altogether (identified at times when he declares language no more important than 'birdsong'), or if he wants to reveal the messianic, deconstructive element *within* language that shadows language at every turn. As his analysis makes clear, one cannot dispense with sovereign power if one does not also dispense with language, since both maintain the same sacramental 'origins'. At least this is the conundrum that often appears to readers of his work: how are we to be done with all apparatuses like language (*logos*) and law (*nomos*) that shape and control humanity (hence their possible *anti-nomos*, or antinomian, quality) so that our being is no longer simply presupposed and a form-of-life can emerge?

We can at least note that Agamben tries on occasion to resolve this aporia of language and existence through recourse to the way in which a messianic element within language deconstructs language, as well as all identities, representations, institutions and so forth. Hence, he is certainly focused on the *anomic* element latent within every structure, institution, history or identity. As I have and will continue to argue, such a claim is a major philosophical issue that needs to be further clarified in his work. As Agamben will illustrate, philosophy begins its operations by putting 'in question the primacy of names' and the 'sacramental bond that links the human being to language, without for that reason simply speaking haphazardly, falling into the vanity of speech' (SL 72/OHS 355). This is a move that is parallel to his reading of Plato whom Agamben suggests renounces the 'idea of an exact correspondence between the name and the thing named' (SL 72/OHS 355). Philosophy becomes as such a critique of the oath, a movement of resistance and change that appears to oppose whatever structure or normative order establishes a given part of society.

What is not always as clear, however, is whether or not philosophy is to be equated with the liberalism that antagonises the fiction of sovereignty. At least from one angle, the answer would seem to be that they are not to be equated as the juridical-religious is opposed to the philosophical-scientific, meaning that the former is split by the latter. If the juridical-religious is traversed by the divine name that philosophy rigorously critiques, another question therefore remains: what is left of the divine, and the sovereignty such a figure signifies, within Agamben's project?

As mentioned above, such an expression of the divine name as pronounced in oaths is entirely bound up with an ontology of performance and of operativity, as was formulated eventually in Kant's work as an ontology of command and as the ontology that would come to dominate modernity, according to Agamben (OD 118/OHS 744). As he will discuss matters in *Opus Dei*, we can locate such operations within the role of the will in the West, but also within those who present a monotheistic God who 'speaks in the imperative and to whom one speaks in the same verbal mode in worship and prayer' (OD 119/OHS 745). In essence, these are performative issues surrounding the existence of the monotheistic God and of God's 'having to be' established repeatedly through language – again, the very performance that grounds any sovereign power. This suggestion goes a long way toward helping us understand why proofs for God's existence continuously creep into the centre of Western theological discourse, as these proofs actually provide the foundations *for* God's existence. In other words, God only exists insofar as we strive to prove that God exists *in* our economy of representations, and so *in* our language. And it is the performance of such proofs that ultimately establishes God *as* sovereign (and despite God's complete lack of actual substance).

What is revealed philosophically by Agamben is that Kant's transcendental philosophy 'means precisely that an ontology of having-to-be has already taken the place of the ontology of being' (OD 121/OHS 747). This is a point that Agamben notes repeatedly – with a particular tension embedded within it – that cannot be escaped:

> There are, that is to say, two distinct and connected ontologies in the tradition of the West: the first, the ontology of the command, proper to the juridical-religious sphere, which is expressed in the imperative and has a performative character; the second, proper to the philosophical-scientific tradition, which is expressed in the form of the indicative (or, in a substantivated form, in the infinitive or participle – *esti, einai, on*, 'is,' 'to be,' 'being'). The ontology

of *estō* and of 'be!' refers to a having-to-be; that of *esti* and of 'is' relate to being. Clearly distinct and in many ways opposed, the two ontologies live together, struggle with each other, and nevertheless never cease to intersect, to hybridize, and to prevail over one another by turns in the history of the West. (OD 120/OHS 745–6)

And, as he continues:

> At the threshold of modernity, when theology and metaphysics seemed to definitely cede the field to scientific rationality, Kant's thought represents the secularized reappropriation of the ontology of *estō* in the bosom of the ontology of *esti*, the catastrophic reemergence of law and religion in the bosom of philosophy. In the face of the triumph of scientific knowledge, Kant sought to secure the survival of metaphysics, engrafting the ontology of command and having-to-be into that of being and substance and allowing it to act there. He believed himself to have secured in this way the possibility of metaphysics and to have founded, at the same time, an ethics that was neither juridical nor religious. Yet on the one hand, he welcomed the inheritance of the theological-liturgical tradition of *officium* and operativity without rendering an account of it, and on the other, he took leave of classical ontology in a lasting way. (OD 122/OHS 747)

In essence, Agamben will suggest that Kant 'substituted an ontology of command for an ontology of substance', a movement that ultimately revealed what had been at stake all along within an ontology of command (OD 122/OHS 747): the establishment of a substance utilised to naturalise and legitimate sovereign forms, from God to the King to the self. In a way that Kant was very attentive to, such figures are established through the construction of, and justification given for, the will. Hence, we can note too the way in which the will is developed philosophically to explain the movement from potency (potentiality) to act (actuality) within the history of Western thought:

> The ontology of command and the ontology of operativity are therefore closely bound: as a putting-to-work, the command also

presupposes a will. According to the formula that expresses the prince's command (*sic volo, sic iudeo*) ['I will it, I command it'], 'willing' can only mean 'commanding,' and 'commanding' necessarily implies a will. Will is the form that being takes in the ontology of command and operativity. If being does not exist, but must actualize itself, then in its very essence it is will and command; and vice versa, if being is will, then it does not simply exist but has to be. The problem of the coming philosophy is that of thinking an ontology beyond operativity and command and an ethics and a politics entirely liberated from the concepts of duty and will. (OD 129/OHS 752)

This ontology of the will, as an ontology of *command*, is significantly contrasted in his work with an ontology of *demand*, which will be linked explicitly to Spinoza's elaboration of the *conatus* (the term that Spinoza had once used to signal the pure desire to survive on the part of a being). This is a point that will once again cement not only the importance of a modal ontology in Agamben's work, but his overall indebtedness to Spinoza's way of thinking. Before turning toward the ontology of demand, however, what I want to pursue further at this point is how such a contrast is played out in Agamben's formulations of the tensions that permeate the sphere of political-theological thinking, specifically in the historical notions of the divine that have been constructed either through an ontology of command or an ontology of demand. This tension can be seen, for example, in how Agamben traces the antagonistic dualisms that govern philosophical inquiry far back to the origins of religion in the West.

## ON GOD AND GODS FROM THE POINT OF VIEW OF A MODAL ONTOLOGY

There is no doubt that the conceptualisations and symbols of sovereign power that permeated the ancient Roman world overlap with Christian themes in important ways. As Agamben points out in *The Kingdom and the Glory*, the correspondence liturgically between theological claims and pagan emperors (KG 168–71/OHS 524–6), as well as the acclamations and consensus found in direct democracies (KG 170/OHS 526), is an unavoidable sign that sovereign power managed to make a seamless transition from the one sphere to the other through the implementation of certain theological claims. As with his study of the oath, which went back to an archaic source before the split between magic, law and religion, so too does Agamben's study of glory intend to direct us,

> pushing back the origin of these essentially Christian expressions to a more obscure foundation in which they overlap with the acclamations of the pagan emperors and with the cries that greeted the epiphany of Dionysius in the Orphic rituals, with the exorcisms of the magical papyruses and the formulae of the Mithraic, Gnostic, and Manichean mysteric cults. It also means posing the problem of the origin and significance of the acclamations and their relation with Christian liturgy. (KG 169/OHS 524)

It is from this presupposition that Agamben begins his genealogical analyses of various resonances between the ancient Roman world and Christian liturgical rites. For example, we can note:

- the 'theologico-sacred' character of the divine monarch's relationship with his subjects;
- the kissing of feet, royal robes, crown of laurels, and the throne, the colour purple, specific postures taken with regard to power and other ceremonial objects, including the flag;
- gestures and performative acts that are arranged through the suspension of the normal character of language, which is a signature;
- the fasces as an effective symbol of imperial power;
- the performative aspects of such objects that are not simply for pomp, but 'the key to understanding the decisive transformations of the constitution' – that is to say, it 'is not merely aesthetic', but a political, juridical and public liturgical performance;
- and this list could go on.

There are also those acclamations of Roman emperors related to Christological military symbols:

- the joining of 'ecclesiastical liturgy and profane protocol';
- the link between modern totalitarian regimes and the new holiday of 'Christ the King'; and
- the example of the liturgical chants used in imperial Rome and at the racetracks (see KG 174–92/OHS 529–46 for all of the above examples).[9]

Each of these examples lifts up and secures a fundamental connection between theological justifications for divine power and glory and the power wielded by sovereign authorities entirely within our world.

What all of these examples point toward is the indistinguishable sphere where the religious, the juridical and the magical blur together (KG 188/OHS 542). This is, as suggested by Agamben, portrayed in the Egyptologist Jan Assmann's response to Carl Schmitt's claim that all political concepts are secularised theological ones. In contrast, Agamben avers, all 'significant concepts of theology are theologized political concepts' (KG 193/OHS 547). This intuition further confirms the fact wherein certain periods of history tell us how the Pope and the Emperor adore each other, how glory is where they coincide and how there is really no 'body or substance' to the power they wield. This context is what gives rise to glory, as glory exists primarily to conceal the absence of any substance. It is the mystical aura that cloaks a lack of being. In many ways, this is where we can eventually locate too a modal ontology that will become so important to Agamben in the *Homo Sacer* series. That is, when there is no presumed relation to substance that must be essentially claimed, a 'whatever' mode of being ('form-of-life') can appear in the void of a necessary substance.[10] This is what had made the extreme crises experienced within the historical context of Auschwitz so catastrophic: the normal use of modal categories had collapsed, when the 'impossible is forced into the real' and contingency is cancelled in favour of an 'absolute necessity' become violence itself embodied (RA 148/OHS 859).

What the various acclamations that were exposed through the overlap in religious and political power demonstrate is that the tensions between the monarchy (including the office of the papacy to be sure) and the threatened division of its unity, either through recourse to some primordial polytheism or Trinitarian theology, are eventually resolved by the concept of *oikonomia*. As we have already seen, *oikonomia* is a concept that theologians were not slow to exploit in order to legitimate sovereign power (KG 35–6/ OHS 403–4). And as Agamben will declare through his genealogy of the term, *oikonomia* does not have contradictory meanings but two meanings that are inseparable from each other: 'the internal organization of divine life, and that which concerns the history of salvation', as well as 'ontology and pragmatics, Trinitarian articulation and government of the world' (KG 51/OHS 418). Hence *oikonomia* was first introduced into the history of theology in order 'to avoid a fracture of monotheism that would have reintroduced a plurality of divine figures, and polytheism with them' (KG 53/OHS 419). However, it is in this way that a plurality is preserved at the heart of a unity. The divine being is not fractured forever precisely because it *is* divided on the level of *oikonomia*, and so not in its being or ontology. This is, according to Agamben, the 'secret dualism' he claims was introduced into Christian thought by Gnosticism and that Christianity cannot leave behind, being that which goes beyond simply grafting Aristotle's unmoved mover into a Christian context.[11] As such, Christianity is forced to forever deal with a practical and not ontological problem at its core (KG 54/OHS 420).

> In Gnosis, the opposition between a god who is foreign to the world and a demiurge who governs it is more essential than that between a good and an evil god. Both Irenaeus and Tertullian clearly grasp this 'idle' and 'Epicurean' character of Marcion's and Cerdo's good God, to whom they oppose a God who is, at the

same time, good and active in all creation. Irenaeus writes that 'they found out the god of Epicurus, who does nothing either for himself or others'. And according to Tertullian, Marcion would have attributed 'the name of Christ [to] a god out of the school of Epicurus'. (KG 55/OHS 420–1)

It is interesting here that the figure of Epicurus enters, and not insignificantly, as he represents a movement of resistance within philosophical thought to these theological speculations, and which may play a much larger role in Agamben's thought – as it once did in Spinoza's – than many have taken it to be.

One of the reasons that it is often difficult to trace the philosophical influences upon Agamben's own constructive thought is the fact that he often seeks to efface the reference to a particular author or work so that his own position does not rely upon the authority of another, but is taken at face value within the context of an ongoing argument. Though this technique of erasing citations leaves readers struggling at times to comprehend the background for some of his philosophical, political and theological claims, it is also a technique easily merged with the genealogical methods he utilises and which point toward original, synthetic readings of historical-conceptual developments. For this same reason, however, it is of particular significance when a given author is cited, even (and perhaps especially) in passing, for their entrance signals a reference of meaning that cannot be neglected.[12]

Referring to Epicurus in this context explicitly represents the movement away from divine legitimation for natural activity within our world, as well as, through Lucretius' *On the Nature of Things*, serving as a reminder of the driving force behind much of modern humanist and atheist thought.[13] For Agamben, Epicurus comes to represent one side in a seemingly eternal struggle to describe the dualistic tendencies for characterising the divine which are carried over from antiquity directly into Christian theological attempts to formulate the economic identity of God.[14]

Beyond simply being able to characterise most dualisms within our world as caught up in such divisions – from the left/right, liberal/conservative dualisms, as well as the management versus leadership paradigms in business and politics today – readers of Agamben's work are witnesses to a complete rethinking of Western ontology and all that it presupposes. For example, from this perspective, whatever order we observe in our world is a relation and not a substance, a point that Agamben discerns first at work in Aristotle's *Metaphysics* (KG 83/OHS 445), but which he puts a completely new spin on in his own reflections. The relation of transcendence and immanence is really one between ontology and praxis that has been grafted onto a theological spectrum – this is Agamben's original contribution to the metaphysical debates that have raged for centuries. *Taxis*, or order, is what for Agamben essentially 'names' the 'aporetic relation' between God and world (KG 84/OHS 446). 'Things are ordered insofar as they have a specific relation among themselves, but this relation is nothing other than the expression of their relation to the divine end' (KG 87/OHS 448). There is therefore a trace element (or what he will come to call a 'signature') of order perceptible in our world that keeps together 'substance and relation, ontology and praxis'. Likewise, immanence and transcendence refer to each other as a 'paradoxical coincidence' that defines the economy that binds them together (KG 89/OHS 451). In this sense, order is said to exist because it perpetually heals the permanent fracture between these dualistic ends (KG 90/OHS 452). Through an extended discussion of those relations established between primary and secondary power (KG 102/OHS 462), authority and execution (KG 103/OHS 463) and absolute and ordered power (KG 104/OHS 464), Agamben is able to demonstrate how these distinctions are drawn in a dualistic fashion because God's omnipotence appears as limited at times, leaving theologians to debate *oikonomia* as an attempt to reconcile the world's order with God's omnipotence (KG 105/OHS 465). Accordingly, free will appears as an option to humanity because it offers a response to how 'God's impotence functions to make possible a righteous government of the world' (KG 106/OHS 466).

It is from this point of view that we can best perceive the rise of deism in the modern period alongside the problem of providence and free will (KG 114/OHS 474). As Agamben will remind us, the modern division of powers we see in our world is rooted in a providential machinery wherein 'fate depends on God, and is nothing else but "the economy itself [...]"' (KG 136/OHS 494). Providence is forever linked as such with grace, which is the 'higher' way of governing (KG 136–7/OHS 495). In a more precise sense, divine government has nature and grace as its 'two eminent modes' wherein grace cannot prevent free will from being exercised. As Agamben will conclude, the providential paradigm of government 'is not tyrannical, but democratic'. In other words, 'Providence represents, in the same sense and to the same extent, an attempt to reconcile the Gnostic splitting between a God who is foreign to the world and a God that governs, which Christian theology had inherited through the "economical" articulation of the Father and the Son' (KG 140/OHS 498). At the same time as providence attempts this reconciliation, it also posits the existence of another paradigm of political thought: the democratic one, in contrast with the political-theological one of absolutism, as previously noted (KG 142/OHS 500).

What we observe in Agamben's thought, as much as in the history of the Church generally – such as we see through the existence and challenges of the Gnostics, Cathars, Albigensians, or so many other heretical movements– are the dualisms of operative/inoperative and transcendence/immanence preserved within the heart of theological teachings (KG 78/OHS 441). In this light, we witness the early heretic Marcion as a gnostic supporter who produced another 'Gnostic antinomy between a god who is foreign to the world and an earthly demiurge' (KG 79/OHS 442), but also the Christian *oikonomia* as trying to overcome Marcionism by inserting this division within God's own being so as to reconcile 'the divinity's noninvolvement with the world with its government' (KG 79/OHS 442), much as I already indicated.

Such a dualistic tendency within Christian doctrine is embedded that much further by the incorporation of Aristotelian thought and its categorical dualities that seek to incorporate one side within the other, and vice versa. This is, once again, the logic of presupposition that allows us to see how these doctrines, as with language, are apparatuses that capture and control the beings that they presuppose. They do so by introducing a fundamental, bipolar division within being. In this context, the God who is the immovable mover and the 'thought of thought' illustrates transcendence and immanence as inseparable and as part of the machinery that holds together the two sides. Transcendence 'defined by means of the traditional terms of separation and autonomy' combines itself with a form of immanence that defines order (*taxis*) (KG 80/OHS 443). The immovable mover as transcendent *arche* and immanent order as *physis* are forever combined in an intricate relationship, which is how Aristotle had once himself linked sovereignty to nature (KG 82/OHS 444). (It is also how Aristotle will link the division between potentiality and actuality at the heart of Western metaphysics, as we will later see.)

Such connections are what will further lead Agamben to discern how 'Power – every power, both human and divine – must hold these two poles together, that is, it must be, at the same time, kingdom and government, transcendent norm and immanent order' (KG 82/OHS 444). The existence of these dualisms is how kingdom and government are brought into close alignment, and inseparably intertwined. It is also the formulation of political and ontological thought that is foundational to Western metaphysics. It asserts a linkage between ontology and politics, or being and acting, which cannot be severed (KG 84/OHS 446). Hence, the 'content of the transcendent order is the immanent order' and 'the meaning of immanent order is nothing other than the relation to the transcendent end' (KG 87/OHS 449). Order tries to think a balance in theoretical terms between the extremes of pantheism and a Gnostic foreign deity.

> The perfect theocentric edifice of medieval ontology is based on this circle, and does not have any consistency outside of it. The Christian God is this circle, in which the two orders continuously penetrate one another. Since that which the order must keep united is in point of fact irremediably divided, not only is *ordo* – like Aristotle's being – *dicitur multipliciter* [several answers] [. . .], but *ordo* also reproduces in its own structure the ambiguity that it must face. From this follows the contradiction, noticed by scholars, according to which Thomas at times founds the order of the world in the unity of God, and at times the unity of God in the immanent order of creatures. This apparent contradiction is nothing other than the expression of the ontological fracture between transcendence and immanence, which Christian theology inherits and develops from Aristotelianism. If we push to the limit the paradigm of the separate substance, we have the Gnosis, with its God foreign to the world and creation; if we follow to the end the paradigm of immanence, we have pantheism. Between these two extremes, the idea of order tries to think a difficult balance, which Christian theology is always in the process of losing and which it must at each turn regain. (KG 87/OHS 449)

Pantheism, practically speaking, becomes a form of atheism in that it articulates the position of those who deny divine governance of the world, not God's existence (OD 108–9/OHS 737). Hence, we are told, Leibniz could accurately label Spinoza as an atheist while preserving room for an ethics to develop through the establishment of an *officium* (or that which defines one's duty or service through the position, or 'office', established). Divine governance and human actions are linked, Agamben will further suggest, so that critiques of Spinoza are really a defence of divine governance and human action (OD 110/OHS 738) – a point that, once again, drives home Agamben's defence of Spinoza's philosophy on the whole.

In this sense, liberalism tries to elevate the supremacy of 'the pole of the "immanent order-government-stomach" to the point that it almost eliminates the pole "transcendent God-kingdom-brain"' (KG 284–5/OHS 630), yet they are also inseparable (KG 285/OHS 631). They cannot just be opposed as if 'secularism and the general will' stood opposite to 'theology and its providential paradigm' (KG 285/OHS 630). They secretly need each other, which leads to a situation wherein 'theology can resolve itself into atheism, and providentialism into democracy, because *God has made the world as if it were without God and governs it as though it governed itself*' (KG 286/OHS 631, emphasis in the original). Modernity did not leave God behind, but placed these theological ideas firmly at its core, through the governmental paradigm that still goes unrecognised today within the spheres of politics as we have come to know them.

## AN ONTOLOGY OF DEMAND

What Agamben wants to rehabilitate in order to see things differently arranged within our world is a Spinozistic reading of a modal ontology that may certainly be mistaken for pantheism, but which is not merely a playing out of the pantheism that is generated by the liberal-secular governance of the universe that typically operates in opposition to the sovereign deity's kingdom. The ambiguity of this modal ontology (as it speaks to the variety of the modes of existence), 'insofar as it seeks to think the coincidence or indifference of essence and existence, potential and act', is presented as sometimes ontological and sometimes juridical. Therefore, this ambiguity needs to be thought out further, not simply eradicated (UB 161/OHS 1172–3). This is where Agamben will turn toward the concept of demand (*conatus*) – again following Spinoza's classic portrayal of the *conatus* in his *Ethics* – in order to arrive at a very different conclusion regarding substance (as perceived from the point of view of a modal ontology).[15]

Demand, as he will describe it in *The Use of Bodies*, is the 'most adequate category to think the ambiguity of logic and ontology that the Aristotelian apparatus has left as an inheritance to Western philosophy' (UB 169/OHS 1180). Like sovereign power, there is no substance to demand; it is 'real and not factual, neither simply logical nor completely real'. Spinoza's *conatus* had been his attempt to think ontology *as* demand, leading Agamben to conclude that 'the being that desires and demands, in demanding, modifies, desires, and constitutes itself' (UB 171/OHS 1182). The relationship between substance and modes is thus: 'The modes are the figures in which substance preserves its demand (its *ductus*)' (UB 172/OHS 1182).

In developing a counter-philosophy to those that legitimate sovereign power, it should not be a surprise that Agamben invokes the clinamen in relation to his modal ontology, as the clinamen was the term used by Lucretius to describe the unpredictability of atomistic movements within Epicurean thought. As history well teaches us, such a reference is the primary philosophical move to establish a way of seeing the world other than that provided by the fiction of sovereignty and the plans of a predestined world. Whatever metaphysics had legitimated, our perception of nature has reached its end, much as Nietzsche had once claimed. For what we see here now is how the problem of taste is the problem of individual inclination or judgement, the unpredictability of preference that Lucretius had used to describe the atomism of Epicurus.[16] For Agamben, it is also the pure arbitrariness or contingency of human life and of a choice that escapes the realm of sovereign decision (parallel to the difference between *demand* and *command*) and so is opened toward recognising how form-of-life is lived outside the law. In his words:

> It is not a matter of attributes or properties of a subject who judges but of the mode in which each person, in losing himself as subject, constitutes-himself as form-of-life. The secret of taste is what form-of-life must solve, has always already solved and displayed – just as gestures simultaneously betray and absolve character. (UB 231/OHS 1237)

## Religious and Political Implications

Such a way of proceeding philosophically has significant implications for rethinking politics as well as ethics, for

> If every body is affected by its form-of-life as by a clinamen or a taste, the ethical subject is that subject that constitutes-itself in relation to this clinamen, the subject who bears witness to its tastes, takes responsibility for the mode in which it is affected by its inclinations. Modal ontology, the ontology of the *how*, coincides with an ethics. (UB 231/OHS 1237)

It is from this angle that we might note how Agamben takes up and praises Lucretius' Epicurean views as what points toward a liberating use of a thing freed 'from every established teleology' (UB 51/OHS 1075). In accord with his previous comments in *The Coming Community* on the liberation of persons from their theological signatures and teleological ends, Agamben suggests rather a 'reversal of the relation between organ and function' that 'amounts to liberating use from every established teleology' (UB 51/OHS 1075). As he continues the thought in such a way as to expose the significance of use over function (which he develops in-depth in *The Highest Poverty*):

> The meaning of the verb *chresthai* [to use] here shows its pertinence: the living being does not make use of its body parts (Lucretius does not speak of organs) for some one predetermined function, but by entering into relation with them, it so to speak gropingly finds and invents their use. The body parts precede their use, and use precedes and creates their function. (UB 51/OHS 1075)

The quest that Agamben places before us is one attempting to formulate a relational, non-substantial self that has no 'predetermined telos' (UB 54/OHS 1077). It has shed its theological signature in order to escape an otherwise destined form. This suggestion will eventually culminate in the opposite of the sovereign tautological performance of power: an 'intimacy without relations' that seeks to make contact, or touch, the other form-of-life before them without trying to inscribe them within a given order where they might serve as a presupposition for a metaphysical division of their being.

This 'intimacy without relations' will be described further in *The Use of Bodies* as bound up with a presentation of the self as a use-of-oneself, or more specifically, a use of oneself that precedes being (UB 55–6/OHS 1078–9). It is what he had suggested in *Remnants of Auschwitz* was a proximity or 'promiscuity that never becomes identity' (RA 125/OHS 845) – what in *The Use of Bodies* was an 'intimacy without relations' and what, I would suggest, in *The Time that Remains* was a 'nearness to the word' (TR 136). It is this formulation that allows us to conceive of being not as substance but as the use of oneself. This is a proposition that, I believe, runs parallel with his analysis of *oikonomia* earlier where he concluded that there is no substance of power but only an economy of power (KG 141/OHS 499). From this vantage point Agamben will draw up the significance of the modalities of being as well as a Pauline messianic formulation that does not call a new substance into being, but only a new use of being (e.g. the Pauline 'as not' that stresses use over ownership) (UB 57/OHS 1080). As such, the discussion of the fiction of sovereignty, understood through traditional arguments and representations of the divine being and its substance in the West, gives way in Agamben's thought to a (Pauline) weak messianic force that seeks a form-of-life beyond the inscriptions of sovereign power.

To further expose the contours of an ontology of demand, Agamben will also recall Walter Benjamin's formulation about what demands to be remembered, even if it has been forgotten – the very nature of exigency that upends historical representation:[17]

> But what does it mean to demand that something be, without it necessarily being? Hence the peculiar ontological status of demand: it is not of the order of essence (it is not a logical implication contained in essence), but neither does it coincide with actual reality. In the onto-logical, it consists of the threshold – the hyphen – that unites and at the same time separates the ontic and the logical, existence and essence. (UB 169/OHS 1180)

Through the poetic rhythm that language produces within life, humanity is able to establish its being through demand and not substance, providing an infinite number of modes of existence – or 'singular existences' – that are not a particular substance, but 'an infinite series of modal oscillations, by means of which substance always constitutes and expresses itself' (UB 172/OHS 1182). There is an incredible flexibility within such singular existences wherein:

> Mode expresses this 'rhythmic' and not 'schematic' nature of being: being is a flux, and substance 'modulates' itself and beats out its rhythm – it does not fix and schematize itself – in the modes. Not the individuating of itself but the beating out of the rhythm of substance defines the ontology that we are here seeking to define. (UB 173/OHS 1183)

As Agamben had noted previously in his remarks on the way that the force of the messianic is connected to rhythm and to the core of Christianity, we see here the messianic nature of a modal ontology that is one of the most significant and original conclusions he asserts within the entirety of the *Homo Sacer* series. It is one, as I have been arguing throughout, that also presents a unique combination of Epicurean-Spinozistic philosophy and Pauline theology. Seeing the modal nature of ontology rather than an allegedly fixed essence is, he concludes, what allows one to take up a space 'within time' from which to create a new flux, a new rhythm and a new use for things (hence its messianic nature). There can be no doubt that every ethical relation must be reconfigured upon such grounds of respect for the singular existences, or forms-of-life, lived beyond every established order.

# 2

# On Aristotle, Actuality and Potentiality

## ARISTOTLE AND THE PROBLEM OF 'POTENCY'

As noted in the previous chapter through Agamben's genealogical exploits, the various efforts to manufacture substance through the necessary fiction of sovereignty are exposed for what they are through the history of the Christian liturgy and its focus on how (divine) mystery brought substantiality and effectiveness to be identified together (OD 40/OHS 683). This creates a situation which allows effectiveness itself to become, in the terms that Agamben utilises in his genealogical study of the liturgy, *Opus Dei*, a 'new ontological dimension', as well as the only representation of being today that we have (OD 41/OHS 684). The conditions of such an established ontology are based on a distinction made by Aristotle between *energeia* ('work' or actuality) and *dynamis* ('ability' or potentiality) (OD 43/OHS 685). Referenced frequently by Agamben, this Aristotelean distinction sought directly to actualise potential and thereby establish effectiveness as a primary category of Western political and philosophical thought. This split between potentiality and actuality became the fundamental metaphysical distinction in the West, and that which allowed the logic of presupposition to capture being and render it subject to the operations (operativity) of the apparatuses that subsequently came to govern over it. In this way, Agamben discerns, the 'dislocation of being into the sphere of praxis, in which being is what it does, is its operativity itself' (OD 44/OHS 687). Here, as he makes clear, the dualism *potentia-actualitas* in Latin becomes a rendering of the Greek pair *dynamis-energia*, which the Latin Fathers also translated as *possibilitas-efficacia* (OD 46/OHS 688). By embracing the mystery that unites these polarities, and which is part of the presupposition or capturing of being, these pairs enter into a space of undecidability that *is* the apparatus of the liturgy, offering another byway from which to view the political and philosophical through the lens of the theological (OD 47/OHS 689).

Despite the reality that medieval theologians were often searching for a 'third thing' between form and material, or potential and act (a lineage that Agamben here traces only to develop in wholly new directions), these dualisms proceeded to gain traction within theological circles for the pronounced political currency they often displayed. Divine being was made operative in the Son – that is, actualised (hypostatised) in Christ – which became not only the basis for Christological justifications for the divine right to rule, but also portrayed a reality wherein the Christian sacraments, or what were material moments of divine grace, could do nothing other than 'effect what they signify' (OD 52–3/OHS 692–3). The political valences of these doctrinal positions were then all too easily deployed as justifications for papal, and later monarchical, sovereignty, just as they embodied previous embodiments of sovereign power during Aristotle's time.

Though ethics slowly began to initiate a distinction between the subject and their actions (OD 54/OHS 694), what was clearly introduced into Western thought via theological assertion and liturgical praxis was the mystery of liturgical action as the effect itself. Agamben will describe this association as a combination of mystery and effectiveness intended to legitimate relations between being and action: 'what is mysterious is effectiveness, insofar as in it being is resolved into praxis and praxis is substantiated into being. The mystery of the liturgy coincides totally with the mystery of operativity' (OD 55/OHS

694–5, de-emphasised from the original). Operativity, as effectiveness, is legitimated by the apparatus of liturgy and provides a cover for divine being itself. Liturgical mystery exists because of 'an economy of divine being', which in turn legitimates the liturgy (OD 55/OHS 695). Building off of his previous creative genealogical analysis of economy and glory, Agamben is subsequently able to discern the implications of such an ontological positing for ethical constructions of the subject by determining how 'There is an *oikonomia* – that is, an operativity – of the divine being: this and nothing else is the mystery' (OD 55/OHS 695, de-emphasised from the original). In other words, we have only experienced being *as* operativity, and not as some abstracted state beyond the politics and economic relations of our world. We have not beheld our form-of-life, but only understood being as that which was created through the apparatuses that captured being. In this sense, Agamben builds directly off of Heidegger's attempts to more accurately elucidate the contours of being, while also departing from Heidegger's account in order to elaborate upon the ways in which being has been captured – a tactic he borrows expressly from Foucault's genealogical efforts.[1] From this point of view, operativity can be discerned not as the site of our being, but only as a virtual reality that lacks any substance (OD 64/OHS 701). This is an argument that is clearly to be equated with the fiction of sovereignty established only through its own effectiveness or operativity.

Agamben's critique of the Aristotelian categories that have dominated Western metaphysics and theology (e.g. potentiality/actuality, contingency/necessity and so on) lead him further to interrogate the use of dualisms in Western thought insofar as they are used to legitimate traditional political and ethical relations. Each dualism is itself the result of the capture of being that is now presupposed by the split within being that gives rise to the dualistic structure we ceaselessly seek to overcome, but which we seemingly cannot. It is for this reason that analysing Aristotle's interpretation of the relationship between potentiality and actuality is of the utmost importance, as it is the lynchpin of metaphysical, dualistic thought in the West and it is that which actually prevents us from embracing our being (as a form-of-life that remains uncaptured by a logic of presupposition). This is the reason why Agamben returns to Aristotle and this categorical dualism on multiple occasions in his writings in order to contest this division and propose a fundamental rereading of the history of being in relation to metaphysics (again along the lines of a merger of the insights of Heidegger with Foucault). The configurations of politics and economics that dominate Western history are determined by the tensions that this dualism generates and so, in order to critique the entirety of their reach and to consider another reality as possible, his criticism must be directed here.

This particular dualism is referred to repeatedly in the *Homo Sacer* series, including as the metaphysical basis for the foundations of power locatable in the distinction between constituted and constituting power (where Carl Schmitt's work was particularly illuminating), as well as between governance and sovereignty (where Foucault held the reins of the conversation). It is also revisited in the context of the habit of potential or *hexis* in *Opus Dei* (OD 92–3/OHS 725). Here habit joins the potential and the actual together in that it regulates the passage between them (OD 94/OHS 726). Habit functions like a certain grace, or glory, to keep the two polarities in relation to one another, while they are also permanently kept separate: 'The strategic meaning of the concept of habit is that, in it, potential and act are separated and nonetheless maintained in relation' (OD 94/OHS 726). And, as Agamben will immediately go on to state, 'Only insofar as habit is also habit of a privation can potential endure and have mastery over itself, without always already losing itself in action' (OD 94/OHS 726). In other words, there may be *another* way to think of habit, as a form of privation (which will lead to weakness, poverty and so forth), that will ultimately lead to perhaps *another* form of sovereignty – as I will describe it later on.

## Giorgio Agamben's Homo Sacer *Series*

To get to this space, Agamben demonstrates how habit was developed in the history of Western theology, and its accompanying monastic practices, as a concept that might allow one to stay within the realm of potential alone and not merely capitulate to action, hence as distinct from the form of habit that had served to unite potential and actual. This is where we can locate Agamben's insistence that we find a way to embrace a form of potentiality that does not cross over into actuality, a 'pure potentiality' that refuses to be part of the dualistic split brought about by presupposing being. With explicit reference time and again to Aristotle's classic distinction between potentiality and actuality as lying at the heart of Western metaphysics, Agamben wants rather to think a form of being (a form-of-life) that regresses back to a space before the split between potentiality and actuality occurred (see P 177–84). This split, as with so many others, is really what results from the presupposition of being and the dualistic metaphysical-philosophical systems that result from its capture. Pure potentiality, by his reckoning, is the *other* form of habit that was joined to the concept of use in order to find a way to break the Aristotelian dualistic impasse between potentiality and actuality:

> Only if we think habit not only in a negative mode, beginning from impotential and from the possibility of not passing into act, but rather as habitual use, is the aporia, against which Aristotelian thought on potentiality has made shipwreck, dissolved. Use is the form in which habit is given existence, beyond the simple opposition between potential and being-at-work. (UB 60/OHS 1082)

In this formulation, the self is portrayed not as a subject, but appears as it is established in relation to use and to potential. It is ultimately what will point to a self beyond subjectivity, or toward a form-of-life, at the end of the series as well. Here it is this 'habit of privation', or poverty, that is of great interest to Agamben, as this formulation holds the key toward understanding how we might break through the dualistic impasses that characterise Western thought. It is only through the ability to enter into a privative state, to regress toward one's potentiality, or to *use* but not *possess*, that one is capable of maintaining a relation with one's impotentiality. As occasional readers of his work will note, Agamben always frames the discussion of potentiality as one concerning impotentiality at the same time. In a short essay on 'What We Can Not Do', for example, he describes it in detail:

> 'Impotentiality' does not mean here only absence of potentiality, not being able to do, but also and above all 'being able to not do,' being able to not exercise one's own potentiality. And, indeed, it is precisely this specific ambivalence of all potentiality – which is always the power to be and to not be, to do and to not do – that defines, in fact, human potentiality. This is to say that human beings are the living beings that, existing in the mode of potentiality, are capable just as much of one thing as its opposite, to do just as to not do. This exposes them, more than any other living being, to the risk of error; but, at the same time, it permits human beings to accumulate and freely master their own capacities, to transform them into 'faculties'. (N 43–4)

It is precisely our impotentiality that allows us to be defined as human beings capable of transcending our biological vocation – or our genetic coding, as he will call it on occasion – in such a way. This is how Agamben will even concretely define the human being in evolutionary terms: we were the animals capable of rejecting our instincts, and it is this, and this alone, that makes us distinct from the other animals (cf. IP 95–8 and O 33–8). Or, in the words of the Portuguese poet Fernando Pessoa, it is our artificiality that is perhaps most natural to us.[2]

There is a definite logic to such an argument, and it is one that Agamben pursues relentlessly throughout his oeuvre, from his commentaries on Pauline messianism as a suspension of our identities as human beings to his remarks on animality in the context of Heidegger's thought in his study *The Open*. Humanity can be viewed anew from this perspective as it recognises its own impotentiality. This is what Agamben will illustrate through Melville's figure of Bartleby the scrivener, a Christlike figure of contingency and resistance in that he fully exercises his impotentiality through only responding to commands with the phrase 'I prefer not to' (see his essay 'Bartleby, or On Contingency' in P 243–71, which is itself indebted to a dialogue he maintained on the subject of contingency with the work of Gilles Deleuze). Or, again, as he will elaborate on this concept further:

> Nothing makes us more impoverished and less free than this estrangement from impotentiality. Those who are separated from what they can do, can, however, still resist; they can still not do. Those who are separated from their own impotentiality lose, on the other hand, first of all the capacity to resist. And just as it is only the burning awareness of what we cannot be that guarantees the truth of what we are, so it is only the lucid vision of what we cannot, or can not, do that gives consistency to our actions. (N 45)

The ability to choose 'not to' do something is precisely what constitutes the power of resistance, inasmuch as it also constitutes something of the form of sovereignty itself. In suggesting this, a certain aporia of sovereignty must be confronted in Agamben's thought, as well as the possibility for *another* form of sovereignty to arise, though not the one typically associated with those sovereign powers active, and effective, in our world. As we learn in the first volume of *Homo Sacer*, constituting power is the problem of potentiality, which needs to be rethought in relation to sovereignty and the 'primacy of actuality' (HS 43–4/OHS 39–40). But it is not always clear whether maintaining one's impotentiality can also be a sign of sovereignty within the individual who resists the movement from potentiality to actuality, whether or not it stakes out its own space of autonomy free from the normative orders that otherwise define our world. That is, would not the exercising of one's impotentiality retain sovereignty within the individual self that is now removed from the dualistic dynamics of power as they are publicly displayed?

## On Aristotle, Actuality and Potentiality

It is clear that Agamben is searching for a form of 'pure potentiality' beyond the actual-potential dualism that Aristotle originated in the West, but the question remains in Agamben's work as to how this form of 'pure potentiality' avoids making a form-of-life sovereign precisely through its autonomy as established apart from the political, dualistic configurations of power in our world. Would not its ability to remove itself from all particular configurations of sovereign power not create the conditions for a new form of sovereignty through this heightened and increasingly isolated autonomy?

As Agamben stresses from the outset of the series, what is apparent is that Aristotle's foundational dualism is inherently linked with the metaphysical basis of sovereign power. Subsequently, any attempt to go beyond the dualism itself will have significant repercussions for politics on the whole.

> In thus describing the most authentic nature of potentiality, Aristotle actually bequeathed the paradigm of sovereignty to Western philosophy. For the sovereign ban, which applies to the exception in no longer applying, corresponds to the structure of potentiality, which maintains itself in relation to actuality precisely through its ability not to be. Potentiality (in its double appearance as potentiality to and as potentiality not to) is that through which Being founds itself *sovereignly*, which is to say, without anything preceding or determining it (*superiorem non recognoscens*) other than its own ability not to be. And an act is sovereign when it realizes itself by simply taking away its potentiality not to be, letting itself be, giving itself to itself. (HS 46/OHS 42)

Potentiality/actuality are two faces of 'the sovereign self-grounding of Being'. This is the reality that allows Agamben to claim in *Homo Sacer* that pure actuality and pure potentiality are indistinguishable from one another and that the sovereign is the zone of indistinction between them. It is in this confusion of a pure potentiality that never leaves the realm of potential (or how, say, God is defined in the writings of certain Christian mystics) and a pure actuality that never leaves the realm of action (and which, we should recall, had defined God as 'pure act' for a theologian like Aquinas) that Agamben notices Aristotle's attempt to access the 'thinking of thinking' as a possible solution to this impasse between them (HS 46/OHS 42). Later on, Agamben's conjectures on the 'thinking of thinking' return in a parallel stress placed upon the significance of the Idea itself, something that he will come to defend as the location of real political reform and what suspends or renders inoperative the anthropological machinery of our world. Hence, the abstraction of thought thinking about thought is both linked to metaphysical justifications for divine being (and the doctrinal apparatuses that try to capture our being), but *also* the liberating resistance of the Idea in the face of these apparatuses.

The zone of indistinction is a point Agamben will return to on occasion in order to locate within one's impotentiality the key to solving the dilemma of the impasse between potentiality and actuality. In short, the power to both act and not act that is a recognition of the impotentiality (or impotence) within every potentiality (or potency) is the 'supreme power' sovereignty searches for. Furthermore, it is the locus of another form of sovereignty beyond the one that determines politics most typically in our world:

> Thanks to this potentiality to not-think, thought can turn back to itself (to its pure potentiality) and be, at its apex, the thought of thought. What it thinks here, however, is not an object, a being-in-act, but that layer of wax, that *rasum tabulae* that is nothing but its own passivity, its own pure potentiality (to not-think): In the potentiality that thinks itself, action and passion coincide and the writing tablet writes by itself, or, rather, writes its own passivity. (CC 37)

And, as he continues to elaborate on this possibility for a pure potentiality, he suggests that:

> The perfect act of writing comes not from a power to write, but from an impotence that turns back on itself and in this way comes to itself as a pure act (which Aristotle calls agent intellect). This

is why in the Arab tradition agent intellect has the form of an angel whose name is *Qalam*, Pen, and its place is an unfathomable potentiality. Bartleby, a scribe who does not simply cease writing but 'prefers not to,' is the extreme image of this angel that writes nothing but its potentiality to not-write. (CC 37)

One's power, one's *true sovereignty* we might say, comes not from acting or performing the appearance of having to act – as a duty or obligation even, such as what monarchs have been subject to – but from refraining from action. It comes from the weakness or impotency 'that turns back on itself' and becomes a 'pure act' in another sense altogether from that which defines traditional forms of sovereign power and the divine. Such an establishment of *another* form of sovereignty, however, retains the tautological structure of self-grounding in that it 'turns back on itself and in this way comes to itself as a pure act'.

Such formulations are very intriguing to find in Agamben's work, especially as they coincide with certain theological definitions of the divine as either 'pure act' or 'pure potential' beyond the dualistic split of potentiality/actuality. But these are suggestions that Agamben does not develop in any great depth, preferring rather to assess genealogically the dualisms that have undergirded political power in the West. Following on the heels of Heidegger's efforts to think the destruction of ontology in Western metaphysics (OD 60/OHS 698), Agamben is rather trying to think ontology and politics 'beyond every figure of relation', beyond then too every attempt to presuppose being at the foundations of every dualistic split in our being (HS 46/OHS 42). Hence his efforts to try to think a modal ontology that moves beyond the positing of sovereignty through substance (as ontology, but also politics, has traditionally proceeded) are directed toward a realm of pure potentiality that crosses over into the realm of pure act in order to demonstrate what we might call *another* form of sovereignty – one removed from the dualistic tensions that characterise humanity and its politics in our world.

However, questions are raised by the possibility for such a form of sovereignty, such as: whether or not this resistance to political forms of sovereignty merely recreates the conditions for sovereign autonomy, though at another level, and whether such attempts to avoid sovereign forms are merely revealing how deeply they are already intertwined with sovereign power. We are returned to one of the major issues occasionally appearing within contemporary philosophical debates regarding what is in excess of identity, institution and law – the limit-experiences that appear to go beyond these domains and the possibilities of a presence beyond all representation. As we will see, these are the foundational questions of the *Homo Sacer* series and the ones Agamben returns to most often.

## POTENTIALITY AS A FORM OF RESISTANCE

We can begin to access this *other* form of sovereignty through recourse to a figure who, for Agamben, works counter to the dualistic split between potentiality and actuality. The nature of resistance to the political as a new form of politics is defined by one of Herman Melville's characters, Bartleby, and his resistance given through the exercising of his impotentiality (HS 48/OHS 43). It is as such that Bartleby becomes for Agamben the 'perfect cipher of the aporias of Aristotelean ethics' (OD 97/OHS 728). Bartleby issues a challenge to the fundamental Aristotelian dualism through his 'preference not to' which is ultimately a refusal to be inscribed within the political operations that normally give rise to both action and ethics as we know them. Bartleby refuses to be lured into the dualistic split between the potential and the actual, preferring instead to regress into his own being.

However, the question that remains perplexing for Agamben is whether or not resistance itself – such as figures like Bartleby, and even Christ, put before us – can be inscribed into the heart of existing political structures. Can genuine and desired forms of resistance be put into law? Can the right to resistance be included in the constitution itself (SE 10/OHS 175), which is to speak too of *anomie* being possibly inscribed into the heart of law and order (SE 23/OHS 185)? Or, as Agamben phrases the question in more concrete terms, does only Parliament have the right to dissolve the constitution (SE 12/OHS 176)?

Agamben's conclusion to these questions is quite revealing, not only to the central questions being asked regarding the possibility of another form of sovereignty in his thought, but also regarding the many accusations of antinomianism as a latent force within his work on the whole:

> It is certain, in any case, that if resistance were to become a right or even a duty (the omission of which could be punished), not only would the constitution end up positing itself as an absolutely untouchable and all-encompassing value, but the citizen's political choices would also end up being determined by juridical norms. The fact is that in both the right of resistance and the state of exception, what is ultimately at issue is the question of the juridical significance of a sphere of action that is in itself extra-juridical. Two theses are at odds here: One asserts that law must coincide with the norm, and the other holds that the sphere of law exceeds the norm. But in the last analysis, the two positions agree in ruling out the existence of a sphere of human action that is entirely removed from law. (SE 11/OHS 175)

If resistance were inscribed into the law, the law could only be of a totalitarian nature, as the right to resistance must be extra-juridical, or beyond the law, by definition. But also beyond the law is the state of exception upon which sovereignty is founded. Once again, these contrasting positions bring into view the overlap between two different forms of sovereignty – the one heavily critiqued by Agamben and the other subtly alluded to as *another* possible form of sovereignty – a positive form perhaps even subtly aligned with *other* forms of glory and *other* forms of grace that also escape the dualistic machinery that produces the human being and politics as we commonly know them. What *is* evident at least is that genuine resistance, whether in the form of Bartleby or of a certain Christic messianism, cannot be brought about entirely removed from the existence of law. The state of exception, as we well know from the second volume of the *Homo Sacer* series, is what founds the law, leaving resistance to see to the law's undoing without ever being able to actually depart in its relationship to law.

This is what is meant when Agamben speaks about how the messianic – a term he takes from both Pauline thought and from Walter Benjamin – as with one's private life, shadows the law, or one's public life. It is also what he means when he suggests that there is not another state beyond the law waiting to be discovered and lived as a new, utopian existence. Rather, the messianic experience can only be found in rendering the law inoperative, though not in doing away with it once and for all. Again, we encounter only the messianic vocation as the revocation of all vocations, as an undoing of law and of identity (cf. TR 23–7).

> The word of faith manifests itself as the effective experience of a pure power of saying that, as such, does not coincide with any denotative proposition, or with the performative value of a speech act. Rather, it exists as an absolute nearness of the word. One therefore understands why, for Paul, messianic power finds its *telos* in weakness. The act itself of a pure potentiality of saying, a word that always remains close to itself, cannot be a signifying word that utters true opinions on the state of things, or a juridical performative that posits itself as fact. (TR 136)

While not formerly part of the *Homo Sacer* series, but heavily linked to the conclusions arrived at in *The Use of Bodies*, within Agamben's study of Pauline thought in *The Time that Remains* we see a 'pure potentiality of saying' brought through messianic weakness to be a form of 'pure power' that signals perhaps *another* form of sovereignty – something like a *pure* sovereignty that dwells in proximity (here a 'nearness', and what he will later call, in *The Use of Bodies*, an 'intimacy') to the word. It is this conclusion that reconfigures, using one of Agamben's favoured illustrations, what we have historically taken the Church to be in the world, as it cannot be an institution that depends upon a politically sovereign power. Likewise, faith is not what we have taken it to be either; it is rather something like the displacement of sovereignty itself toward another form of its possible appearance.

In the same context, this line of inquiry leads Agamben to declare the absence of anything like a 'content of faith', one of the sharpest critiques given to the institutional Church founded upon the messianic teachings of Paul:

> There is no such thing as a content of faith, and to profess the word of faith does not mean formulating true propositions on God and the world. To believe in Jesus Messiah does not mean believing something about him, *legein ti kata tinos*, and the attempt of the Councils to formulate the content of faith in *symbola* can only be taken as a sublime irony. 'Messianic and weak' is therefore that potentiality of saying, which, in dwelling near the word not only exceeds all that is said, but also exceeds the act of saying itself, the performative power of language. This is the remnant of potentiality that is not consumed in the act, but is conserved in it each time and dwells there. If this remnant of potentiality is thus weak, if it cannot be accumulated in any form of knowledge or dogma, and if it cannot impose itself as a law, it does not follow that it is passive or inert. To the contrary, it acts in its own weakness, rendering the word of law inoperative, in de-creating and dismantling the states of fact or of law, making them freely available for use. *Katargein* and *chrēsthai* are the act of a potentiality that fulfills itself in weakness. That this potentiality finds its *telos* in weakness means that it does not simply remain suspended in infinite deferral; rather, turning back toward itself, it fulfills and deactivates the very excess of signification over every signified, it extinguishes languages (1 Cor. 13: 8). In this way, it bears witness to what, unexpressed and insignificant, remains in use forever near the word. (TR 136–7)

What we witness in Agamben's commentary on Pauline faith is a direct challenge to the Aristotelian, categorical duality that governs Western thought, as well as the institutional *ecclesia* founded upon Paul's claims. What we see at work in Paul's reformulation of a messianic faith is how this possible *other* form of sovereignty – posited through a 'turning back toward itself' that mirrors the tautological nature that defines sovereign power – must proceed through weakness and not in order to produce something appearing as strength made effective through a dualistic configuration of sovereign power as is typically deployed in our world in order to presuppose and so suppress the fullness of our being. This nod toward weakness gives us a first hint as to why the concept of poverty becomes such a central one in the *Homo Sacer* series, most prominently evident in his discussions of Franciscanism and the tensions between possession and use.

Agamben's analysis of Pauline thoughts on language is therefore also resonant with his critique of the significance of language in *The Sacrament of Language* where he suggests, quite provocatively, that language is no more important than birdsong. What we are to know about Jesus Messiah, he claims, is not some Christological distinction or doctrine, but only that he stands for rendering inoperative the effectiveness of the law, or even of one's identity. This is a messianic gesture pointing toward the kenotic weakness of being that 'does not simply remain suspended in infinite deferral', but rather, as we just heard, 'bears witness to what, unexpressed and insignificant, remains in use forever near the word' – what he will describe later in the *Homo Sacer* series as form-of-life (TR 137).

For example, we see this linkage made directly in his collection of essays *The Fire and the Tale* in relation to the act of contemplation (a subject that returns in *The Use of Bodies* as well, UB 214ff/OHS 1221ff), and which maintains something of the 'thought of thought' that suspends normal (economic) operations and produces another path through which to walk toward *another* form of sovereignty. In this case it is manifest in the 'anonymous living beings' who do not seek public glory, but possibly maintain *another* form of glory, and so too *another* form of grace, beyond the sovereignty, glory and grace that configure the political and social spheres in which we live.

> Certainly, the contemplation of a potentiality can only be given in an opus; but, in contemplation, the opus is deactivated and made inoperative and, in this way, given back to possibility, opened to a new possible use. A truly poetic form of life is the one that contemplates in its opus its own potentiality to do and not to do, and finds peace in it. A living being can never be defined by its opus but only by its inoperativity, that is, by the way in which, maintaining itself, in an opus, in relation with pure potentiality, it constitutes itself as form-of-life, in which what is at stake is no longer either life or opus but happiness. The form-of-life is the point in which the work on an opus and the work on oneself perfectly coincide. The painter, the poet, the thinker – and, in general, anyone who practices an 'art' or an 'activity' – are not the appointed sovereign subjects of a creative operation and of an opus; they are rather anonymous living beings who, contemplating and making at each turn inoperative the opus of language, of vision, and of bodies, try to experience themselves and keep in relation with a potentiality, that is, to constitute their life as form-of-life. (FT 137–8)

This *other* form of sovereignty, contrary to the glory (or celebrity) that mainly accompanies our world's sovereign powers, is *anonymous*. Its anonymity is part and parcel of its weakness in terms of the representations of identity and naming we are commonly familiar with. It returns to itself, but only through a deactivation of the potentiality/actuality dualism that takes place through the practice of contemplation. This is precisely where Agamben will locate a form-of-life as it is lived beyond the law. Form-of-life is lived as an exemplary life akin to the figure of the saint who is at once lifted out of the normative order but is also not excluded as a form of bare life produced by the anthropological machinery that gives us forms of sovereign power as sources of our strength.

The distinctions that Agamben subsequently draws in *The Use of Bodies* between the typical forms of mastery that characterise sovereignty and the *other* form of sovereignty that he seeks to recover are essential to comprehend at this point. Traditional forms of sovereign power place an emphasis on the act of deciding for the sovereign element in order to put potential in one direction or another (UB 61/OHS 1083). Here habit becomes an act wherein 'subjectivity seeks to make itself master of being', using a 'perfect circularity' and appropriates being to itself (UB 61/OHS 1084). Hence, according to this way of being in the world, 'Having is nothing but the appropriation of a being' (UB 61/OHS 1084). As previously noted, Agamben's emphasis will rather be placed upon the manner in which use, and not having or not possessing, is 'beyond both being and having' (UB 61/OHS 1084). Developing *another* form of habit, 'Use, as habit, is a form-of-life and not the knowledge of faculty of a subject' (UB 62/OHS 1084, de-emphasised from the original). It is imperative, for Agamben, to think a form of 'being-in-use' as such and as opposed to 'being-in-act' (UB 58/OHS 1081).

Such a contrast will lead him to depict *another* form of mastery and so *another* form of sovereignty as expressed in *The Fire and the Tale*: 'Contrary to a common equivocation, mastery is not formal perfection but quite the opposite: it is the preservation of potentiality in the act, the salvation of imperfection in a perfect form. In the painting of a master or on a page of a great writer, the resistance of the potentiality-not-to is marked in the work as the intimate mannerism present in every masterpiece' (FT 42). For Agamben, tastelessness is the inability to refrain from something, the compulsion to have to actualise everything one desires, and so the opposite of the artistic master who retains the ability to *not* do something. Therefore, such mastery is the opposite of a tastelessness that characterises sovereignty, which 'is always being incapable not to do something' (FT 43). It is in passages such as these that we see him subtly pointing toward *other* forms of mastery and sovereignty, though he does not develop these insights in any great depth in the *Homo Sacer* series itself, which spends the vast majority of its time producing genealogical analyses of various historical concepts.

The inability to not do something that characterises sovereignty is what also characterises tastelessness – a point that not only explains the poor taste of dictators, but also aids the rethinking of art, the very purpose of which is called into question on these grounds. There must remain a tension between inspiration and the potentiality-not-to in order to present a work of art, he will claim, and it is a ceaseless dialectic between 'a non-individuated part and an individual and personal part. The pre-individual is not a chronological past that, at a certain point, is realized and resolved in the individual: it coexists with it and remains irreducible to it' (FT 44). Here the impersonal element ('potentiality-to' or 'genius') is dialectically balanced by the personal element ('potentiality-not-to'). Yet potentiality-not-to is also the inoperativity of the potentiality/actuality dichotomy – what he will label, with one of his most sought-after phrases, as a form of 'pure potentiality' (FT 47, 49). Consequently, it is through this return to a pure potentiality that we are able to link contemplation and inoperativity as perhaps the most significant concepts that define the human being as such:

> Contemplation and inoperativity are, in this sense, the metaphysical operators of anthropogenesis, which, freeing the living human being from any biological or social destiny and from any predetermined task, make him available for that particular absence of work we are used to calling 'politics' and 'art'. Politics and art are neither tasks nor simply 'works': they rather name the dimension in which linguistic and bodily operations – material and immaterial, biological and social – are deactivated and contemplated as such. (FT 54–5)

The acts of contemplation and inoperativity are thus essential for art, politics, ethics and philosophy, though our failure to think them more fully has brought about the dominance of particular forms of sovereignty, glory and grace that have repeatedly suppressed alternative experiences of each concept. In the end, this is why Agamben will return to each concept in order to rework them into *other* possible forms that we had missed latent within the actual forms we had been subject to previously. This move is made possible by the internal division of the already divided (social, political, theological and linguistic) forms that rely upon the presupposition of being (and its accompanying dualistic splits). This is where the Pauline 'division of division itself' – Paul's division of the Jew/Gentile split into a second flesh/spirit division, making every Jew potentially a Jew 'in the flesh' or a Jew 'in spirit' – plays a prominent role in his philosophical methodology (TR 49–53). It is also why he does not seek after a state *beyond* politics, ethics, philosophy or community, but only those new 'coming' forms, or new *uses*, of those things that already exist.

For example, in this same context from *The Fire and the Tale*, Agamben will reiterate the possibility for a new form of grace to appear through one's resistance to the dualistic impasse that Aristotle bequeathed to the West. Again, as I have suggested already, it is only through an ontology of demand that such a resistance might be developed:

> What poetry accomplishes for the potentiality to say, politics and philosophy must accomplish for the potentiality to act. Rendering inoperative economic and social operations, they show what the human body is capable of; they open it to a new possible use. Spinoza defined the essence of each thing as desire, the *conatus* to persevere in one's being. If I might express a minor reservation with regard to a great thinker, I would say that it now seems to me that we need to insinuate a small resistance even in this Spinozian idea – as we have seen with the act of creation. Certainly, each thing desires to persevere in its being; but, at the same time, it resists this desire; it renders it inoperative at least for an instant and contemplates. Once again, this is a resistance internal to desire, an inoperativity internal to the operation. But it alone confers on *conatus* its justice and its truth. In one word – and this is, at least in art, the decisive element – its grace. (FT 55–6; see also his remarks on contemplation in UB 214–19/OHS 1221–6)

Though he refrains from delivering a positive conceptualisation of grace in the *Homo Sacer* series itself, instead focusing on those versions of grace that have been deployed as part of the political-theological apparatuses of our world (KG 137/OHS 495), his reconsideration, and redefining, of the same term bears noting. As in so many other contexts in his work, Agamben walks the reader toward a complete redefinition of a commonly (mis)used concept in order to enable us to think a new use of it – a technique of reinvention that he inherited explicitly from Walter Benjamin, but which he puts to new use time and again.

## CONTEMPLATION OF THE INAPPROPRIABLE

It is within such a setting as well that we can understand anew the significance for Agamben of Spinoza's reflections on the contemplation of the self, as well as the self that the modern subject has usurped (UB 62–3/OHS 1085). As he will describe this significance:

> Use is the form in which habit is given existence, beyond the simple opposition between potential and being-at-work. And if habit is, in this sense, always already use-of-oneself and if this latter, as we have seen, implies a neutralization of the subject/object opposition, then there is no place here for a proprietary subject of habit, which can decide to put it to work or not. The self, which is constituted in the relation of use, is not a subject, is nothing other than this relation. (UB 60/OHS 1082–3)

The 'proprietary subject of habit' is displaced by *another* form of habit *as* use, one that allows form-of-life to ultimately appear in a clearer light. This displacement is what will allow Agamben to conclude that 'habitual use is a contemplation and contemplation is a form of life', which he notes is directly affirmed in the works of both Gilles Deleuze and Maine de Biran (UB 63/OHS 1085). Seen from this Spinozistic point of view, contemplation is confirmed as a 'use-of-oneself' that makes possible the deactivation of the subject and of the dualisms that gave rise to it (UB 64/OHS 1086).

As we have just seen, what likewise becomes abundantly apparent is that contemplation plays a significant role in the regression toward one's impotentiality because it indicates the possibility of *use* rather than *possession*. This is the crucial ontological distinction that Agamben introduces in *The Highest Poverty* and which is brought to bear on his development of a modal ontology in *The Use of Bodies*. As he will clarify the relationship in the latter text:

> Contemplation is the paradigm of use. Like use, contemplation does not have a subject, because in it the contemplator is completely lost and dissolved; like use, contemplation does not have an object, because in the work it contemplates only its (own) potential. Life, which contemplates in the work its (own) potential of acting or making, is rendered inoperative in all its works and lives only in use-of-oneself, lives only (its) livability. We write 'own' and 'its' in parentheses because only through the contemplation of potential, which renders inoperative every *energia* and every work, does something like the experience of an 'own' and a 'self' become possible. The self – whose place the modern subject will usurp – is what is opened up as a central inoperativity in every operation, as the 'livability' and 'usability' in every work. And if the architect and the carpenter remain such even when they are not building, which they can also not put to work, but because they habitually live in use-of-themselves as architect or carpenter: habitual use is a contemplation and contemplation is a form of life. (UB 63/OHS 1085)

This site is where we can locate the *other* form of sovereignty that Agamben does not directly acknowledge as such. It is present in the favouring of the self over the subject and in the way Agamben still has recourse to an 'own' and an 'it', though he feels compelled to put them in parentheses and quotation marks so as to downplay their potential conversion into substance. Contemplation is the 'use-of-oneself' that is also a 'zone of nonconsciousness', allowing for contemplation to be defined as a habit that occupies a form-of-life. It is at this point that the Franciscan emphasis placed upon both poverty and use becomes relevant in determining *another* mastery of the self that is not predicated upon the Aristotelian dualism of potentiality/actuality, but is grounded only in itself and its own weakness.

What is especially interesting in Agamben's discussion of use in relation to virtue is that use, beyond all sense of possession, effectively does away with the idea of virtue as something that one possesses. Agamben develops instead a theory of virtue as only use, 'beyond being and acting' (UB 65/OHS 1087). In his words:

> Use, insofar as it neutralizes the opposition of potential and act, being and acting, material and form, being-at-work and habit, wakefulness and sleep, is always virtuous and does not need anything to be added to it in order to render it operative. Virtue does not suddenly develop into habit: it is the being always in use of habit; it is habit as form of life. Like purity, virtue is not a characteristic that belongs to someone or something on its own. For this reason, virtuous actions do not exist, just as a virtuous being does not exist: what is virtuous is only use, beyond – which is to say, in the middle of – being and acting. (UB 65/OHS 1087)

To revert to use instead of possession (as with potential instead of actual, as we saw earlier) is a refusal of the paradigm of action and effectiveness that has governed Western ethics. To truly be virtuous means to embrace use over possession and so, in a manner similar to Derridean deconstruction where a true gift removes itself from the economy of gifting, it is essentially to efface the category of virtue altogether.[3] To truly be virtuous means not to identify with the virtuous act, or to appropriate the virtue to oneself. By only engaging the use of a thing, one embraces a form of life that attempts to remove itself from whatever economy of virtuous living identifies a given community and the boundaries that inscribe it.

It is for this reason that, for Agamben, the Franciscan movement rises to an elevated prominence within the *Homo Sacer* series. The simple act of renouncing ownership emphasises not the will of the subject, but merely the 'nature of things' (UB 80/OHS 1100). As such, and following Benjamin in describing the natures of both possession and its relationship to injustice, Agamben tries to imagine an experience of the world as 'absolutely inappropriable', as that which cannot be owned, but only used. This is a proposition Agamben illustrates through the Franciscan call to embrace a life of poverty beyond all acts of possession. For example, he will suggest that 'If we recall that justice [. . .] coincided with the condition of a good that cannot be appropriated, to make of the world the supreme good can only mean: to experience it as absolutely inappropriable' (UB 81/OHS 1101). The Francisican ideal of poverty is incorporated into Agamben's thought through the category of the inappropriable as the very basis through which justice might enter the world. But it must be assumed that, as Benjamin had already foreseen, justice cannot be accessed through a notion of possession completely aligned with particular forms of sovereign power and its inherent decisionism:[4]

> poverty is not found on a decision of the subject but corresponds to a 'state of the world.' And if, in the Francisican theorists, use appeared as the dimension that is opened when one renounces ownership, here the perspective is necessarily reversed and use appears as *the relation to an inappropriable*, as the only possible relation to that supreme state of the world in which it, as just, can be in no way appropriated. (UB 81/OHS 1101)

This suggestive elaboration of what exactly constitutes the poverty of existence that Agamben sees modelled in the Franciscan renunciation of possessions becomes the means by which he extends an analysis of the 'inappropriable' as the embodiment of use. The body, language and landscape, for example, constitute 'the inappropriables' as that which cannot be brought into one's possession, but which remind humanity of its precarious and ultimately impoverished existence.

Turning briefly to focus on what has been received from the phenomenologies of Edmund Husserl, Edith Stein and Emmanuel Levinas, Agamben is able to focus on how the body is fundamentally an experience of oneself, comprehended only as a distinction between the 'I' and the body of the other (UB 82–3/OHS 1102–3). Since the body always 'casts a shadow' over experience, we are able to see nudity and shame as the most improper things, the 'most foreign things' that we hide, but which also are part of us – what is inappropriable to us (UB 85/OHS 1105). Analogous to our experience of the body is likewise language, which cannot be possessed and reminds us of what we can only use as it moves beyond us.

As the third example given of the inappropriable, Agamben determines landscape the ultimate illustration because it is an external image of what cannot be possessed, only viewed. In the viewing of landscape, being itself, we are told,

> is suspended and rendered inoperative, and the world, having become perfectly inappropriable, goes, so to speak, beyond being and nonbeing. No longer animal nor human, to the one who contemplates the landscape is only landscape. That person no longer seeks to comprehend, only look. If the world is the inoperativity of the animal environment, landscape is, so to speak, inoperativity of inoperativity, deactivated being. And negativity, which inhered in the world in the form of the nothing and non-openness – because it comes from the animal closure, of which it was only a suspension – is now dismissed. (UB 91/OHS 1109–10)

Landscape is 'the outstanding form of use' for Agamben, as it is here that 'use-of-oneself and use of the world correspond without remainder' (UB 91/OHS 1110). True justice is possible in this space, and is decisive but not in the sense that we might typically take as the decisionism of the sovereign, for here there is no chance of a possession taking place. 'Landscape is a dwelling in the inappropriable as form-of-life, as justice. For this reason, if in the world the human being was necessarily thrown and disoriented, in landscape he is finally at home' (UB 91/OHS 1110).

Though it may sound in many ways like the epitome of romanticism, Agamben determines the act of love within such a context as one's relationship to what is other than it and simply cannot be appropriated. Love becomes, in this formulation, an activity of framing the portrait (as landscape) of what is inappropriable within the other (as nature) at the same time as it is a sharing of what is inappropriable between persons (UB 93/OHS 1112). To love is thereby to cease using others to experience nature (through appropriating others, dominating over them and so forth) instead of experiencing nature ourselves as inappropriable. It is from this place, and this place only, that intimacy and privacy are located as the constitution of oneself (UB 91–2/OHS 1110), offering us a political portrait of intimacy as a counter force to sovereign power (UB 92–3/OHS 1111).[5] In his short but profound definition, 'We can call "intimacy" use-of-oneself as relation with an inappropriable' (UB 91/OHS 1110).

Making clear the philosophical stakes within Western thought on the whole, Agamben concludes his discussion of use versus possession by returning it to the context that could be said to have birthed it: Aristotle's distinction between potentiality and actuality. Situating the use/possession debate within this metaphysical-speculative register allows us to sense the significance of Agamben's thought for Western politics on the whole. As he will conclude, use is what renders the potential/actual division itself inoperative, stressing potentiality over actuality and allowing for new possibilities of use to come forth into our world (UB 93–4/OHS 1112). The new possible use of something, like of one's body, for example, is only made possible through this suspension of the division (potential/act) that has traversed Western anthropogenesis (i.e. the capturing of being in order to create the 'human being') and its metaphysical grounds. As such, this suspension is the foundation for new forms of intimacy, love and even something like grace – all of which are brought to our attention through the possible enactment of what I have termed *another* form of sovereignty in our world.

## DEMAND, MEMORY AND THE PLACE OF THOUGHT

I want to return to the ontology of demand at this point to underline some of the most significant points that Agamben has arrived at, especially insofar as they circle back and repeat their trajectories in ever new and expanding contexts of thought. His emphasis on demand can be understood at this point to represent and illustrate the importance of inoperativity, potentiality and the inappropriable in ways that unite much of his earlier suggestions.

For example, in a short essay, 'On the Concept of Demand', Agamben interweaves all of what we have gone over so far in order to link memory to demand and the exigencies of history, as Walter Benjamin once defined their relationship. Memory, in Benjamin's parlance, is capable of upending an 'accomplished' representation, even within one's *own* memory, in order to allow justice to be present.

> Even memory, insofar as it gives incompleteness back to the past and thus somehow makes it still possible for us, is something similar to demand. Leibniz's stance on the problem of demand is here reversed: it is not the possible that demands to exist, but the real – what has already been – that demands its own possibility. And what is thinking if not the capacity to give possibility back to reality, to belie the false claim of opinion that it is founded only on facts? To think means first and foremost to perceive the demand of what is real to become possible again, to do justice not only to things but also to their tears. (WP 30)

Therefore, Agamben will argue that certain memories are unforgettable, even if they are forgotten, because they contain a demand within them that cries out beyond them. 'The unforgettable is, in this sense, the very form of demand. And this is not the claim of a subject: it is a state of the world, an attribute of substance – that is, in Spinoza's words, something that the mind conceives of substance as constituting its essence' (WP 30–1). What grabs hold of us in the memory crying out for justice is precisely the material substance of Spinoza's *conatus* that is identified as demand itself, one that goes beyond 'factual reality'. 'It is not that being simply is: it demands to be. Once again, this means that desire does not belong to the subject, but to being' (WP 32). We should recall that the subject is what was created through the dualistic split brought about through the presupposition and capture of being at the hands of those apparatuses that define and control humanity (or what we will look at soon as what lies at the heart of anthropogenesis).

Agamben is also suggesting that thinking itself – the domain of the Idea – is what enables humanity to transform reality. Thinking allows us to make what appears as 'real' reappear as only 'possible' and so to offer the possibility for transformation of whatever reality to take place. The demands of matter are capable of being reread and taken into account in new ways so that reality might be realigned into new forms and relationships.

Moreover, matter itself makes a demand upon us and is what breaks through the dualistic structures of power within our world, for matter is 'the demand that interrupts the false alternative between the sensible and the intelligible, the linguistic and the non-linguistic: there is a materiality of thought and language, just as there is an intelligibility in sensation' (WP 33). It is at this point that Agamben returns to the inappropriableness of the body itself, as an illustration of what we can only use, but never possess. Here the body makes a demand as a (political) form of 'its most intimate potentiality' (WP 33). In this manner, and not without significant theological implications, the possible demands to become material matter (or substance), allowing us to reread the history of God as really 'the taking place of bodies, the demand that marks and materializes them' (WP 33).[6] God is understood as that which guarantees the existence of the inappropriable, and our relationship to it, within our world.

In the end, demand is described by Agamben as 'more original than the very distinction between essence and existence, possibility and reality', and it is from this place that the entirety of ontology is rethought from the ground up (WP 31). It is in this fashion too that he will go on to ask, 'What if being itself were to be thought of as a demand, of which the categories of modality (possibility, contingency, necessity) are only the inadequate specifications, which we decidedly need to call into question' (WP 31)? Not only is God in need of being rethought, as so much speculation on the nature of the divine has been based upon the historical categories of modality, but the (sovereign) *subject* needs to be reconceived as well through a modal ontology that makes room for forms-of-life lived beyond the law. This necessary rethinking is due to the (sovereign) subject being the modern location of sovereignty par excellence. To reiterate, whatever we are to allow of intimacy, love and grace is predicated upon humanity's ability to go beyond its inscription within particular configurations of sovereign power and imagine anew the possibilities latent within the pure potentiality of existence itself.

> We should not conceive of the subject as a substance but as a vortex in the flow of becoming. He has no other substance than that of the single being, but, with respect to it, he has his own figure, manner, and movement. And it is in this sense that we need to understand the relation between substance and its modes. Modes are the whirlpools in the endless field of substance, which, by collapsing and swirling in itself, is subjectivized, becomes aware of itself, suffers and enjoys. (FT 61)

Going beyond even this, while also making clearer why the history of political-theological thought is so important, Agamben describes how this shift in emphasis upon matter and demand opens up another perspective on faith. Like demand, faith calls out for the existence of, and even provides a reality for, something that does not actually exist. This is the importance of hope within theological realms.

> In this sense, faith is similar to demand, yet on condition of specifying that it is not the anticipation of something to come (as it is for the believer) or that needs to be realized (as it is for the political militant): the thing we hope for is already completely present as demand. For this reason, faith cannot be a property of the believer, but a demand that does not belong to him and reaches him from the outside, from the things he hopes for. (WP 32)

And so, for the faith of the believer as well, there is only a demand that calls out for a reality that does not yet exist, but which comes to be only through the actions that attempt to posit a sovereign power within the world. *Or* they exist only through the messianic force of a potentiality that never actually becomes reality. The demand is the source of critical thought itself – of the *idea* that lies beyond any concrete political action or decision. This is precisely what will allow Agamben to conclude that 'The idea – and demand – is the sleep of the act, the dormition of life' (WP 34).[7]

# 3

# *Glory and the Significance of Political Theology*

KINGDOM, GOVERNMENT AND SOVEREIGNTY

The strength of Agamben's analysis of economic-governmental forms in the *Homo Sacer* series lies squarely in his ability to discern the ways in which a particular political-theological nexus of relations ultimately founded and legitimated the Western subject as we know it. This is something routinely enacted through the presupposition and division of being, which lies at the heart of sovereign power, that I have been discussing. Quite profoundly, he concludes that what we typically regard as philosophical and theological speculation (such as Aristotle's distinction between potentiality and actuality) is, in truth, a highly political discourse with genuine consequences for how our political reality is lived out. What the fields of theology, politics, economics and philosophy today are to make of themselves after such a rereading of their primary (metaphysical) operations remains to be seen. This is why Agamben is also always calling for a 'coming politics' or a 'coming community', as he well knows the implications of his analyses are significant and long-reaching. I will turn in the chapter that follows to Agamben's *The Kingdom and the Glory* because it offers us the opportunity to re-examine relations between these fields and to provide another reading of reason, logic and order altogether. I will begin with the division he introduces between kingdom and government, as this distinction is pivotal for comprehending the scope of Agamben's rearticulation of the relationship between these fields.

From the start, the split between kingdom and government is one that is based on the division, introduced in historical-theological discussions of Trinitarian *oikonomia*, between Being and Act (or praxis). In time, this became the essential division that established the Trinitarian formulation of God's being in three separate but related 'persons', as defined by early theologians (though such forms of subjectivity, in Agamben's reasoning, could also be considered as 'actions', though no one has actually labelled them as such). The resultant dualism predicated upon a certain Christological political-theological interpretation of reality is what ultimately split formulations of the Trinity into ones that were dependent upon a binary representational system, precipitating a movement from an inherently ambiguous Trinity to a Binity.[1] We are left here, historically, with a Christology imposed upon the Trinity. Though there are certainly theologies that would contest this presentation of concepts, an imposed Christology is a point that Agamben is quick to demonstrate as being historically active in various political configurations throughout the West. In his estimate, 'This is the secret dualism that the doctrine of the *oikonomia* has introduced into Christianity, something like an original Gnostic germ, which does not concern the caesura between two divine figures, but rather that between God and his government of the world' (KG 53/OHS 419).[2]

Agamben's reference to an original Gnostic duality, and the concomitant distance which the divine could be said to display with regard to the sovereign's subjects who are governed with a bureaucratic efficiency and discipline, is what forces the division between the kingdom and the government into stark relief within the history of antagonisms that have continued to define the fundamental operations of political theology. From the perspective of Carl Schmitt, whom Agamben utilises as his starting point for his genealogical study of the embedded dualistic structure of Western politics, there was the person of the sovereign, 'he who decides'. However, the sovereign simply could not be eradicated from the foundations of liberal-democratic society, no matter how hard such a society might wish to eliminate their trace altogether.[3] Though Schmitt may have been somewhat dismissive of a liberal society and the way it tries to litigate the everyday affairs of its citizens through the rule of law – what Schmitt decried as an 'endless conversation' – there is nonetheless an inseparable nature to their relationship. Sovereign power, embodied in the kingdom, exists in a permanent struggle with its bureaucratic operations of governance – what Foucault had termed governmentality, and what Agamben takes up directly in relation to Schmitt's formulation of sovereignty. This analysis by Agamben brings to light a tension that neither Schmitt nor Foucault had fully theorised in their respective works.

The uniqueness of Agamben's study in this particular relationship is what grants a heightened urgency to his volume *The Kingdom and the Glory*, for it is there that he most clearly describes the exact relationship between sovereignty and governmentality, as well as the many attempts to suture them together throughout the history of theological discourse. If sovereignty can be understood as an externally imposed will upon the people being governed, and governmentality as an internal power that shapes the governed through their own actions, the notion of order (*ordo*) itself was in fact developed in the medieval period as an attempt to 'suture this division by reproducing it inside itself as a fracture between a transcendent and an immanent order (and between *ordinatio* and *executio*)' (KG 111/OHS 472). As such, the providential and transcendent hand of the sovereign may have established the rule of law and brought to life the tedium of governance. However, it is the immanent regulation of life (governmentality), which appears itself as if it were a grace fatefully given to humanity that undergirds the normative, operational and bureaucratic order of society (KG 126, 136–7/OHS 485, 494–5). We can then assert that the co-existence of these mutually antagonistic spheres in the resultant *oikonomia* of this world is testimony to an unending attempt to 'heal' the fracture between being and praxis that cannot ever be fully healed, much like the split between philosophy and poetry, which Agamben takes up repeatedly in other contexts (KG 89/OHS 451).

Once again, the presupposition of being and the fracture or scission of being into a duality that accompanies its capture by a given apparatus is on full display in political terms. At any rate, we are certainly left with the impression that the two go hand-in-hand and that their appearance in this world is given in such a way as to offer themselves as automatically legitimated as if by God's hand. As Agamben will summarise the situation, 'In other words, the governmental machine functions like an incessant theodicy, in which the Kingdom of providence legitimates and founds the Government of fate, and the latter guarantees the order that the former has established and renders it operative' (KG 129/OHS 488).

For his part, Schmitt had rightly discerned the necessity of a political theological conceptualisation of sovereignty, but he had been too dismissive of the liberalism with which it was inherently, and seemingly eternally, locked in tension. His temptation to emphasise one side over another, however, is not one that easily goes away; it is the temptation that lingers in every denunciation of those powers that tend in one direction or the other, in many ways, constituting the backdrop of all-too-facile binary partisan politics. From this point of view, there are, and seemingly will always be, 'conservative' elements that stress the authority of decision and any resultant communal identity, and there are 'liberal' elements that counter with an emphasis upon the democratic rule of law that provides equality for all (and so frequently deconstructs dominant identities and narratives in order to achieve such ends). This tension is considered by Agamben as a permanent split between the 'providential-economical paradigm' as the democratic option and the 'theological-political paradigm' as that of absolutism (KG 142/OHS 500). Yet the suspension of rule that guaranteed the sovereign's power was fundamentally at odds with the legal structures upon which liberal society was based, though such a rule of law was not possible without a declared state of exception that allowed laws to appear in the first place. A quasi-aporia appears to us from this point of view through the existence of a highly effective binary machinery within which we are prevented from resolving the tension that defines much of Western politics. Furthermore, this is a tension that we are unable to shed because it is what has captured and shaped our being as we know it.

The figure of the sovereign does maintain a distance from the everyday affairs of governance through their ability to render a decision that institutes the sphere which makes possible the rule of law, though the sovereign does not subsequently govern subjects directly. This is the implicit meaning of the phrase analysed by both Agamben and Foucault that 'the king reigns but he does not govern'.[4] The sovereign is, *de potentia ordinata* (through an ordained power only), subject to the law. Simultaneously, the sovereign is, *de potentia absoluta* (through absolute power), not bound by it. This is a principal distinction, as Agamben shows us, first drawn up by canon lawyers with regards to the limits of papal sovereignty (KG 105/OHS 465). The decisions of the sovereign will appear henceforth as that which occur as if by necessity, while liberal-democratic processes will always, by definition, appear as if entirely contingent – despite their necessary existence as the correlate of sovereign power. As Agamben has honed in on this concept, the situation that results is one wherein 'Power – every power, both human and divine – must hold these two poles together, that is, it must be, at the same time, kingdom and government, transcendent norm and immanent order' (KG 82/OHS 444). The sovereign will always appear at a certain distance from the everyday operations of the world, while bureaucratic governance will only ever be able to imply that the divine is disseminated and dispersed throughout all of creation – an analysis that in many ways Foucault laid out clearly for Agamben to follow.

This conclusion introduces a perpetual temptation that one must either choose between an utterly transcendent Gnostic or deistic sovereign deity *or* assume the implications of an entirely immanent pantheism (KG 87/OHS 449).[5] This choice, we are given to understand, must be rejected as a facile dichotomy, one that does not reflect the real stakes of the game: Gnosticism and pantheism are but two extreme positions embedded within the same machinery that produces the terrain of Western political theology. As such, Agamben will conclude – and here extending his investigations beyond those of Foucault – theology will never entirely be rid of either extremity. The present task for theology is to discern why such positions seem to recur cyclically as the outgrowth of a permanently wedded tension between sovereign power and governance that can neither be severed nor eradicated.

In this inspection of what can only appear as perpetually recurring theological heresies, we must also not forget that the constant temptation we are faced with is one located between the symbolic poles of Gnosticism and pantheism. It is one that parallels the modern fluidity that would see the divine will 'annulled in the freedom of men (and the latter in the former)' so that 'theology can resolve itself into atheism, and providentialism into democracy, because God has made the world just as if it were without God and governs it as though it governed itself' (KG 286/OHS 631, de-emphasised from the original).[6] Various theories of secularisation are still trying to resolve the implications of such movements that would see the modern rise of atheism alongside the elevation of the human will into its own divinity (as Ludwig Feuerbach had once already, and correctly, noted).[7] However, Agamben is most concerned about the political-theological implications of such movements. If God can be said to create the world through a sovereign gesture of creation *ex nihilo* and then to let it govern itself such that modern humanity might begin to mistake itself for the divine sovereign and replicate sovereign power within its own structures and institutions, what are the political implications of particular theological formulations concerning God and what are the metaphysical implications for various political formations? Moreover, what remains of a possible divinity beyond such concerns – a wholly *unknown* God to be sure? And what can be said of a humanity that does not seek to imitate its projections onto an external sovereign deity?

## THE DESIRE FOR ORDER

I will return later to questions of a possible humanity and divinity beyond their historical-theological manifestations (or the 'signatures', as Agamben will call them, behind each manifestation that unify them all together and that the genealogist seeks to locate). First, I turn here to the construction of a political-theological order meant to ceaselessly unite that which is forever kept separate: the kingdom and the government. The attempt to conceal and yet maintain such a tension is instructive beyond what I have already gestured toward above in that the order (*ordo*) it articulates is one that defines the role of rationality itself, and in far greater terms than most have understood it. In short, the entire dualistic representational fabric of politics and theology, as much as of language itself, is given its particular *raison d'être* through this political-theological act. That is, the logic of presupposition that captures our being and produces these dualistic splits is what constructs an ordering of reality itself.

> Although the providential machine is unitary, it articulates itself [. . .] into two different planes or levels: transcendence/immanence, general providence/special providence (or fate), first causes/second causes, eternity/temporality, intellectual knowledge/praxis. The two levels are strictly entwined, so that the first founds, legitimates, and makes possible the second, while the second concretely puts into practice in the chain of causes and effects the general decisions of the divine mind. The government of the world is what results from this functional correlation. (KG 141/OHS 499)

As we will eventually see, this capturing of our being hinges upon an exclusionary inclusion (or inclusionary exclusion) that depends upon its sacrificial machinery – the very foundations of the entire *Homo Sacer* project that Agamben has undertaken.

The dichotomous logics that Agamben enumerates are only the tip of the iceberg, as careful readers of Agamben's work have long known. There are the dualisms of potentiality/actuality, *zoē/bios*, constituent/destituent, *potestas/auctoritas*, law-preserving/law-creating, representation/presentation, word/gesture, necessity/contingency, and so on, each appearing at various crucial junctures throughout the *Homo Sacer* series. A particular apparatus creates each of these dualistic frameworks and each brings an order to bear upon an irreconcilable split. Hence, Agamben can say that '*Ordo* names the incessant activity of government that presupposes and, at the same time, continually heals the fracture between transcendence and immanence, God and the world' (KG 90/OHS 452). In truth, it attempts to 'heal the fracture' between each of these dualistic pairings inherent to humanity's linguistic and representational efforts. However, it can never *fully* do so, so instead must perform a temporary suture that actually retains and sustains the problematic split.

What Agamben wants, however, is to re-evaluate (in hopes that there is a potential to overcome) the split through particular movements of regression back toward a given duality's hold upon our representational, linguistic and so ultimately also political contexts. Agamben wants to regress to the original site of being before it was captured by an apparatus, while also recognising that such a regression is not a utopian hope for some primordial state of being or the location of an actual, historical point in time. This is why his turn to form-of-life, as something of a site of pure potentiality, must always exceed the boundaries of such constructed dualities and the order they represent.

The existence of order in our world inherently conjures an ontology, and, concurrently, an ethics and a politics – all things that appear as permanent, though which are anything but eternally fixed.[8] Theology has served historically as a pivotal legitimating discourse for the various complex networks of relations that comprise such orders or cosmologies, hence

Agamben's seemingly endless fascination with it through the series as well as in a number of shorter essays that quickly followed its publication. As one might expect, mythology serves a significant role in configuring, narrating, justifying and transmitting these relations throughout space and time. The theologian James Alison, for one, has noted how the construction of a normative order relies upon a (sacrificial) mythological narrative and the anthropological machinery of an exclusive inclusion (or a 'scapegoat' in the Girardian idiom in which Alison writes) much in the manner that Agamben articulates.[9] The history of theology that Agamben genealogically investigates is one indebted to such mythological structures and their liturgical rites of both power and glory. Much as the work of René Girard focuses on the manifestation of false forms of sacrality in our world in order to expose their violent mechanisms of domination and oppression,[10] Agamben's aim is to reveal the emptiness that order founds itself upon and which itself is

> an empty concept, or, more precisely, it is not a concept, but a *signature*, that is, as we have seen, something that, in a sign or a concept, exceeds it to refer it back to a specific interpretation or move it to another context, yet without exiting the field of the semiotic to construct a new meaning. (KG 87/OHS 449, de-emphasised from the original)

It is transferable and easily imposed upon the subjects who inhabit a given field of social and political representations as the price to be paid for a shared (symbolic) intelligibility.

The implication of such reasoning is that the transcendent order only refers to the immanent order and the immanent order only points back toward the transcendent. In short, they mutually reinforce each other and establish a series of relations that constitute the order of the universe (or *cosmos*), to put it in its most generally conceivable terms. Though the stress may fall from time to time upon one end of this spectrum, and often for politically partisan reasons, they are inseparably intertwined and cannot be effaced. They are the representational coordinates that underlie the tension between kingdom and government, or the sovereign and democratic-liberalism.[11]

This discussion of the metaphysical foundations of order, or of reason itself, is a major implication of Agamben's thought that grants us a complete rereading of modernity and its quest to liberate the (sovereign) subject through recourse to reason alone. Kant's definition of Enlightenment (*Aufklärung*) was, we should recall, dependent upon one's ability to overcome a state of immaturity or 'self-incurred minority' (*Unmündigkeit*). This is an interesting way to phrase things in light of Agamben's contention that order founds itself on the exclusive inclusion of a marginalised (minority) figure (cf. RA 33–4/OHS 783–4). In Kant's words, 'Minority is inability to make use of one's own understanding without direction from another.'[12] In reality, the formulation of autonomy, and of establishing reason itself as the axis of one's subjectivity, involves subordinating one's immaturity in order to reign sovereign over oneself and so to constitute the subject *as* sovereign. What Kant denounced as oppressed and in need of liberation was a state that had not yet attained personhood (i.e. true liberation), at the same time subordinating the non-person to the person who *is* a subject that dares to reason without being dependent on another's understanding. The one who is rationally sovereign over themselves, who has no lack of resolution and who therefore dares to know (*Sapere aude!*) is the one who maintains complete freedom, while the non-person (the minority) remains in chains (and which became all-too-real in the dismissed subaltern non-persons who were subsequently deemed inferior, immature and to be colonised). As Agamben has demonstrated time and again, the modern machinery of personhood and the humanisms that accompany it in the West have been very active in establishing a certain percentage of the population as non-persons through the link established between sovereignty and the autonomous individual who reigns over themselves through the exercise of reason, as of a particular mythological order.[13]

## SOVEREIGN GLORY

There is a circularity of reasoning – the tautology behind every sovereign power – that cannot be ignored as foundational to this logic. Jacques Derrida beautifully isolated this dynamic in his exposition of sovereignty in his study *Rogues*, where he explained how this tautology served to legitimate that which cannot ever really be legitimated and which is, in reality, an empty concept as within a political-ontological reality, a bringing to life of the emperor's 'new clothes'.[14] As Agamben demonstrates in parallel fashion, this is the case because order, like glory, is both an essential attribute of the divine and also that which must be rendered to the divine by the humans who bear the *imago dei* through the act of worship (KG 214/OHS 566). This is the index of reciprocal relations that defines the inscription of power in relationships of domination and in no way leads to their deactivation. For example, in the context of discussing Karl Barth's theological inscription of power within his definition of glory, Agamben discerns how 'The circularity of glory here attains its ontological formulation: becoming free for the glorification of God means to understand oneself as constituted, in one's very being, by the glory with which we celebrate the glory that allows us to celebrate it' (KG 215/OHS 567). This circularity ends only through obedience, inculcated and concluded through the institution of the Church – the very same collective that, as Agamben says elsewhere, has sought determinately to neutralise the messianic gesture that Paul once found within the 'new experience of the word' that deactivated, or rendered inoperative, its old use (P 88). One's 'dignity and the highest freedom' are to be located in such an act of obedience to the glory of sovereignty, which is glorified *because it is glorious* (KG 216/OHS 216–17). From Roman imperial rites to mythological liturgies within the Church that draw from and mirror their Roman forerunners, we might be correct to conclude from Agamben's genealogical analysis that sovereign glory becomes manifest as that which is rendered to God at the same time as

105

it is what emanates from the divine. This offers the Church a self-legitimating narrative for its own existence and its exercise of sovereign power. If this conclusion has any merit, it should not be restricted to the Church either. This conclusion posits the same dynamics that lie at the heart of all political, cultural, social and economic institutions as well, as each maintains itself as an apparatus seeking to capture and control being in some way through the orders they impose upon humanity.

However, it is important to note – especially insofar as this will illuminate a general comprehension of what is ultimately at stake in Agamben's thought – that he does give us an alternative vision of the Church, again through reference to Pauline thought. Agamben offers the reader something like a messianic vision of a Church that is locked in a permanent tension with the governing economic force of law or state. As Agamben elsewhere contends, the Church must realise its messianic vocation or risk being 'swept away by the disaster menacing every government and every institution on earth' (CK 41). This menacing threat would seem to be something inherent to any given structure, and it is not entirely clear whether this somewhat Derridean gesture is a uniquely modern development or whether it will always haunt any given structure or institution. Nonetheless, by placing his critique of the Church alongside the possibility for another, messianic Church to appear from within its mythological edifice is intriguing to say the least (and also insofar as it echoes some of the foundational objections of the Protestant Reformation). It also gives rise to the suggestion that any given human collective must always have a narrative before it, though hopefully one more conscious and aware of its own ideological investments, in order to lessen the injustices and violences that will undoubtedly affect the shared domain of intelligibility.

The distinction between these two forms of reciprocal glory – what has been historically understood as a division between external and internal forms of glory – is maintained, as Agamben claims, in order to conceal God's true substance, what he further calls God's 'nudity' (KG 221/OHS 572). It is not entirely clear if this is a reference to an ambivalence concerning God's existence, God's *in*existence, God's capriciousness or (perhaps) weakness or even a sense that God does not know what God is doing. What *is* clear is that this formulation parallels humanity's (specifically, historically, *man's*) attempt to conceal a lack of power, a lack of justification for the dominance it wields over other humans, women, particular races of persons, animals and even itself. In this sense, the reciprocal nature of glory mirrors the reciprocal foundations of governance itself.[15] This is the fulcrum upon which Agamben's critique depends.

What is revealed through the analysis of the two forms of reciprocal glory is the fact that there is no secret to God's being, only an encounter with a reality that ceases to entice us into the machinery that produces the human subject, and which appears deceptively to us as that which is beautiful. As with Agamben's remarks elsewhere on nudity and the beautiful, what we are actually searching for is an encounter with the human body shorn of the conditions of beauty – an existence, as Walter Benjamin suggests to Agamben, 'beyond all beauty' and what registers as an encounter with the sublime. We are searching for our being before its capture into an apparatus. It is where nothing appears, an encounter with 'only the veil itself' (N 85). Here, Agamben will conclude that 'It is in this way that, in nudity without veils, appearance itself appears and displays itself as infinitely inapparent, infinitely free of secret. The sublime, then, is an appearance that exhibits its own vacuity and, in this exhibition, allows the inapparent to take place' (N 85–6). We are hereby returned to the empty gestures of sovereignty, but also to the emptiness that remains in 'whatever being' or as with a form-of-life lived beyond the confines of representation that we seek to encounter in the authentically ethical relation that Agamben is after. Such an encounter is something like the sublime possibility of grace in our world.[16]

The reciprocal glory that grounds the violent mechanisms of power underneath a community's sense of itself are really no more than a thin veil that attempts to conceal a chasm of emptiness, its particular nudity as it were – a point that Agamben is not hesitant to expose as such: 'Does the distinction between internal and external glory, which reciprocally respond to one another, really constitute a sufficient explanation? Does it not rather betray the attempt to explain the unexplainable, to hide something that it would be too embarrassing to leave unexplained?' (KG 224; OHS 575). Like order itself, glory is an attempt to suture the divide between kingdom and government, immanent and economic models of the Trinity, as well as Being and action (KG 230/OHS 580). The gesture Agamben makes is to suggest that the glorification of prayer that takes place doxologically and liturgically in order to conceal the gap between these various dualisms is the same gesture made through prayer that sacrifice also makes. As sacrifice is central to the anthropological machinery that Agamben wants to condemn, so too does prayer, through its glorification of the divine, maintain the apparatus that would construct the human subject in a particular nexus of power relations (KG 226/OHS 577).

In his short essay 'What Is an Apparatus?', Agamben summarises and contextualises his archaeology of glory as one that revolves around deactivating the apparatuses that create and sustain the human being, such as language itself. Here we find a link to sacrifice even more fundamentally asserted than in *The Kingdom and the Glory*. However, before stating this link to sacrifice explicitly, Agamben first reiterates the very terms by which the apparatus captures our being. In his words:

> apparatuses are not a mere accident in which humans are caught by chance, but rather are rooted in the very process of 'humanization' that made 'humans' out of the animals we classify under the rubric Homo sapiens. In fact, the event that has produced the human constitutes, for the living being, something like a division, which reproduces in some way the division that the *oikonomia* introduced in God between being and action. (WA 16)

Again, we are privy to the political-theological justifications and doctrines that are as much an attempt to construct the human being in relation to language and its being dominant over the animal world (and nature itself) as they are about the divine, though their focus, as with Trinitarian economic models, is often squarely displaced upon the transcendent realm. The distance which the human being now enjoys vis-à-vis its environment mirrors the distance that God takes from the created world. And here is where sacrifice enters his analysis of the role of apparatuses:

> From this perspective, one can define religion as that which removes things, places, animals, or people from common use and transports them to a separate sphere. Not only is there no religion without separation, but every separation contains or conserves in itself a genuinely religious nucleus. The apparatus that activates and regulates separation is sacrifice. Through a series of minute rituals that vary from culture to culture [. . .] sacrifice always sanctions the passage of something from the profane to the sacred, from the human sphere to the divine. (WA 18–19)

The relationship between sacrifice and the creation of order, both facilitated through the discourses of religion, is cemented as the central machinery of Western subjectivity. It is for this reason that any subject or identity exists in the first place and why the maintenance of the subject, theologically or philosophically, is so significant. The task of profanation, for Agamben, is tantamount to rendering the apparatuses that fabricate the human subject inoperative – that is, suspending their operations indefinitely (PR 73–92). Only in such a way might we accede to a new understanding of a life that is lived without being inscribed into such (dominant and potentially unjust) relations, the concluding form-of-life that the entire *Homo Sacer* project has been aiming toward from its inception.

In light of the reality that Agamben's *Homo Sacer* series is guided by the presupposition that articulates the process of anthropogenesis at the hands of a machinery that seeks to create the human being *as* a sovereign subject, we are forced to inquire as to how reason itself, inherent in the processes that give us order through a particular cosmos against an apparent chaos, is indebted to the same forces of sacrifice that demarcate the 'exclusionary inclusion' that defines the figure of the *homo sacer*. This compels us furthermore to ask: to what degree is reason itself, or whatever rationality we employ, utilised to keep the chaos of our own animality at bay, to repress its truth still further through the apparently mysterious existence and implementation of language? To give an order to human existence, to institute a hierarchical, categorical rationality of any sort, is little more than an outworking of the same forces that allow humanity to dominate the animal world external to it at the same time as it dominates its own animal nature within itself. The concept of hierarchy in the West, after all, originates in the mystical theological writings of Pseudo-Dionysius[17] and his attempt to sacralise a form of power that 'descends from the Trinity, via the angelic triarchies, to the earthly hierarchy', something easily extended in principle to the hierarchy of humanity over animality as well (KG 153/OHS 509–10).

In *The Open*, another instance where Agamben tries to clarify this relationship, he has described the human being's animality as a zone 'outside of being', a space of *agnoia* or non-knowing, yet *within* whatever knowledge the human being constructs and not apart from it. Agamben is not trying to forge a new creation between the human and the animal, nor positing a dialectical synthesis of the two even. Rather, Agamben is rendering inoperative the machinery that ceaselessly divides the one from the other in order to legitimate the human's mastery over the animal. His conclusion on anthropogenesis in *The Open* is therefore entirely parallel with his suggestions made in *The Kingdom and the Glory*:

> man has always been the result of a simultaneous division and articulation of the animal and the human, in which one of the two

terms of the operation was also what was at stake in it. To render inoperative the machine that governs our conception of man will therefore mean no longer to seek new – more effective or more authentic – articulations, but rather to show the central emptiness, the hiatus that – within man – separates man and animal, and to risk ourselves in this emptiness: the suspension of suspension, Shabbat of both animal and man. (O 92)

This 'suspension of suspension', or what Agamben will call in the context of Pauline thought the 'division of division itself', is what renders identity as we know it inoperative – a suspension of the suspended lives humanity embodies in a recognisable political-representational sense (TR 49).[18] Logic, ontology and politics are all opened up anew thanks to this Pauline negative dialectic that Agamben continues to reformulate and articulate in new genealogical contexts as the real solution capable of being pronounced in our world today. The capacity to reason, as humanity defines it, ceaselessly legitimates and justifies such an endeavour through its unending exercise. It is for this reason that logic itself must always rest on a metaphysical (anthropogenetic) foundation or ground. This understanding was certainly apparent to Heidegger in his lectures on *The Metaphysical Foundations of Logic*, wherein ontological difference itself – between *Being* and *beings* – was what grounded logic.[19] However, what we see in Agamben is that such facile dualisms are precisely what legitimate political relations of dominance and oppression because they are what has been provided in order to legitimate the presupposition of being taking place within every constructed dualism.

If we follow Agamben more closely, we see that the apparatus of language has introduced a nexus of guilt and punishment into the realm of human existence. As he will conclude elsewhere, the fact that the human being stepped outside of its genetic coding in order to speak and thus to remove itself from the other animals around it, is what has subsequently become the human species' 'original sin' (FT 16–17). Language, sharing a particular affinity with the pluralistic liberal order that we cannot remove ourselves from, is part of the 'mysterium burocraticum' that Agamben sees humanity dwelling within and that we cannot dispense with. Not until we 'get to the bottom of' this mystery that finds us immersed in the bureaucratic apparatuses of language itself: 'the mystery of language and of guilt, that is, in all truth, of his being and not yet being human, of his being and no longer being an animal' (FT 18). Language is ultimately that which allows us to provide an order to veil our dominance of our own animality and the animal world around us.

As we see in a number of studies of Agamben's that reach their culmination in the *Homo Sacer* project (and also recall from Chapter 1), the political, performative power of the oath is inextricably linked to the sacrament of language, with both playing vital roles in the maintenance of the anthropological machinery of the West and developing the political-theological nexus that legitimates its dominance through the formation of the human subject (SL 66/OHS 350–1). According to Agamben, whose originality of argumentation leads the way in this context, the time has come to render profane this sacramental bond that has been so central to Western legal codes (such as the use of oaths in legal and political matters). The deactivation of this machinery – our capacity to render it inoperative – will be possible only through a secondary messianic suspension of the primary suspension (or state of emergency) that undergirds the decisive power of the sovereign. Here it is the Pauline influence that allows him to reread the Schmittian state of exception as that which itself can be suspended. Uniquely it is philosophy that, for Agamben, will be able to provide such a critique, as he illustrates in another genealogical study, *The Sacrament of Language*:

> Philosophy is, in this sense, constitutively a critique of the oath: that is, it puts in question the sacramental bond that links the human being to language, without for that reason simply speaking haphazardly, falling into the vanity of speech. In a moment when

all the European languages seem condemned to swear in vain and when politics can only assume the form of an *oikonomia*, that is, of a governance of empty speech over bare life, it is once more from philosophy that there can come, in the sober awareness of the extreme situation at which the living human being that has language has arrived in its history, the indication of a line of resistance and of change. (SL 72/OHS 355–6)

# 4

# *Economy and its Inoperativity*

### THE BIPOLAR SOVEREIGNTY OF IDENTITY

Christianity's implicit indebtedness to acts of exclusionary inclusion – the basis for establishing such figures as the *homo sacer* – has resulted in the perpetual re-articulation and justification of God's, humanity's and the Church's employment of sovereign power in very real and worldly political terms. These political terms, and the divisions they rest upon, are not exclusively the domain of the Church, but the foundations of order itself as we know it. The question that lingers, and will presumably linger throughout any analysis of Agamben's work in general, is: to what degree such a messianic suspension of governing institutional norms could ever become a history in and of itself? Or, in a much more Derridean sense: will the weak force of the messianic be that which haunts every institution or normative structure without ever positing a (grand narratival) history for itself, as to declare such a force for the majority is to dominate over another and to cease the radically deconstructive act that is the force of the messianic?

Though I will ultimately argue that we cannot do away with narrative, identities and communities altogether, we are still able to discern the difficulty of attempting to resolve this question through some of the political-theological examples that Agamben takes up. Furthermore, these examples hinge upon historical-theological efforts to avoid the problem altogether by positing the sovereignty of God as the ultimate solution (or ultimate denial of a political reality, depending on one's perspective). Such an investigation, from Agamben's point of view, includes a critique of the attempted transfer of the sheer power and domination that glory attempts to mask and maintain into the sphere of the aesthetic through the concept of the beautiful, what he senses at work in the theological aesthetics of Hans Urs von Balthasar and Karl Barth alike (KG 212–13/OHS 564–5).

To give a glimpse of this connection between glory and beauty as evident and lingering justifications for sovereign power, whether vested in God or in humanity, we might look to von Balthasar's theological aesthetics as it is taken up in his *The Glory of the Lord* – a movement that is made parallel to Barth's attempts to ground God's sovereignty in his distance from any worldly affairs.[1] Consequently, this distancing offers a permanent critique of all political and religious forms. As Agamben illustrates in the context of their works, the problem with such a manoeuvre – no matter whether this is ultimately what von Balthasar and Barth are doing in their writings where things may at times be more nuanced – is that the effort to identify God with glory and beauty, and to ignore the political elements latent within such a vision, is to wager a more significant risk of repeating the worst aspects of political glory and its potentially authoritarian liturgical operations. As Agamben articulates, 'The attempt to exclude the very possibility of a Christian "political theology," so as to found in glory the only legitimate political dimension of Christianity, comes dangerously close to the totalitarian liturgy' (KG 193/OHS 546).

It is perhaps no surprise that Barth's theology, which serves as a source of inspiration for von Balthasar in many respects, is inherently Christocentric, and so fundamentally dependent upon the precise binary nature of Jesus's alleged being. As we have already seen, this precise binary nature is what sustains a certain outworking of political theology, which had been signaled by Ernst Kantorowicz, a contemporary of Barth.[2] Much of Western political theology has been concerned throughout the centuries, especially in its Roman-imperial and medieval contexts, with stressing particular political instances of Christomonism which had been utilised to justify and legitimate Western imperial impositions through a link forged between Christ as king and an actual, earthly monarch. As a critique of such links, we witness Agamben's claims regarding how divine Trinitarian economy was actually turned into a Christomonistic machine that ultimately created the Western subject.[3] This 'Binity', or Two-ness of sovereign power – though Agamben does not himself use this term – places an extreme emphasis on the bond between the Father and the Son in order to combat the historical heresy of Arianism, though it was never really eradicated from the sphere of politics and has come in many ways to define Western theological articulations of the Trinity as well.[4] The reciprocal relations of the Father and the Son in this way refuse to be disrupted by the entrance of a third term – the Holy Spirit – in order to deconstruct their attempt to dualistically posit themselves as sovereign. There is certainly another theological possibility of reading the Trinity as a potential undoing of the Binity that dominates Western political theology. But this is something that remains relatively unexplored in most political theological contexts, including in Agamben's own critique, which certainly makes little room for the Holy Spirit either.[5]

The linkage that von Balthasar posits between glory and sovereignty is the inevitable conclusion drawn from Barth's restoration of God's sovereignty through Christ's dual nature. It is in this fashion that Agamben declares, 'Glory is precisely the place at which this bilateral (or bi-univocal) character of the relation between theology and politics clearly emerges into the light', and so presumably is the reason that it becomes the focal point for the subsequent Barthian theology of von Balthasar (KG 193/ OHS 547). The human being is caught up in the glory offered to God through the praise of God's glory – the reciprocal relationship of glory that signals the wholescale incorporation of sovereign power within a theological paradigm. Rather than depart from the fundamental gestures of sovereign power in the human, political sphere, such theologies seem to do little more than legitimate such powers in ecclesial terms.[6]

The modern theological positions that Agamben's critique of the Binity mirrors is therefore not that of von Balthasar or Barth, but rather that of feminist, queer and other contextual theologians who have mounted a vast critique of the oppressive heteronormative and strictly binary forms of gender and sexuality that are utilised to oppress particular minority persons or groups. It should equally be noted, these are often theologies that are frequently denounced as antinomian – a charge that resonates with Agamben's philosophy as well, as I have already suggested. Therefore, it should come as no surprise that the messianic visions of a Trinity beyond the Binity, of a Trinity that cannot be reinscribed back into a Binity but rather which ceaselessly deconstructs it, are favoured by queer theologians in particular for its radical subversive possibilities. The radical liberationist and 'indecent' theologian Marcella Althaus-Reid, for example, favourably cited Agamben's work as a central philosophical attempt to move past the binary systems of thought that have guided Western politics from its inception.[7]

## SUBJECTS AND THE SUSPENSION OF IDENTITY

The meditation that Agamben's critique opens up to us at this point is much wider than might be expected in *The Kingdom and the Glory*, which is mainly restricted to its genealogical methods and so refrains from drawing connections to the larger oeuvre of Agamben's writings. However, what Agamben does chart dovetails nicely with his broader considerations regarding numerous political-theological topics that all centre around the issue of a suspension of normative order and everyday activity that seems to accompany, not only reflections on the Sabbath in the Judaic and Christian traditions, but also speculations on what the heavenly afterlife might resemble in its unending praise and glory of God other than what ostensibly appears to be an acute, ironic, infinite and even torturous boredom. Theological discussions on the afterlife, and an eternity of glorification of God's glory, are really a political-theological laboratory for humanity's configuration of itself in relation to sovereign and governmental power, as Roberto Esposito also has phrased it. In this dynamic, not even the angels are safe from our political conclusions:

> It is now comprehensible why [. . .] the perfect cipher of Christian citizenship is constituted by the song of praise, and the pleromatic figures of the political is bestowed upon the angels who have become inoperative. The doctrine of Glory as the final end of man and as the figure of the divine that outlives the government of the world is the answer that theologians give to the problem of the end of economy. The angelic ministries survive the universal judgment only as a hymnological hierarchy, as contemplation and praise of the glory of the divine. With every providential operation exhausted and with all administration of salvation coming to an end, only song remains. Liturgy survives only as doxology. (KG 162/OHS 518)

The only thing that such theological conjectures on the angelic hierarchies and eternal liturgies reveal is the empty centre that humanity ceaselessly tries to conceal. Such activities only serve the purpose of sustaining a very worldly legitimation of reciprocal glory, which tries to suture together the kingdom and the government as a single political-theological mechanism. In such images, God simply sits on the throne in heaven, ostensibly doing nothing other than exist so as to fully embody the glory of the sovereign. This leaves unanswered the apparent eternal torment of having to take part in endless liturgies of power and glorification, as well as the question of what God was occupied with before the creation of the world. As we are led to understand things, God is really concealing, through reference to Being and Act, an abyss of potentiality and inoperativity that cannot be ignored, but must be ceaselessly covered over: 'glory is what must cover with its splendor the unaccountable figure of divine inoperativity' (KG 163/OHS 518, de-emphasised from the original).

Perhaps the ultimate model of what theologians contemplate when they consider the suspension of normal economic relations is the Sabbath, or the suspension of the normal working day (as a marker for order itself) in lieu of celebration and feasting. Giving a face to the dynamics of inoperativity that Agamben seeks to formulate, the Sabbath, or, in general, any feast day, grants us a look into the messianic deactivation that would become an alternative to the economic order that governs our world and its many representations. As Agamben makes clear:

> The feast day is not defined by what is not done in it but instead by the fact that what is done – which in itself is not unlike what is accomplished every day – becomes undone, rendered inoperative, liberated and suspended from its 'economy,' from the reasons and aims that define it during the weekdays (and not doing, in this sense, is only an extreme case of this suspension). (N 110–11)

The characteristic feature of the Sabbath suspension is its ability to deactivate an already operative economy and to declare such a suspension of economic and rational order as the messianic task par excellence. Again, Agamben is deftly relocating this Pauline notion of the messianic suspension within a philosophical context thanks to the resonance Paul's thought shares with the philosophical speculations of Walter Benjamin on a 'weak messianic force' moving throughout history.

The historical-theological image that every noteworthy task points toward within Agamben's thinking is that of the Sabbath, or the religious notion of a suspension of the everyday that results in a thing being rendered inoperative and so open to a new use. The Sabbath, he notes, originating in the Jewish scriptures and tradition, is the most sacred day because it is 'the day on which all work ceases', and for this reason, 'the name of what is most proper to God' (KG 239/OHS 588). Likewise, it is what could be said to identify the Kingdom of

God in Christianity (KG 240/OHS 589). As Agamben unfolds the dynamics that have distorted the proper name of God in *The Kingdom and the Glory*, we eventually see how glory comes to take the place of the inoperativity of power, which is unthinkable and unsayable in the vacuum it occupies (KG 242/OHS 591). From this point of view, one can easily imagine how the empty throne which could otherwise symbolically indicate the suspension of power, comes to represent the glory of God and of the kings and popes who would sit upon such thrones throughout the centuries (KG 243–4/OHS 592). Comparable to the vacuity of the state of exception upon which sovereignty and humanity is founded:

> the center of the governmental apparatus, the threshold at which Kingdom and Government ceaselessly communicate and ceaselessly distinguish themselves from one another is, in reality, empty; it is only the Sabbath and *katapausis* – and, nevertheless, this inoperativity is so essential for the machine that it must at all costs be adopted and maintained at its center in the form of glory. (KG 242/OHS 591–2)

Glory is what attempts to conceal this fundamental emptiness that characterises the true 'purpose' (as purposelessness) of the human being. In fact, it is this purposelessness that allows for any sense of purpose to be created at all within a human being's life.

> Human life is inoperative and without purpose, but precisely this *argia* and this absence of aim make the incomparable operativity of the human species possible. Man has dedicated himself to production and labor, because in his essence he is completely devoid of work, because he is the Sabbatical animal par excellence. And just as the machine of the theological *oikonomia* can function only if it writes within its core a doxological threshold in which economic trinity and immanent trinity are ceaselessly and liturgically (that is, politically) in motion, each passing into the other, so the governmental apparatus functions because it has captured in its empty center the inoperativity of the human essence. This inoperativity is

the political substance of the Occident, the glorious nutrient of all power. (KG 245–6/OHS 594–5)

This purposelessness is sensed as powerfully present in Pauline thought as the messianic force that renders inoperative every given vocation or identity. In fact, it is precisely the messianic life that maintains 'the impossibility that life might coincide with a predetermined form' (KG 248/OHS 597). Therefore, the Sabbath inherently calls forth a form of inoperativity that Agamben wants to recover as a messianic suspension of identity that differs significantly from the theological notions of the eternal and of a glorious life that were frequently posited as substitutions for the messianic vocation (KG 249/OHS 597). By charting this originary proclamation of Pauline thought, he hopes as well to make abundantly clear how inoperativity functions in Western thought alongside contemplation as the sites of possibility which make politics conceivable in our world (KG 249–51/OHS 598–600). It is also the force, however, that will undo the very political coordinates that have established our given political relations throughout history.

What such figures of eternal contemplation and praise call to mind is the very real suspension of entirely human norms and rules, orders and principalities that give rise to new forms of thought. This is the philosophical procedure that Agamben discerns latent within these many theological genealogies of figures of inoperativity, but which is all-too-often suppressed so that sovereign power might be somewhere maintained. Indeed, it is even possible to co-opt the Sabbath itself, not as an act of deactivation, de-creation or destituent potential, as Agamben variously labels such acts throughout the *Homo Sacer* series, but as a potential site of (false) sacrality which extracts the radical, messianic force from it and domesticates it for institutional power.

> This does not mean that the human activities that the feast has suspended and rendered inoperative are necessarily separated and transported into a more elevated and solemn sphere. It is possible,

in fact, that this separation of the feast into the sacred sphere, which certainly came about at a certain point, was the work of the Church and the clergy. (N 111–12)

This is a portrait of the Church and its supposed minions (i.e. its clergy) who serve an exclusionary-inclusive mechanism – the Western anthropological machinery – by stamping each subject (or identity on the whole) with a particular theological signature. It is precisely such forces that fight against the apparent growth of the secular sphere and defend the inscription of a false form of sacrality that would merely replicate the order and rationality that Agamben is explicitly calling into question. His repeated calls for an act of profanation beyond the secular/sacred dichotomy run fairly directly across these lines:

> We should, perhaps, try to invert the familiar chronology according to which religious phenomena are placed at the origin, only to be secularized later on, and instead hypothesize that what comes first is the moment in which human activities are simply neutralized and rendered inoperative during the feast. What we call 'religion' (a term that, in its current meaning, is missing from ancient culture) intervenes at that moment by capturing the feast in a separate sphere. (N 112)

It is such religious gestures that must be resisted as they seek to isolate and identify, or simply *create*, the religious subject through the presupposition of one's being. What we are left with in Agamben's critique of such falsely religious acts of sacralisation is the sense that a new use of the human body is possible beyond its theological legacy (signature), one that is strangely identifiable in the modern world, as we will now see.

## NEW USES OF THE BODY

The first example Agamben gives us of such possible new uses of the body – the very topic upon which the *Homo Sacer* series concludes – is actually in an earlier work outside of the *Homo Sacre* series, *The Coming Community*. Herein, he finds, the emergent capitalist processes of reification (or objectification) are also strangely liberating in that they, at least, remove the theological meanings that had been placed upon the body. As such, the female body – as the outstanding example of cultural objectification he takes up – is freed from its enslavement to the theological signatures of virginity and biological reproduction at the same time that it is sexually objectified (CC 47–50). The second example is made available through the rise of pornographic films and the bodies engaged therein that introduce a new use for the body beyond its theological signature. This is a new use that in fact parallels the glorious, resurrected body that theologians have long contemplated as existing beyond the register of everyday bodily functions. The lack of lived bodily economies within the glorious body could only ever mirror the body of the porn star, as neither are forced to engage in the basic economies of everyday life that the body must otherwise attend to (N 91–103). In both examples, we witness a new possible use of the body beyond its theological signature, while also sensing certain limitations that keep us at a distance from truly rendering our representations of the body inoperative.

A third, very different example arises in the final volume of the *Homo Sacer* series, *The Use of Bodies*, where the task of contemplation provides another byway from which to view the operation of deactivation with regard to the theological signature placed upon the human body, and so too its possible liberation. Referencing Plotinus, Agamben seeks to expand upon the former's notion of life as an immediate form of contemplation and is as such able to conceive of contemplation as a 'paradigm for use' instead of its obverse partner, possession (UB 215/OHS 1222; for more reference on an Aristotelian exchange, see Chapter 2). We are able to access something like form-of-life through the (both theological and philosophical) act of contemplation because it is this act in particular that restores us to our ownmost potentiality:

> Like use, contemplation does not have a subject, because in it the contemplator is completely lost and dissolved; like use, contemplation does not have an object, because in the work it contemplates

only its (own) potential. Life, which contemplates in the work its (own) potential of acting or making, is rendered inoperative in all its works and lives only in use-of-itself, lives only (its) livability. (UB 63/OHS 1085)

It is this 'livability' that Agamben is particularly attentive to because it seems to offer humanity an opportunity to glimpse life beyond its inscription in the anthropological machinery. Bearing testimony to the possible deactivation of the human subject, contemplation promises the inoperativity of the human being and an access to 'whatever being' appears in its stead.[8] The centrality of contemplation and its inoperativity, here taken as synonymous terms, is what Agamben links explicitly to form-of-life, 'the properly human life' that

> is the one that, by rendering inoperative the specific works and functions of the living being, causes them to idle, so to speak, and in this way opens them into possibility. Contemplation and inoperativity are in this sense the metaphysical operators of anthropogenesis, which, in liberating living human beings from every biological and social destiny [their 'theological signature'] and every predetermined task, render them available for that peculiar absence of work that we are accustomed to calling 'politics' and 'art'. (UB 277–8/OHS 1278)

Agamben's remarks on contemplation as another form of inoperativity – specifically in relation to a new use of the body beyond its historical-theological legacy (again, which he considers as a 'signature'), and so the glory that has frequently obscured the very real bodies underneath the objectifying veil (what the 'glorious body' signalled) – bears a remarkable overlap with those critical-political theorists who would advocate for not taking action in the face of what appears to be a looming need for political action or decision. These are positions staked in opposition to the Schmittian necessity for a decision. For example, we see this call to 'think' in the work of both Slavoj Žižek and Theodor Adorno, who both resist the Schmittian call to decisive action as yet another reinscription into the political and anthropological machinery that presents sovereign decision as a necessity and is thus incapable of thinking a more authentic revolutionary potential for transformation.[9] Adorno, who was significantly challenged and upset by the student protests of the late 1960s, was adamant about the role of critique and of the space for thought itself in the face of the demand for political praxis. Calling thinking a 'force of resistance', he was quite clear on why we must politically maintain a space for critical thought: 'Thinking is not the intellectual reproduction of what already exists anyway. As long as it doesn't break off, thinking has a secure hold on possibility. Its insatiable aspect, its aversion to being quickly and easily satisfied, refuses the foolish wisdom of resignation.'[10]

This call to thinking as a force of resistance is perhaps best illustrated through the work of Derrida whose hesitancy to engage any direct form of politics was often a source of discouragement to those more inclined to political praxis – especially from the side of Marxist theorists. Derrida's insistence on providing a critique of sovereignty alongside what appeared to be an endless deferral of meaning through the play of *différance* captured something of the 'endless conversation' that liberalism represents, at least according to Schmitt. Derrida's refusal of the either/or nature of the decision that produces the sovereign subject (à la Kierkegaard) left him searching for other ways to institute the subject – through something like a 'passive' decision, as Geoffrey Bennington has recently put it.[11] Such an alignment might also go a long way toward explaining why a good many academics intent on certain, even scientific, forms of decisionism – and here a good many philosophical and theological communitarians should be included – protested Derrida's work so vehemently as it seemed to constantly evade the moment of decision (and so too *definition* or *order*) that typically grounds a community's autonomously established sense of sovereignty. If the pluralistic, endless discourses of liberalism are already opposed by definition to the decisionism of those wishing to be sovereign, then Derrida's dalliances in language were almost bound to fail with the latter crowd from their inception.

## MESSIANIC OR HYPERNOMIAN

Agamben's relationship with Derrida was not always amicable and not always clear either. It seems that, at times, they mirror each other while also simultaneously disavowing any possible connection between their respective works. What is minimally clear is that the only new possible use of the human body is made available from the deactivation of the old body, the one we had thought we possessed. In some sense, this is akin to Derrida's insistence that the deconstructive act is only possible from within a pre-existing structure or identity, not external to it.[12]

Though Agamben clearly shares with Derrida a certain critique of sovereignty, it is also clear that Agamben's preferred source for discussing the potential for theo-political transformation is Pauline thought, which offers him the chance to reread philosophical operations through a theological lens. Pauline messianism offers the most direct model for contemplating the deactivation of subjectivity and personal identity that one can imagine, though the Church has also historically domesticated it on occasion. In Agamben's reading of things, Pauline messianism 'acts as a corrective to the demonic hypertrophy of angelic and human powers. The Messiah deactivates and renders inoperative the law as well as the angels and, in this way, reconciles them with God' (KG 166/OHS 522). Jesus Christ, an identification between individual and messianic (Christic) vocation so strong that no article is inserted between the two words, becomes for Paul an entrance into the deactivation of all social, political, economic *and* religious identities, including the Judaic one that had seemed to identify Jesus from his birth. 'The ultimate and glorious telos of the law and of the angelic powers, as well as of the profane powers, is to be deactivated and made inoperative' (KG 166/OHS 522).

However, rather than offering a rejection of Judaic law, Jesus's attempt to surpass the literal requirements of the law through claiming to be its 'fulfilment' introduced something like a *hypernomian* moment (to borrow a phrase from Elliot Wolfson)[13] within the seemingly unbridgeable dualism between *nomos* and *anomie*. What is interesting to note in this formulation of things is the difficulty that arises in locating and defining a position *as* hypernomian. This struggle is reflected by the awkwardly invented and infrequently utilised term itself, which indicates a force we still do not know what to do with, or even how to think about its potential for de-activating law. Establishing a hypernomian position, which Agamben seeks to access through a number of differing terms – such as pure potentiality or the 'division of division itself' – all seem to involve a quasi-negative dialectic that promises to subdivide the division introduced by the pre-existing social division that grants the individual a sense of identity. It is also what introduces the messianic suspension of identity as a threshold of indifference to already existing, and often firmly reinforced, social, political and religious dichotomies: 'In Paul, the messianic community as such is anonymous and appears to be situated on an undifferentiated threshold between public and private' (KG 175/OHS 530, de-emphasised from the original). The characteristic of anonymity is essential here too, because it is this *lack of identity* that allows it to contest the articulation of sovereign power and its resultant identifications produced through those apparatuses that constitute the anthropological machinery in our world. As he describes this formulation more recently in a short essay:

> The form-of-life is the point in which the work on an opus and the work on oneself perfectly coincide. The painter, the poet, the thinker – and, in general, anyone who practices an 'art' or an 'activity' – are not the appointed sovereign subjects of a creative operation and of an opus; they are rather anonymous living beings who, contemplating and making at each turn inoperative the opus of language, of vision, and of bodies, try to experience themselves and keep in relation with a potentiality, that is, to constitute their life as form-of-life. (FT 138)

Contemplation, as the medium of inoperativity, becomes the essential path toward one's potentiality and consequently the hope for embodying a form-of-life lived beyond the sovereign subject and its indebtedness to the realm of representation.

Paul, for his part, does not engage in formulating the necessity for a Trinitarian economy to found and legitimate a given cosmological ordering, which comprises acts of 'reciprocal glorification' intended to cement sovereign power (as we saw at the beginning of this chapter and throughout Chapter 3). Rather, he engages in the task of messianic redemption which sees the veil that both conceals and reveals the divine glory erased, allowing glory to be transmitted from God to humanity (KG 203–4, 211/ OHS 556–7, 563–4). It is only in this fashion that Paul can think the de-activation of a reciprocal glory that otherwise seeks to sustain the connection between economy and glory, as between the kingdom and government (or sovereignty and liberalism, in Schmitt's parlance) (KG 210/OHS 562).[14]

A more sustained subversion of glory comes about through multiple rereadings of the (Pauline) theological tradition, including the realisation that glory attempts to cover over the true nature of the human being. This is what the notion of the Sabbath perfectly captures: its inoperativity. God's glory, as is noted in *The Kingdom and the Glory*, 'coincides with the cessation of all activity and all works' (KG 239/OHS 588). The true holy day is the day when all activity has been suspended, and whose suspension must be rigorously maintained. 'Sabbatism is the name of eschatological glory that is, in essence, inoperativity' (KG 240/ OHS 589). What had concerned the governmental apparatus above all else is the very thing that defines both humanity and the divine being, but which must, for this very reason be concealed at the same time that it is revealed: the inoperative nature of divine and human existence. As he describes the situation, 'Man has dedicated himself to production and labor, because in his essence he is completely devoid of work, because he is the Sabbatical animal par excellence' (KG 246/OHS 594). Agamben's task, which becomes manifest through his elucidation of Paul's messianic politics, is to begin to think inoperativity outside of the apparatus of glory that has defined Western political theological relations (KG 247/OHS 595). This is a task that involves exposing the nudity of God as much as the nudity of the human being, with both taking place beyond the meanings that have been placed upon them (or to whose existence one might be reacting). It is a movement toward vulnerability, precariousness and poverty, not a reinscription back into a matrix of (either established or newly minted) power relations.

This trajectory of critique will take Agamben down a brief tour of Pauline thought in *The Kingdom and the Glory* and a much lengthier exposition of this 'weak messianic force' in *The Time that Remains*, among other places where Paul appears as the apparent solution to the impasse that such a hypernomianism is attempting to overcome. At its most basic level, what takes place in the messianic suspension of all vocations and identities is a displacement of the subject that actually gives rise to the possibility for life itself to emerge from underneath its inscription in the anthropological machinery: 'In the same way that the Messiah has brought about the law and, at the same time, rendered it inoperative [. . .] so the *hōs mē* ['as not'] maintains and, at the same time, deactiviates in the present all the juridical conditions and all the social behaviors of the members of the messianic community [. . .]' (KG 248/OHS 597).

This messianic politics is possible through its ability to produce a gap between every identity and itself, a permanent caesura that divides any pre-existing social division. Hence, the Jew lives *as if not* a Jew and the Gentile *as if not* a Gentile, producing a new form of universality through the negation of a prior negation (of an ultimately undefinable fullness of a particular existence) that was yet constitutive of one's identity. The Christian, Paul will proclaim, is the person who does not possess an identity, but only makes use of identities – the major investigative claim of the finale of his *Homo Sacer* project, articulated in both *The Highest Poverty* and *The Use of Bodies* – thereby rendering one's relation to law as not quite a negation of the law, but rather a fulfilment of it in the sense that one can make use of it without possessing or being possessed by it (its particularly *hypernomian* flavour) (UB 274/OHS 1275; see also the commentary on use and possession in HP 123–43/OHS 985–1000, as well as the discussion about the inappropriable in Chapter 2). Agamben's project is not antinomian in the sense of trying to exist apart from law or state or governance, which is what monasticism and Franciscanism had tried, but ultimately failed, to do. Rather, he wants to follow Paul in trying to think the element of *anomie* as it lies *within* every law, the anarchy *within* every power, the unrepresentable *within* every representation and form-of-life exposed 'as the inoperativity immanent in every life' (UB 275, 277/OHS 1276, 1278). It is with this realised form of inoperativity that we find something like a new form of prayer as a contemplation of potentiality (as a 'destituent potential'). This form of inoperativity opens up the space for a new joy to take place within the life that is being lived beyond all given forms of representational life (the 'forms of life' as opposed to forms-of-life) (UB 278/OHS 1279).

More specifically still, Agamben considers how 'The messianic life is the impossibility that life might coincide with a predetermined form, the revoking of every *bios* in order to open it to the *zōē tou Iesou*. And the inoperativity that takes place here is not mere inertia or rest; on the contrary, it is the messianic operation par excellence' (KG 248–9/OHS 597). As such, there is the possibility of accessing life itself – life (*zoē*) through Jesus, identified *as* Jesus – beyond the social forms of life (*bios*) that have been inscribed upon us. This is not bare life, which is the result of the sacrificial machinery that violently reduces human being to a form of life lived outside the *polis*; it is rather the form-of-life that can only be accessed by rendering inoperative the identities that had been foisted upon humanity by the exclusionary acts that define social relations. It is Agamben's desire to escape through taking up a type of 'intimacy without relation', or a bond without the prescribed social representations being placed upon it (UB 236/OHS 1242). In essence, this is what is to be sought as the only authentic way to represent something by demonstrating precisely our failure to represent the 'thing itself'. This is the only possible way to achieve a presentation beyond representation. It is not through the mythical suggestion of an almost magical entity or encounter, but rather by showing (or exposing) the failure itself as the only 'true' representation (see IP 131–3).[15]

It is in this place of an experience of failure that is paradoxically our only hope of success that we encounter glory once again, but this time in a radically different form. Agamben will later describe this as a means of (entirely immanent) grace beyond the (falsely) sacralised forms of grace that the Church has too often peddled: a form-of-life lived beyond its inscription in any representational matrix (see his remarks on grace in FT 56). This is the 'eternal life' (*zōē aiōnios*) that Paul promises through the messianic suspension of all existing, worldly identities. It is a life that predates our inscription into the anthropological machinery that religion, as a fabricator all too often of the (false) sacred, has fostered (KG 251/OHS 599–600). There is in such gestures an apparently *kenotic* nihilism reconceived as a form of negative dialectics that undoes the divide between sovereign power and governmentality, and which introduces us to our own poverty as forms-of-life. But it is also that which must be recognised as the only way to move beyond the impasse that such political, representational dualisms present us with.[16]

# 5

# *The Border between the Human and the Animal*

## THE FICTION OF THE HUMAN BEING

The best illustration of the necessary illusion of sovereignty that permeates our spheres of political interaction can be made through recourse to the establishment of the human subject in relation to its own animality. This is a point that Agamben returns to again and again in order to demonstrate how sovereign power operates. In a prominent example, he enters a discussion in *The Use of Bodies* regarding the border between animality and humanity through an examination of Heidegger's thoughts on 'the open', or the space that is taken up as the centre of anthropogenetic activity (UB 183–6/OHS 1192–5). Here, the open, as the rightful site of our poverty of being, helps humanity to rethink possibility as a fundamental ontological category (UB 188/OHS 1197). Yet, contrary to Heidegger, who tries to envision the human being as the one who responds to the call of Being from within the ambiguity of the thrownness of Dasein, Agamben suggests rather that:

> The anthropogenetic event of appropriation on the part of Being can be produced only in a living being, whose destiny cannot fail to be in question in Dasein. Only a conception of the human that not only does not add anything to animality but does not supervene upon anything at all will be truly emancipated from

the metaphysical definition of the human being. Such a humanity nonetheless could never be thought as a task to be 'taken on' or as the response to a call. (UB 183/OHS 1192)[1]

We can note in this context that Agamben's solution to the Heideggerian problem of the 'anthropogenetic event' is that we must not add anything to our animality (e.g. the typical definition of the human as above and beyond the animal, as sovereign over one's own animality, or as something like a 'super-animal' then). Humanity must not attempt to create any new form at all – the very thing the apparatuses in our world do through the presupposition and division of being – in order to access our 'emancipation from the metaphysical definition of the human being' (UB 183/OHS 1192). The obvious parallel here is to his suggestions elsewhere (e.g. KG 246/OHS 595) that the new form of politics is not a utopian ideal, but is another way of reading the human form that is already before us. Or, to restate my assertions made thus far, it is not the eradication of sovereignty that is sought after, but finding another use for it. This is why I locate in Agamben what I have been calling *another* form of sovereignty available to humanity.

True to Agamben's themes and the construction I have presented thus far, it should come as no surprise that the key to this emancipation can only be located within the act of suspension or inoperativity. But, to clarify, this suspension is not necessarily of one's own animality, which is the typical manner in which the human being is constructed as sovereign over the animal world. It is usually by ignoring one's own animality that humanity is capable of being dominant over the entirety of the animal world. With reference to Heidegger's comments on the animal's 'poverty of world', Agamben suggests that:

> The human being thus appears as a living being that, in suspending its relations to things, grasps beings in their self-refusal as possibility. It is an animal that, in becoming bored, has awoken from and to its own captivation and can now grasp it as such, a moth that,

while the flame is consuming it, notices the flame and itself for the first time. This means that Dasein is an animal that has grasped its animality and has made of this the possibility of the human being. But the human being is void, because it is only a suspension of animality. (UB 186/OHS 1195)

There is thus 'no content' or substance to the human being as such, as we have already noted, in Agamben's development of a modal ontology and in his critique of historical-doctrinal faith. But this time the absence of content is established in the context of the division between the animal and the human. We see again the fiction of a sovereign form operating without any particular, fixed substance behind its claims (or that which frequently poses as 'natural'). The fiction of the human being *is* the fiction of sovereignty – they are in fact the *same* fiction. The anthropological machinery, with its empty centre as a state of exception that Agamben wants to suspend, has been extremely effective in creating such fictions in a political sense. This time it is the human being as sovereign who fabricates itself over the animal world by suspending its own animality. The human being includes its animality by excluding it from itself (or 'banning' it, to use the language from the first volume of the series) in order to establish itself as dominant over all other life forms.

The zone of indistinction, or the boundary that separates humanity from its animality but which also renders their relationship unclear, is therefore to be understood as a zone of fiction. It does not exist in a substantial sense; it is perspective and activity alone. This zone does not produce a particular substantial form as if determined by the divine or by nature, as the human being is usually presumed to be. It does not produce either a hybrid or utopian substantial form. It only produces mythological creatures. Agamben in fact analyses the werewolf as the legendary symbol of sovereign power in the first volume of the *Homo Sacer* series. Here, he stresses, the werewolf does not exist in substance, but only serves to express a profound truth about humanity's perceptions of itself. As a result, mythological figures such as this one (and one might also add a host of others, including zombies, vampires and the like) express a very significant condition of sovereignty, namely its utterly fictitious nature.

As we have already explored, there is a polarised dualistic tension brought forth by the anthropological machinery that tries to create the substance of the human being. But it is a tension that must be kept separate, preventing the two opposing poles from coinciding as they existed prior to the presupposition of being. Understanding this task is what allows the division between the human and the animal to become a major philosophical and political issue, not just an anthropological one. It functions through the same dynamics that institute any politically sovereign form in our world and it is what legitimates any violence enacted in order to sustain such a tension. In Agamben's words:

> But if it is possible to attempt to halt the machine, to show its central fiction, this is because between violence and law, between life and norm, there is no substantial articulation. Alongside the movement that seeks to keep them in relation at all costs, there is a countermovement that, working in an inverse direction in law and in life, always seeks to loosen what has been artificially and violently linked. That is to say, in the field of tension of our culture, two opposite forces act, one that institutes and makes, and one that deactivates and deposes. The state of exception is both the point of their maximum tension and – as it coincides with the rule – that which threatens today to render them indiscernible. To live in the state of exception means to experience both of these possibilities and yet, by always separating the two forces, ceaselessly to try to interrupt the working of the machine that is leading the West toward global civil war. (SE 87/OHS 241)

It is only through their separation, and not through a synthesis of any sort, that the symbiotic relationship between such forces can be broken apart in order that the tension itself remain.

Moreover, and as I will pursue further below, Agamben's remarks on the state of exception are directly applicable to the boundary that separates humanity from its animality, especially insofar as this boundary refers to the fictional nature of the state of exception (as a 'zone of indistinction'):

> If it is true that the articulation between life and law, between anomie and *nomos*, that is produced by the state of exception is effective though fictional, one can still not conclude from this that somewhere either beyond or before juridical apparatuses there is an immediate access to something whose fracture and impossible unification are represented by these apparatuses. There are not *first* life as a natural biological given and anomie as the state of nature, and *then* their implication in law through the state of exception. On the contrary, the very possibility of distinguishing life and law, anomie and *nomos*, coincides with their articulation in the biopolitical machine. Bare life is a product of the machine and not something that preexists it, just as law has no court in nature or in the divine mind. Life and law, anomie and *nomos*, *auctoritas* and *potestas*, result from the fracture of something to which we have no other access than through the fiction of their articulation and the patient work that, by unmasking this fiction, separates what it had claimed to unite. But disenchantment does not restore the enchanted thing to its original state: According to the principle that purity never lies at the origin, disenchantment gives it only the possibility of reaching a new condition. (SE 87–8/ OHS 241)

The fiction that is maintained through the deployment of the state of exception is one that is joined with the construction of morality and religious vocation (or office, *officium*) in the West. As he will explore in greater depth in *Opus Dei*, moral codes based on duty are grounded in a distinction between acting and being in order to elevate the role of efficacy in a political sense and of the priestly office in a religious context specifically. That is, ethics has been legitimated by recourse to the position that one performs or acts, as well as one's duty to it, rather than through any substantial articulation of our being. As Agamben will express repeatedly in the series, trying to ground ethical imperatives on the *imago dei* (image of God) within the human being is a fictive exercise – as theologians have not been hesitant to assert over the centuries – though it is also one whose form cannot necessarily be eradicated altogether simply by disproving God's existence. The desire to ground ethical norms within such a foundation cannot be removed, but only seen from another perspective (much as modern forms of humanism and human rights often rest on a presumed, though undisclosed, metaphysical foundation).

Agamben's attempts to disenchant the ethical constructs and vocations, or offices, we typically depend on does not bring about a new position, a new being or a new ethics to replace the old one. His perennial task is to find a new use for an old thing. This is contrasted with finding a new thing, or synthesis, to replace the old one. Hence Agamben's repeated searches for a *pure* law, a *pure* language, a *pure* violence, a *pure* means without an end, and a new *use* of human praxis are always found among what *already* exists (and thus giving precedence to genealogical methods in his work, not positive-constructive philosophical programmes). These quests are meant to deal only with what already exists and not to create (sovereignly) a new form that must be legitimated through a political, ethical and religious nexus of actions (or praxis) and the fictions that all too frequently accompany them. Rather, as Agamben will determine in the context of Pauline thought, there is only the revocation of every vocation that is the messianic task par excellence, and not the institution of a utopian kingdom as one might otherwise expect (TR 23). As he will further describe this state of affairs in their decidedly political terms:

> To show law in its nonrelation to life and life in its nonrelation to law means to open a space between them for human action, which once claimed for itself the name of 'politics.' Politics has suffered a lasting eclipse because it has been contaminated by law, seeing itself, at best, as constituent power (that is, violence that makes law), when it is not reduced to merely the power to negotiate with the law. The only truly political action, however, is that which severs the nexus between violence and law. And only beginning

from the space thus opened will it be possible to pose the question of a possible use of law after the deactivation of the device that, in the state of exception, tied it to life. We will then have before us a 'pure' law, in the sense in which Benjamin speaks of a 'pure' language and a 'pure' violence. To a word that does not bind, that neither commands nor prohibits anything, but says only itself, would correspond an action as pure means, which shows only itself, without any relation to an end. And, between the two, not a lost original state, but only the use and human praxis that the powers of law and myth had sought to capture in the state of exception. (SE 88/OHS 242)

For Agamben, it is important to understand that the establishment of the human being as dominant over its own animality – as also over the entire animal world – is not a one-time event, but an ongoing process wherein such acts of sovereignty must be constantly reasserted. Because we are able to make the movement from potentiality to actuality (for example: through habit, as Agamben will discuss this process in *The Use of Bodies*), we are able to traverse the ground from animality to sovereignty. Not only do we establish the human form, but we also enter into the dualistic contestations for power that characterise politics. However, what this configuration also reveals is the primacy of potentiality over actuality. This insight will prove most helpful in determining a way to think possibility beyond the form of the human-as-sovereign. In his words:

> If the interpretation of the genesis of the human being from animality that we have delineated here is correct, then possibility is not one modal category among others but is the fundamental ontological dimension, in which Being and the world are disclosed by the suspension of the animal environment. And it is because Being reveals itself above all in the form of the possible that Heidegger can write that 'the human being, which as existent transcendence is thrown before in possibility, is a being of distance'. The human being is a being of distance because it is a being of possibility, but insofar as the possibility to which it is

assigned is only the suspension of the immediate relation of the animal with its environment, it contains the nothing and non-being as its essential traits. And precisely because being human is given to it only as possibility, the human being is continually in the act of falling back into animality. The privilege of possibility in Heideggerian ontology is indissoluble from the aporia that assigns humanity to the human being as a task that, as such, can always be mistaken for a political task. (UB 188/OHS 1197)

Though he refrains from commenting directly upon Heidegger's failure to accurately think the complexity of politics, something that certainly would have given pause to any rethinking of Heidegger's understanding of (the sovereignty of) Being, Agamben does determine how possibility is the mode that allows for the human being to construct itself upon the nothingness and non-being that truly rests within it. Taking account of possibility as removed from the dualistic scenario of potentiality and actuality that Aristotle had utilised can undo the entire edifice upon which the human being is constructed and also reduce the distancing that characterises the sovereign office (which is best captured in the image of a deistic God who works only at a great, possibly even infinite, distance from our world). The removal of this distance said to characterise the human being – but which really only legitimates it *as* sovereign, and so is what Agamben will seek to de-activate – is what will ultimately give rise to an 'intimacy without relations' that he points toward at the conclusion of the entire *Homo Sacer* series as one of the overarching and original goals of the project.

The implications of comprehending how sovereign power is constituted in the act of anthropogenesis involve both metaphysical presumptions (again, the logic of presupposition), and so the entire history of ontology, and also political and religious forms that have likewise depended upon the construction of bare life in order to operate.[2] This is the anthropological machinery that Agamben wishes to see rendered inoperative. The stakes of Agamben's analysis are thereby quite high. We would do well, for instance, to recall the conclusion to the first volume of the series, *Homo Sacer*, where Agamben declared quite bluntly how:

> it may be that only if we are able to decipher the political meaning of pure Being will we be able to master the bare life that expresses our subjection to political power, just as it may be, inversely, that only if we understand the theoretical implications of bare life will we be able to solve the enigma of ontology. Brought to the limit of pure Being, metaphysics (thought) passes over into politics (into reality), just as on the threshold of bare life, politics steps beyond itself into theory. (HS 182/OHS 149)

Anthropogenesis has, for far too long, been dependent upon the fabrication of bare life – a configuration whose time has come to be revealed for what it is: a violence that masks the fictive nature of sovereign power and so has served to prevent its deconstruction throughout the centuries.

## THE PROBLEM OF ANTHROPOGENESIS

The lingering problem of anthropogenesis, according to Agamben, is that we have traditionally constructed the human being as sovereign and as master through a process of what some might call (though Agamben does not) 'othering', or the creation of bare life that can be marginalised, manipulated and controlled. For example, notice how the concept of *oikonomia*, which we explored in Chapter 3, is described as what is able to 'manage, govern, control, and orient – in a way that purports to be useful – the behaviors, gestures, and thoughts of human beings' (WA 12). *Oikonomia* functions, liturgically and theologically, as an apparatus that seeks to capture one's animality in order to produce and legitimate the presupposition of being through language. As Agamben will define it in an essay devoted to exploring the topic, an apparatus is

> literally anything that has in some way the capacity to capture, orient, determine, intercept, model, control, or secure the gestures,

behaviors, opinions, or discourses of living beings. Not only, therefore, prisons, madhouses, the panopticon, schools, confession, factories, disciplines, juridical measures, and so forth (whose connection with power is in a certain sense evident), but also the pen, writing, literature, philosophy, agriculture, cigarettes, navigation, computers, cellular telephones and – why not – language itself, which is perhaps the most ancient of apparatuses – one in which thousands and thousands of years ago a primate inadvertently let himself be captured, probably without realizing the consequences that he was about to face. (WA 14)

The difficulty of removing such apparatuses from our lives is made clear as language itself is implicated in the anthropogenetic process that inscribes humanity within the heart of all that is living in our world. The linguistic, but so also inherently religious, political and ethical, subject is what results from the 'relentless fight' between living beings and apparatuses.

Agamben here again relies upon the work of Foucault as the major inspiration for the genealogical studies of the *Homo Sacer* series, and Foucault's descriptions of the power wielded over bodies through the disciplinary movements of such apparatuses is quite clearly the main influence over Agamben's own analyses.[3] Nonetheless, Agamben wants to push somewhat beyond Foucault in order to address the very inscription into language that religion, especially Christianity, has divinised through its relationship to the *logos*. I argue that this is the same reason why Derrida had once suggested that even our use of language was a moment of 'bloodless violence' as it conscripts us into a dualistic politics from which we seemingly cannot escape and gives a new meaning to his celebrated declaration that 'there is nothing outside the text'.[4] As Agamben will characterise this state of apparatuses, of which language is one:

> The fact is that according to all indications, apparatuses are not a mere accident in which humans are caught by chance, but rather are rooted in the very process of 'humanization' that made 'humans' out of the animals we classify under the rubric Homo sapiens. In

fact, the event that has produced the human constitutes, for the living being, something like a division, which reproduces in some way the division that the *oikonomia* introduced in God between being and action. This division separates the living being from itself and from its immediate relationship with its environment – that is, with what Jakob von Uexküll and then Heidegger name the circle of receptors-disinhibitors. The break or interruption of this relationship produces in living beings both boredom – that is, the capacity to suspend this immediate relationship with their disinhibitors – and the Open, which is the possibility of knowing being as such, by constructing a world. But, along with these possibilities, we must also immediately consider the apparatuses that crowd the Open with instruments, objects, gadgets, odds and ends, and various technologies. Through these apparatuses, man attempts to nullify the animalistic behaviors that are now separated from him, and to enjoy the Open as such, to enjoy being insofar as it is being. At the root of each apparatus lies an all-too-human desire for happiness. The capture and subjectification of this desire in a separate sphere constitutes the specific power of the apparatus. (WA 16–17)

Like the analysis of contemplation in Chapter 4, boredom indicates a suspension of our disinhibitors, and so an opening toward 'constructing a world'. Within such a world, humanity is offered the chance to experience something like happiness through a distancing offered by each apparatus, from one's own animality. It is here that the 'all-too-human' desire for happiness, which every human seeks to fulfil within themselves, 'constitutes the specific power of the apparatus'. As such, the image of the sovereign may easily become the image of one who has fulfilled all of their desires, gratified themselves with every happiness and dominated over their enemies (i.e. over bare life and the *homo sacer*) in order to return only to oneself and one's own happiness. This state of the sovereign returning only to their own context should remind us of Adorno's claim that the dictator is really only ever able to speak about the one thing that they truly love, *themselves*, because every authoritarian is really a narcissist at heart.[5]

Yet how are we to profane such apparatuses, which are traditionally and routinely sacralised, as in the history of an intertwined religion and politics (*as* political theology), through separation and sacrifice, the marginalisation of particular persons (as *homines sacri*)? As Agamben documents throughout the entirety of the *Homo Sacer* series, so many apparatuses control and shape the human being, making it incredibly difficult to embrace the messianic vocation that would suspend each of these established vocations brought about by the apparatuses of our world. This was his critique of the office and of ministry (OD 65/OHS 703), of being bound to one's office in life no matter what it is (OD 72/OHS 708) and of the evolution of the category of duty in the West in order to maintain humanity's ties to its office (OD 72–3/OHS 709), which certainly derives from a 'condition or a status' of the human being. It is these anthropological dimensions that come to the surface in his analyses of the office of the human as it is distinguished from the animal *through* its office (OD 74/OHS 710). As he will phrase things in *Opus Dei*:

> If human beings do not simply live their lives like the animals, but 'conduct' and 'govern' life, *officium* is what renders life governable, that by means of which the life of humans is 'instituted' and 'formed'. What is decisive, however, is that in this way, the politician and the jurist's attention is shifted from the carrying out of individual acts to the 'use of life' as a whole; that is, it is identified with the 'institution of life' as such, with the conditions and the *status* that defines the very existence of human beings in society. (OD 74–5/OHS 710)

As Agamben will continue, the role of the office not only allows for the governance of life, but it implicates the human condition as fundamentally political. This harkens back to Aristotle's distinction between *bios* and *zoē* that is so central to the analysis of life offered in the first volume of the series: '*Officium* thus constitutes the human condition itself, and human beings, insofar as they are *membra . . . corporis magni* (parts of one great body), are beings of *officium*' (OD 75/OHS 711, emphasis in the original). The office renders life governable for human beings, creating the 'institution of life' as the condition of sociality itself (and of language too, as we saw earlier). In addition to this insight, we must note that the way in which *officium* constitutes humanity *as* humanity, as a whole, reaffirms the *officium* through the tautological circularity that defines the establishment of any sovereign power. It is precisely in order to break this circular hold of power that Agamben becomes fascinated with the history of monasticism. It presents an attempt to break the hold of an acting that can only be done first (as with the priestly office or vocation) by reversing the terms of the relationship and claiming that one can only obtain a position through their ability to enact or embody it, as with monastic vocations.

The all-important philosophical distinction between the monk and the priest is crucial here, for the priest can be unworthy and still perform their duties as a priest through their office *ex opere operato* (HP 84/OHS 955–6). Yet, as monasticism will seek to understand, if liturgy is transformed into life, the configuration of *opus operatum* 'cannot hold'. Hence an 'unworthy monk is simply not a monk' whereas an unworthy priest is still a priest (HP 84/OHS 956). This is the logic that is eventually extended into Protestantism where an unworthy Christian is declared not to be a Christian. Conversely, an unworthy Catholic, for many even today, is still undoubtedly a Catholic, whereas an unworthy Protestant runs the risk of not even being considered as a Christian. As Agamben notes, this was Martin Luther's attempt to bring 'monastic liturgy against the Church liturgy', thereby also minimalising 'the eucharistic and sacramental Office' and utilising monasticism as a counter-force to priestly liturgy.

The significance of this analysis for the scope of the *Homo Sacer* project is that it is through monasticism's challenges to the illusory sovereign substance of being that we are able to approach the *forma vitae* (form-of-life) that Agamben has been long seeking to elucidate (HP 86/OHS 957). Monasticism, through its conceptualisation and embodiment of a figure who brought its being about through its actions and not through its position, allows us to proceed one step closer to accessing a form-of-life apart from the liturgical activity that had tried to produce an ontological substance. 'Form-of-life is, in this sense, what must unceasingly be torn away from the separation in which liturgy keeps it' (HP 87/OHS 958).

## ANTHROPOGENESIS AND METAPHYSICS

The implications discovered through the recognition of the tensions that undergird any distinction between the priest and the monk are no less true for the other boundaries that characterise human life. At its most fundamental level, what Agamben is suggesting has grave consequences for the way in which the human being constructs itself vis-à-vis the animal world. At the conclusion to the first volume of the series, Agamben lists the three theses that he has arrived at throughout his initial study, and these are helpful to enumerate insofar as they set the stage for rethinking the relationship between the human and the animal. First, the original political relation is the ban, or the divide established between inclusion and exclusion. Second, sovereign power produces bare life through an inclusive exclusion – where it is considered part of a given order only insofar as it is also excluded from normative relations – and so articulates the divide between nature and culture at the same time. (It is helpful to remember that the opposite of this *inclusive exclusion* will be the *exclusive inclusion* that ultimately defines the form-of-life.) And, third, the camp (concentration, but also potentially refugee or immigrant, wherever the *homo sacer* is being constructed today) is the fundamental political paradigm in the West (HS 181/OHS 148). What we can glean from these conclusions is that the border between the animal and the human, as between nature and culture, is itself produced by the ontological split between potentiality and actuality, as also between inclusion and exclusion, as touched on in Chapter 2. These conclusions find their correlate in the six theses delivered in section 17 of *The Open*, where Agamben elaborates further upon how these divisions relate to the processes of anthropogenesis, and also to the border between the animal and the human. Taking each thesis in order, as I will in the narrative that follows, we see a continuous unfolding of the human/animal distinction as bound up with the maintenance of sovereign power, illustrating quite deftly the fundamental conclusions arrived at in the *Homo Sacer* series.

As Agamben initialises his claims regarding the construction of humanity through the anthropological machinery that has dominated the West for centuries: '1. Anthropogenesis is what results from the caesura and articulation between human and animal. This caesura passes first of all within man' (O 79). As we have already seen, it is the entrance of the Aristotelean dualistic categories through the logic of presupposition that produces endless scissions across our bodies and through our every identity. Every identity, especially the human being, is characterised by this fundamental division or separation that is regulated by an anthropological machinery (for example: as we see in the way sacrifice has functioned religiously as a generator of the sacred self). Marking the boundary between the human and the animal is what allows humanity to conceive of the self-determining boundary between the human and the divine, as if merely repeating the immanent division of the human-animal became the foundation of another, transcendent division.

Next, Agamben moves toward the implications such a border suggests for the history of metaphysical thought:

> 2. Ontology, or first philosophy, is not an innocuous academic discipline, but in every sense the fundamental operation in which anthropogenesis, the becoming human of the living being, is realized. From the beginning, metaphysics is taken up in this strategy: it concerns precisely that *meta* that completes and preserves the overcoming of animal *physis* in the direction of human history. This overcoming is not an event that has been completed once and

for all, but an occurrence that is always under way, that every time and in each individual decides between the human and the animal, between nature and history, between life and death. (O 79)

Anthropogenesis is what motivates every ontological formulation that presents itself as a 'first philosophy'. Metaphysics is what we call the attempt to legitimate the human being in distinction from the sphere of animality, as the human is constructed parallel to the divine (the 'distance' mentioned earlier) at the same time as it is separated from its animal nature. What is striking in this formulation is that anthropogenesis is not a one-time event that is now permanently established once and for all; rather, it is an ongoing event that must be confirmed and reconfirmed again and again. Ongoing debates about the priority of nature or culture, as well as theological discussions of natural or revealed truth, are seen for what they are in this light: political contestations for power as much as they are efforts to establish a particular form of subjectivity or image of humanity.

Agamben's analysis is extended in the following thesis toward the suspension of one's animality in order to construct the human being:

> 3. Being, world, and the open are not, however, something other with respect to animal environment and life: they are nothing but the interruption and capture of the living being's relationship with its disinhibitor. The open is nothing but a grasping of the animal not-open. Man suspends his animality and, in this way, opens a 'free and empty' zone in which life is captured and a-bandoned in a zone of exception. (O 79)

As Heidegger had isolated and developed in the poetry of Rainer Maria Rilke, the concept of 'the open' is revealed to be precisely the emptiness or the void that characterises humanity and which seemingly calls for a fictive form of sovereignty to conceal its vacuity (O 57).[6] The open is the space that we have sought to cover over, as with nudity and the clothing created to cover it (as Agamben details in his essay on 'Nudity', see N 55–90), as with glory and grace which hold the dualistic machinery together at the same time as they keep them separate (as Agamben explores further in *The Kingdom and the Glory*) and as the state of exception conceals in order to ground sovereign power (which Agamben, of course, outlines in *State of Exception*). However, this is the cost of having a world, a language, an identity or a representation in the first place. It is also the result of not being inhibited by our genetic coding; therefore, it is what frees us to pursue the artificiality that leads, in some instances, to a liberation of the human being from its theological signature, as Agamben had once explicated in *The Coming Community* (CC 47–9).

The fourth thesis lays bare the hollowness that constitutes the state of exception as it gives rise to the sovereign human being in the first place, thus acknowledging the fiction of both human being and sovereign power at the same time. '4. Precisely because the world has been opened for man only by means of the suspension and capture of animal life, being is always already traversed by the nothing: the *Lichtung* [clearing] is always already *Nichtung* [destruction]' (O 80). What this proposition illuminates is the way in which the production of the open is inherently also a destruction, a 'suspension and capture of animal life' that allows humanity to reign sovereign over itself and others. The use of violence in order to preserve the fictive construct of sovereignty is nowhere more apparent than in this suggestive remark on the origin of destruction.

The construction of the border between humanity and the animal world is not merely a biological or scientific distinction. It is a political praxis that continues to give foundation to sovereignty in our world. As Agamben will suggest in the next thesis: '5. In our culture, the decisive political conflict, which governs every other conflict, is that between the animality and the humanity of man. That is to say, in its origin Western politics is also biopolitics' (O 80). Bringing to light one of the more significant insights of his analysis concerning anthropogenesis, Agamben, following Foucault's insights in many respects, points toward the role of biopolitics as a continuance of the division that separates the human and the animal, because it is this initial boundary that expresses most clearly the core divisions of politics. With this in mind, we can begin to see why Schmitt's definition of politics – as founded on the opposition of the friend and the enemy – resonates so deeply with Agamben. It also illuminates why one's enemies are often reduced to the status of animals – the ultimate act of creating a figure of the *homo sacer* (or the creation of one's 'enemy').[7] Understanding this division will also help us to understand why living out a form-of-life will have a lasting (counter)impact upon politics in our world, as it refuses the dichotomies that shape traditional political divisions and institutions.

Finally, Agamben's last thesis brings us to consider the significance that his analysis holds for the complete rethinking of human-animal relations as a political reconfiguration: '6. If the anthropological machine was the motor for man's becoming historical, then the end of philosophy and the completion of the epochal destinations of being mean that today the machine is idling' (O 80). Quite suggestively, Agamben contends that we are in a unique historical position. For the first time within humanity's collective memory, we are able to contemplate the 'end of history', the 'end of religion', the end of 'metaphysics' and the end of 'onto-theology' along with whatever other apparatuses that have been used to legitimate sovereign power in our world. For Agamben, arriving at this stage in history means that we are able to contemplate our humanity in such a way as to suspend, or render inoperative, the machinery that has for centuries produced the human being as the sovereign-dominant being that it has performatively been. Now, and only now, we can begin to think new forms-of-life lived beyond the sovereign human forms we have mainly known and constructed.

These theses and comments certainly mirror those given in *The Use of Bodies* where he considers ontology as anthropogenesis and as an event that never stops happening. There Agamben merely reiterates that we live in a time of the impossibility of metaphysics (UB 113/OHS 1128), as well as in a time not defined by any historical a priori (UB 114/OHS 1129). Such a suspension from teleological ends and established presumptions means that we are uniquely situated to reconsider human being from a perspective heretofore neglected. Still following the Heideggerian trail he had set upon, he contemplates two possibilities for the future. In this context, they are even more suggestive in light of the genealogical studies of the office (of humanity) that preceded them:

> At this point, two scenarios are possible from Heidegger's perspective: (*a*) posthistorical man no longer preserves his own animality as undisclosable, but rather seeks to take it on and govern it by means of technology; (*b*) man, the shepherd of being, appropriates his own concealedness, his own animality, which neither remains hidden nor is made an object of mastery, but is thought as such, as pure abandonment. (O 80)

The first is what Agamben will critique in *The Use of Bodies* as the instrumental rationality that dominates technological advancements in the modern world and which proceeds undisclosed in most contexts. It is parallel to humanity's past enslavement of others and it merely displaces the problem of failing to confront ourselves onto an inert technology that becomes an extension of ourselves (though truly also a further distancing of ourselves from ourselves). In many ways, and though Agamben does not note this directly, his analysis here reflects his comments on the displacement of the religious into the secular, an historical movement that refuses to embrace the inoperativity of profanation which he is rather seeking to articulate (PR 77).

The second option, the one that he is eager to employ, is one wherein humanity neither hides its animality nor seeks to master it, but rather lives it in 'pure abandonment' (or what will be the act of profanation, among the many other names he gives it). Like 'pure potentiality', 'pure abandonment' is a suspension that goes beyond the dualistic tensions underlying all forms of political engagement in which we have traditionally participated. Here we see such a 'pure abandonment' become the suspension of the anthropological machinery, as invested in the messianic 'division of division' that suspends every identity and law, but which does not eradicate law or identity once and for all. If this is a type of nihilism concordant with the overcoming of onto-theology and of the end of metaphysics and history as we have known them – at least within the Nietzschean and Heideggerian contexts that he typically pursues such thoughts – it is also the possibility of living life in a form that we have never socially recognised. It is here that a new use for the body is to be located, as well as new uses for politics, law, religion, language and so on. Indeed, there may appear a new use for every apparatus that had captured humanity within its snares, each promising happiness but bringing only an increasingly frustrating act of distancing from both ourselves and others. The apparatuses that have held humanity in their power do not bring with them a renewed sense of an intimacy, but only an intensifying of pre-established relations and identities.

Interestingly, and insofar as it aids the analysis I have been pursuing thus far, it is at this point that Agamben begins to contemplate something like a form of salvation for our being. But this salvation is different than those theological notions of salvation that are caught up within a particular economy of salvation that actually reinscribes humanity back within the anthropological machinery. It is locatable in the non-coincidence of one with one's self – Benjamin's famous conceptualisation of 'dialectics at a standstill' – that breaks the tautological circularity of sovereign power which is a coincidence of self with self.

> What does 'mastery of the relation between nature and humanity' mean? That neither must man master nature nor nature man. Nor must both be surpassed in a third term that would represent their dialectical synthesis. Rather, according to the Benjaminian model of a 'dialectic at a standstill,' what is decisive here is only the 'between,' the interval or, we might say, the play between the

> two terms, their immediate constellation in a non-coincidence. The anthropological machine no longer articulates nature and man in order to produce the human through the suspension and capture of the inhuman. The machine is, so to speak, stopped: it is 'at a standstill,' and, in the reciprocal suspension of the two terms, something for which we perhaps have no name and which is neither animal nor man settles in between nature and humanity and holds itself in the mastered relation, in the saved night. (O 83)

It is only in this place of suspension that the 'saved night' might become possible. From this position alone is humanity able to move beyond the border between the human and the animal, 'in between nature and humanity'.

What we are left with, and here again Agamben follows the lead offered by Benjamin, is a mysterious and uncertain image of this life – what belongs to life, but which also surpasses it. This is what Benjamin had considered as a sexual fulfilment that is not reducible to sexuality alone.

> The enigma of the sexual relationship between the man and the woman [. . .] thus receives a new and more mature formulation. Sensual pleasure and love [. . .] do not prefigure only death and sin. To be sure, in their fulfillment the lovers learn something of each other that they should not have known – they have lost their mystery – and yet have not become any less impenetrable. But in this mutual disenchantment from their secret, they enter, just as in Benjamin's aphorism, a new and more blessed life, one that is neither animal nor human. It is not nature that is reached in their fulfillment, but rather (as symbolized by the animal that rears up the Tree of Life and of Knowledge) a higher stage beyond both nature and knowledge, beyond concealment and dis-concealment. These lovers have initiated each other into their own lack of mystery as their most intimate secret; they mutually forgive each other and expose their *vanitas*. Bare or clothed, they are no longer either concealed or unconcealed – but rather, inapparent. (O 87)

We would do well to read this disenchantment not as a form of secularisation, but as an act of profanation that leaves behind the dualistic split between enchantment and disenchantment altogether. The 'enigma of the sexual relationship' wherein the lovers expose themselves to one another beyond concealment or unconcealment, is precisely a movement of profanation and a hint toward why nudity is so fascinating a topic for Agamben. What he seeks to access and disclose is a form of nudity beyond the hyper-sexualised representations of it, such as we find in the nudity of 'bare life' in the concentration camps (*lagers*), or as a form-of-life is inseparable from its naked body. We might also recall here Saint Francis' own disrobing and his naked body presented to all in order to take up his form-of-life in particular. Each example is what we are seeking to comprehend, but fail to fully understand the implications of at the hands of those apparatuses which capture us through the allure of a happiness merged with a nakedness that is not the nudity Agamben is trying to articulate. Indeed, in Agamben's eyes, this is the abysmal failure of pornography. Pornography, as with various theological speculation on the glorious, resurrected bodies it imagines after Jesus's return, seeks to uphold the mystery that one's nudity, as expressed through a form-of-life, disregards – that is to say, which pornography reveals as not being a mystery at all (see the arguments in his essay 'The Glorious Body' in N 91–103; see also the brief allusion to the pornographic in Chapter 4).

What we are given to consider is instead a profaned relationship between lovers wherein 'In their fulfillment, the lovers who have lost their mystery contemplate a human nature rendered perfectly inoperative – the inactivity and *desoeuvrement* of the human and of the animal as the supreme and unsavable figure of life' (O 87). What lovers can beautifully reveal through their exposure to one another is that there is no mystery underneath the economies, apparatuses, glories and graces that had sought to conceal the empty void of the human being and its body. There is only our nudity, which truly does exist as something of necessary, eternal or natural substance (what he will call its 'theological signature'), though it is incredibly hard to touch in its naturalness beyond all inscribed 'natural-eternal' (fixed) representations, to which many doctors and nurses, care-givers and therapists can attest. Trying to access such a nudity is seemingly impossible to many of us – a situation demonstrated by the clothes we wear both on the street and in the classroom and which we could not imagine shedding in the public domain. And yet *our nudity is still there, underneath our clothing*, a tangible and concrete reality that we have no way of expressing symbolically except, most frequently, as a hyper-sexualised, pornographic image, as a biological instrument subject to medical intervention or as a fixed 'natural' (theological) form (often predetermining one's gender or sexual orientation, for example). In truth, our naked bodies are extremely vulnerable, a material weakness that is constantly covered over with the fiction of sovereignty – a reality that grants real legitimacy to the fable of 'The Emperor's New Clothes'.

Agamben's argument, however, is not necessarily one that would have us parading around naked to one another on a daily basis, in plain public sight. Again, he is not pointing us toward a new, utopian paradise that promises one's ultimate happiness (the antinomian temptation par excellence). Rather, he is drawing our attention toward the emptiness that characterises our human being at its core. Put another way, he is not seeking to demonstrate a new, better relationship that is stronger than the previous one; he is only aiming to demonstrate the failure of every relationship as the only possible authentic relationship. It is this suspension of the relationship that offers us a new possibility for being-together, as undefinable as that might seem to be. As he will summarise this state of affairs:

> However, it is not a question of trying to trace the no longer human or animal contours of a new creation that would run the risk of being equally as mythological as the other. As we have seen, in our culture man has always been the result of a simultaneous division and articulation of the animal and the human, in which one of the two terms of the operation was also what was at stake in it. To render inoperative the machine that governs our conception of man will therefore mean no longer to seek new – more effective

or more authentic – articulations, but rather to show the central emptiness, the hiatus that – within man – separates man and animal, and to risk ourselves in this emptiness: the suspension of the suspension, Shabbat of both animal and man. (O 92)

In congruence with his writings on Pauline theology, this is the site where we encounter the 'messianic banquet of the righteous' that lets humanity be 'outside of being, saved precisely in their being unsavable' (O 92) according to traditional economies of salvation (but for whom a certain 'saved night' might still be possible). Paul had claimed to be separated, and yet the messianic undoes those separations, introducing the division of division itself as the primary activity that undoes a given apparatus's grasp over the potential form of life that has been dominated by its inscription into the human being (TR 44–53).

As we saw a moment ago, bare life is the product of the anthropological machinery and not what precedes it, as in a typical 'state of nature' scenario – something that Agamben certainly rejects out of hand (SE 87–8/OHS 241). Hence the disenchantment he is after, what he will call an absolute profanation, 'does not restore the enchanted thing to its original state' (SE 87–8/OHS 241), as many theologians might wish were the case. It rather undoes the sacred signature that governs the construction of the human being, allowing a new use for the human, *and* its body, to emerge. Agamben captured this point well in *The Coming Community* regarding the rise of objectification and reification at the dawn of industrialisation. In this sense, pornography or the reified images of a body no longer bound to a sacred image of the body (e.g. the pure, virginal body) *are* liberatory in some sense (and as feminist scholars have argued on occasion in defence of pornography or sex workers) (CC 47–50). However, at the same time such images are also thwarted by the fact that they fail to encounter the fragile, precarious bodies that actually live underneath the new, sexualised image. What Agamben is after is a body liberated from its theological signature, but one that also does not reinscribe itself within a new economy of totalised and totalising images. The constellation of images that Benjamin had described in his attempt to give voice to a 'dialectics at a standstill' was one wherein the past image was imposed upon a present image, offering what had been repressed an ephemeral moment of liberation. Instead, what pornography offers us is a present image as *totalised* image, seductive in its false promises for a completed happiness.

However, the space that Agamben is after is one that renders such totalised images inoperative. He seeks to access the void at the centre of human being that can only be seen through suspending our normal representations of ourselves. This explains the repeatedly noted significance of contemplation and of inoperativity in his work. In his words:

> One can therefore understand the essential function that the tradition of Western philosophy has assigned to contemplative life and to inoperativity: properly human praxis is sabbatism that, by rendering the specific functions of the living inoperative, opens them to possibility. Contemplation and inoperativity are, in this sense, the metaphysical operators of anthropogenesis, which, by liberating the living man from his biological or social destiny, assign him to that indefinable dimension that we are accustomed to call 'politics.' Opposing the contemplative life to the political as 'two *bioi*', Aristotle deflected politics and philosophy from their trajectory and, at the same time, delineated the paradigm on which the economy-glory apparatus would model itself. The political is neither a *bios* nor a *zōē*, but the dimension that the inoperativity of contemplation, by deactivating linguistic and corporeal, material and immaterial praxes, ceaselessly opens and assigns to the living. For this reason, from the perspective of theological *oikonomia* the genealogy of which we have here traced, nothing is more urgent than to incorporate inoperativity within its own apparatuses. *Zōē aiōnios*, eternal life, is the name of this inoperative center of the human, of this political 'substance' of the Occident that the machine of economy and of glory ceaselessly attempts to capture within itself. (KG 251/OHS 599–600)

# 6
# *Paul and the Messianic Division of Division*

## A POSSIBLE HERMENEUTIC

We have delayed the conversation long enough and it is perhaps most helpful to take a moment to address Agamben's method for rendering inoperative the apparatuses and the logic of presupposition that ceaselessly divide our world up into those dualistic splits that govern it. To analyse this technique more closely I want to look at a brief passage in a lecture published as *The Church and the Kingdom*, which I will contrast with a possible negative dialectic at work in his commentary on Paul's letter to the Romans in order to more fully elucidate the 'division of division itself'. I believe this is one of the major concepts at work in the *Homo Sacer* series, as well as his characterisations of form-of-life.

In a 2009 lecture at Notre Dame Cathedral in Paris, and in collaboration with various high-ranking members of the Catholic Church, Agamben reflected on the nature of the Church as an institution and the perpetual conflict it feels in relation to its own messianic impulses which cause the Church merely to sojourn in this world, and not to dwell permanently in it. However, this experience of sojourning, or of being in a permanent state of pilgrimage where everyday life is suspended, is not one wherein the Church should anticipate the end of the world. Its sojourning nature implies that there is an experience of the messianic, its peculiar nature of interruption and suspension, which potentially breaks into every present moment. In his words:

> It is important to bear in mind that the term 'sojourn' does not refer here to a fixed period of time: that it does not designate chronological duration. The sojourning Church on earth can last – and indeed has lasted – not only centuries but millennia without altering its messianic experience of time. This point requires special emphasis as it is opposed to what is often called a 'delay of the *parousia*.' According to this position – which has always seemed blasphemous to me – the initial Christian community, expecting as it did the imminent arrival of the messiah and thus the end of time, found itself confronted with an inexplicable delay. In response to this delay there was a reorientation to stabilize the institutional and juridical organization of the early Church. The consequence of this position is that the Christian community has ceased to *paroikein*, to sojourn as a foreigner, so as to begin to *katoikein*, to live as a citizen and thus function like any other worldly institution. (CK 2–4)

But such a position, it should likewise be stated, means that the Church has risked losing touch with its own messianic nature, compromising itself in order to retain the glory of sovereign power in our world: 'If this is the case, the Church has lost the messianic experience of time that defines it and is one with it. The time of the messiah cannot designate a chronological period or duration but, instead, must represent nothing less than a qualitative change in how time is experienced' (CK 4–5).

Messianic time, working as an internal force within humanity's experience of time, 'is a time that pulses and moves within chronological time, that transforms chronological time from within' (CK 12). It is a contracted time, or, as the title of his study on Paul will phrase it, 'the time that remains' (cf. his remarks on time in RA 159, 162–4/OHS 867, 869–70). It is an experience of time that hollows out chronological time, just as the messianic vocation is a revocation of every vocation that 'at once voids and transforms every vocation and every condition so as to free them for a new usage ("make use of it")' (CK 18). As Agamben will continue to describe its experience:

> Just as messianic time is not some other time but, instead, an integral transformation of chronological time, an ultimate experience (an experience of the last things) would entail, first and foremost, experiencing penultimate things differently. In this context, eschatology is nothing other than a transformation of the experience of the penultimate. Given that ultimate realities take place first in penultimate ones, the latter – contrary to any radicalism – cannot be freely negated. And yet – and for the same reason – the penultimate things cannot in any case be invoked against the ultimate ones. For this reason Paul expresses the messianic relation between final and penultimate things with the very *katargein*, which does not mean 'destroy' but, instead, 'render inoperative.' The ultimate reality deactivates, suspends and transforms, the penultimate ones – and yet, it is precisely, and above all, in these penultimate realities that an ultimate reality bears witness and is put to the test. (CK 19)

What develops from this perspective is the Pauline sense of a 'now time' which is not a future time, but rather is what is working *within* the present time. As we have seen in a number of contexts within Agamben's work already, this characterisation of messianic time is not an attempt to posit a new, utopian time outside of everyday time, but rather is another way to view the time that is already present and to make a new use of it. In fact, this re-examination of time becomes a cornerstone of Agamben's philosophy on the whole, and it is a facet of the human experience that must be reckoned with no matter if one is religious or not. What the messianic force working within history as well as within every identity and institutional form represents is a feature of human existence that permeates every living being. Hence, the Church, according to Agamben, has little choice but to bear witness to its own originary observations: 'Living in this time, experiencing this time, is thus not something that the Church can choose, or choose not, to do. It is only in this time that there is a Church at all' (CK 26).

Yet what follows from these insights seems to imply a dualistic, even hermeneutical tension present within our world that more or less blunts or domesticates the radical import of Agamben's calls for the inoperativity or profanation of the ecclesial machinery. It is this dualism, and the tension between each side of the equation, that interests me here especially, as the tension itself is usually portrayed as the result of the presupposition that fractures our being. Indeed, the passage is quite stunning in its admission of an irreducible tension that cannot simply be eradicated or overcome.

> In the eyes of the Church Fathers – as well as the eyes of the philosophers who have reflected on the philosophy of history, which is, and remains (even in Marx) an essentially Christian discipline – history is presented as a field traversed by two opposing forces. The first of these forces – which Paul, in a passage of the Second Letter to the Thessalonians that is as famous as it is enigmatic, calls *to catechon* – maintains and ceaselessly defers the end along the linear and homogenous line of chronological time. By placing origin and end in contact with one another, this force endlessly fulfils and ends time. Let us call this force Law or State, dedicated as it is to economy, which is to say, dedicated as it is to the indefinite – and indeed infinite – governance of the world. As for the second force, let us call it messiah, or Church; its economy is the economy of salvation, and by this token is essentially completed. The only way that a community can form and last is if these poles are present and a dialectical tension between them prevails. (CK 34–5)

There is in this configuration of things a seeming capitulation to the dualistic existence of the Church and its complicity with the presupposition of being, a Church that he unhesitatingly declared to exist most authentically as *without* content or doctrine in *The Time that Remains* (TR 136–7). Agamben claims the Church must maintain a balance of sorts between the economic form and its disruption through an economy of salvation that upends its representation of itself. And even this tension has

## Paul and the Messianic Division of Division

seemed to vanish today, as the crisis of authority and legitimacy has permeated a Church that has seemingly lost contact with its messianic impulses:

> For this reason, the question I came here today to ask you, without any other authority than an obstinate habit of reading the signs of the time, is this: Will the Church finally grasp the historical occasion and recover its messianic vocation? If it does not, the risk is clear enough: it will be swept away by the disaster menacing every government and every institution on earth. (CK 41)

The messianic vocation of the Church, conceiving of a revocation of every vocation, but which yet somehow also maintains a tension with every historically existing vocation, is the focus of Agamben's profanatory task. It is one that the Church has also neglected for far too long throughout the course of its existence, mainly in order to cultivate sovereign power within its institutional-hierarchical forms. Of course, we must also keep in mind that the Church here is merely a cipher for the political-theological foundations of any instituted or normative order, thus pointing toward significant political considerations at the same time.

### THE GESTURE OF POPE BENEDICT XVI

As an example of how the Church might yet embrace its radical messianic force in a contemporary setting, Agamben offers us, in yet another exemplary theological context, the papacy of Pope Benedict XVI. The papacy had seemed at first not to embrace the messianic vocation of the Church, but only to entrench itself further within the culture wars against secularism. However, it was his highly unusual step of abdicating his position as Pope that brought such assumptions swiftly to their end:

> This is why Benedict XVI's gesture appears so important to us. This man, who was at the head of the institution that claims the

most ancient and pregnant title of legitimacy, has called into question the very sense of this title with his gesture. In the face of a curia that, completely oblivious to its own legitimacy, stubbornly pursues the motives of economy and temporal power, Benedict XVI has chosen to use only spiritual power, in the only way that seemed possible to him, namely by renouncing the exercise of the vicarship of Christ. In this way, the Church itself has been called into question to its very root. (ME 4–5)

Though he does not develop it much further in this context, there is a spiritual power at work within the messianic vocation that undoes the sovereign power aligned with every structure, institution, identity, law and language. This is, as I have been calling it, *another* form of power that Agamben wants to isolate and uplift as the weak messianic force we are perpetually called to entertain as a corrective power to whatever established norm governs over humanity's definition of itself. In short, this is why Agamben's reading of Pauline thought, or the history of the Church, is also so provocative for modern philosophical and political formulations.

In another brief essay on the nature of the Church, this time concerning the resignation of the papacy by Pope Benedict XVI, Agamben finds a way to extend his analysis of the illegitimacy of institutions and authorities today within the political fields and questions that comprise a good deal of the *Homo Sacer* series. In this context, he revisits the same possible hermeneutical tension that I noted above, though in slightly different terms. Nonetheless, his analysis locates the precise problematic that our world still faces and for which it must find a solution. For starters, the legitimacy of all institutions today is called into question as we continue to deconstruct the authorities and powers that have been utilised for centuries to maintain and justify sovereign power. As he had noted in Paris, 'I say the following with words carefully weighed: nowhere on earth today is a legitimate power to be found; even the powerful are convinced of their own illegitimacy' (CK 40). It is from this context of the illegitimacy of all institutions that the resignation of Pope Benedict takes on a renewed significance, for here we see how it was precisely this act of stepping down from a position of power and authority that calls into question the entire edifice of power itself and the structures that seek to justify such exercises (ME 2).

The problem of illegitimacy runs much deeper than a simple form of scepticism; it is inbuilt within the structure of every worldly power. Moreover, this is a point that allows Agamben's analysis to embrace a discussion of lawlessness in relation to every law as a tension *internal* to law itself. This formulation runs parallel to earlier discussions of the *anomie* latent within every law and the temptations of antinomianism, as I have noted arise in Agamben's writings, often merely in passing. Theologically, it was Christianity that conceived of the relation between law and lawlessness as held together by a force – the *katechon* or restrainer – that would prevent lawlessness from dominating every structure and institution.

> The structure of eschatological time – this is Paul's message – is twofold: there is, on the one hand, a slowing element (the *katechon*, whether it is identified with the Empire or with the Church, in any case an institution), and, on the other, a decisive element (the messiah). Between the two is situated the appearance of the man of lawlessness (the Antichrist, according to the Fathers), whose revelation, which coincides with the *katechon*'s exiting the scene, precipitates the final battle. The messiah – who, in Paul as well as in the Jewish tradition, renders the law inoperative – inaugurates a zone of lawlessness that coincides with messianic time and in this way frees the *anomos*, the outlaw, who is in this way very similar to the Christian (we do well not to forget that Paul defines himself at one time as *hos anomos*, 'without law' [. . .]. The *katechon* is the power – the Empire, but also the Church, like every juridically constituted authority – that opposes and conceals the lawlessness that defines messianic time and in this way shows the revelation of the 'mystery of lawlessness.' The unveiling of this mystery coincides with the manifestation of the inoperativity of the law and with the essential illegitimacy

of every power in messianic time. (And by all appearances, this is what is happening today under our noses, when the powers of state act openly as outside the law. In this sense, the *anomos* does not represent anything but the unveiling of the lawlessness that today defines every constituted power, within which State and terrorism form a single system.) (ME 33–4)

In a strange reversal of terms, the lawless one, functioning in the space of the messiah, reveals the lawlessness that sustains 'every constituted power', which also allows the messiah and the antichrist to cohere in the same space, perhaps even in the same person. Agamben suggests Paul is the ideal Christian at the same time as he stands outside of the law – indeed, he is the ideal Christian *because* he stands outside of the law, giving him a position from which to call every law and every structure into question. According to Pauline thought, remaining within this tension seems to be the predominant task of the Christian. Furthermore, it is this tension that, for Agamben, defines the politics of our world at the same time.

The schema that Agamben discloses is one wherein an inescapable tension is held together by traditionally opposed theological images – the messiah, the antichrist – so that the Church can maintain itself as a structure, and as a community at all, within our world. This is also the way, philosophically and politically speaking, in which any identity, rationality or order is brought into existence. When one side of the tension is dismissed, reduced or removed from immediate relevance, risks are run that threaten to delegitimate any institution forever, including through its capacity to engage and justify evil within our world. Agamben describes this situation in terms entirely parallel to his previous remarks – and for that reason, all the more significant to note:

In the Church there are two irreconcilable elements, which nonetheless never stop intertwining historically: *oikonomia* – God's salvific action in the world and time – and eschatology – the end of the world and of time. When the eschatological element has been put aside, the development of the secularized *oikonomia* has been perverted and has become literally without end, which is to say, without a goal. From this moment, the mystery of evil, displaced from its proper place and erected into an ontological structure, blocks the Church from any true choice and at the same time provides an alibi for its ambiguities. (ME 38)[1]

To avoid such evil, the tension must be maintained. Similar to his Paris lecture, the hermeneutic that Agamben endorses is one in which the dualisms that construct our world are not forced into a necessarily hierarchical relationship wherein one dominates over another, but a symbiotic relationship where the tension is inescapable and should not be foreclosed upon. By definition, this tension applies to a wide variety of dualistic divisions that appear to suture our world together in a number of ways but which are ultimately the result of the presupposition of being that prevents us from living out a form-of-life. For example, Agamben will defer to some of those scissions within our being that appear with great frequency throughout the *Homo Sacer* series: 'A society's institutions remain living only if both principles (which in our tradition have also received the name of natural law and positive law, spiritual power and temporal power, or in Rome, *auctoritas* and *potestas*) remain present and act in them without ever claiming to coincide' (ME 2–3). They must therefore refuse to be co-opted into a bipolar machinery, as touched on in Chapter 4, such as what is present in the sovereign-governmentality paradigm that Agamben so carefully dissects in *The Kingdom and the Glory*.[2]

This tension appears to be a hermeneutical balance between two opposing forces that must be maintained in order for a given institution to maintain itself politically and historically. At times, however, this vision potentially also undercuts Agamben's more direct critiques of such tensions, which are otherwise constitutive of the anthropological machinery that he wishes to render inoperative. This configuration of relations often leads to a good deal of confusion on the part of Agamben's readers: is he advocating the dissolution of the presuppositional logic that produces dualistic tensions in order to capture being and that are really a justification for sovereign power (such as with the sovereign-governmentality duality)? *Or* is he justifying the existence of certain dualisms, as between *oikonomia* and eschatology, or law and messiah, as we have just seen? Such questions are even more fundamental to ask of the *Homo Sacer* project because the entire series concludes in the quest for form-of-life *beyond* the law.

As this will be an issue not resolved until we examine his considerations of a form-of-life in the last chapter, at this point, I want to take a look at one option presented through a comment he makes in *State of Exception*. It concerns the significance of Benjamin's remark that the law that is studied but not practised is the gateway to justice (SE 63/OHS 220), something we might regard analogously as: the theology that is studied but not practised is the gateway to grace. What Agamben reads into Benjamin's statement is that comprehending the law as the force of a law that has been cancelled (or 'force of ~~law~~' as he phrases it), and so as 'pure means', is the path toward embracing a life lived beyond the law, which both Kafka and Foucault foresaw: 'Kafka's most proper gesture consists not (as [Gershom] Scholem believes) in having maintained a law that no longer has any meaning, but in having shown that it ceases to be law and blurs at all points with life' (SE 63/OHS 220). Not only do we read in this gesture the quest for form-of-life beyond all relation to the law, but it is also a gesture intimately related to Pauline notions of messianic fulfilment, or that which deactivates the law (renders it inoperative) without doing away with it (SE 63–4/OHS 221). Simultaneously, it is Foucault's dream of a 'new law' 'freed from all discipline and all relation to sovereignty' that Agamben finds so appealing, and so revisits when further discussing Foucault in *The Use of Bodies* as well (SE 63/OHS 220).

As we will see in a moment, the status of a law that has been de-activated, or rendered inoperative, is the primary possibility for a life lived anew – the messianic life, or 'life in Christ' as Paul had conceived of it. It is for this reason that Pauline thought merges, in Agamben's reading, with the world of Kafka in order to illuminate a way to live beyond one's inscription in the law. Crucially, he asks:

> What can be the meaning of a law that survives its deposition in such a way? The difficulty Benjamin faces here corresponds to a problem that can be formulated (and it was effectively formulated for the first time in primitive Christianity and then later in the Marxian tradition) in these terms: What becomes of the law after its messianic fulfillment? (This is the controversy that opposes Paul to the Jews of his time.) And what becomes of the law in a society without classes? [. . .] Obviously, it is not a question here of a transitional phase that never achieves its end, nor of a process of infinite deconstruction that, in maintaining the law in a spectral life, can no longer get to the bottom of it. The decisive point here is that the law – no longer practiced, but studied – is not justice, but only the gate that leads to it. What opens a passage toward justice is not the erasure of law, but its deactivation and inactivity – that is, another use of the law. This is precisely what the force-of-~~law~~ (which keeps the law working beyond its formal suspension) seeks to prevent. Kafka's characters – and this is why they interest us – have to do with this spectral figure of the law in the state of exception; they seek, each one following his or her own strategy, to 'study' and deactivate it, to 'play' with it. (SE 63–4/OHS 221)

In this striking passage, finding 'another use of the law' becomes the task Agamben will champion, and one that parallels locating *another* form of sovereignty as an alternative *use* of sovereign power, as I have alluded to throughout. Such a possible re-characterisation is what will allow Agamben to insist that this other, different use is more akin to play (read here as a synonym to 'use') than to possession. In turn, this use becomes that which brings a new form of freedom into the world and makes a new sense of justice possible. In one of the more quoted and rightly illuminating passages from *State of Exception*, we see the stakes unfold exactly as such:

> One day humanity will play with law just as children play with disused objects, not in order to restore them to their canonical use but to free them from it for good. What is found after the law is not a more proper and original use value that precedes the law, but a new use that is born only after it. And use, which has been contaminated by law, must also be freed from its own value. This liberation is the task of study, or of play. And this studious play is the passage that allows us to arrive at that justice that one of Benjamin's posthumous fragments defines as a state of the world in which the world appears as a good that absolutely cannot be appropriated or made juridical. (SE 64/OHS 221)

## TOWARDS A NEGATIVE DIALECTIC

As we have explored throughout, Agamben's reflections on Pauline thought are central to his solution for the anthropological machinery and its incessant division of human life, even the divisions that characterise the existence of the Church as an institution. His reading of Paul is where we are able to situate his major solution to the divisions and fractures that appear through the governance of our being and our world. He will follow Paul in calling for a messianic 'division of division itself' that takes every dualism and further divides it in half, and so neutralising its destructive force (TR 49–53). For example, as Paul will distinctively state in Romans, every identity (e.g. one's Jewish or Gentile identity) is divided from within into flesh *and* spirit, a further division that renders the first division (between the Jew *and* the Gentile) inoperative – though it also does not replace the primary representative division with a new one either. This is a point that echoes the analysis made above regarding Agamben's insistence that the messianic event not lead to a new, utopian state of existence, but only to a new use of a current one. This 'division of division itself' is what Agamben reads Paul as advocating above all else, and this logic is how Agamben will ultimately deal with the tensions that traverse the Church, as with any institution or identity.

In rendering this Pauline operation more visible, Agamben recognises that Paul's comments on the law sound to many ears as being antinomian, since faith stands opposed to law in order to render its normative force inoperative (HS 110–11/OHS 93). Nonetheless, there is also within Paul's articulation of the law a possible new understanding of faith that one must not overlook. Agamben describes it as such:

> Paul is able to set the *nomos pisteōs*, the law of faith, against the *nomos tōn ergon*, the law of works. Rather than being an antinomy that involves two unrelated and completely heterogeneous principles, here the opposition lies within the *nomos* itself, between its normative and promissive elements. There is something in the law that constitutively exceeds the norm and is irreducible to it, and it is this excess and this inner dialectic that Paul refers to by means of the binomial *epaggelia* / *nomos* (the first corresponding to faith, the second to works). This is how, in 1 Corinthians 9:21, having stated that he made himself *hōs anomos*, 'as without law,' along with those who are without law (meaning *goyim*), he immediately rectifies this affirmation specifying that he is not *anomos theou*, 'outside God's law,' but *ennomos christou*, 'in the law of the Messiah.' The messianic law is the law of faith and not just the negation of the law. This, however, does not mean substituting the old *miswoth* [commandments] with new precepts; rather, it means setting a non-normative figure of the law against the normative figure of the law. (TR 95)

Paul's argument links the force of messianic activity with the 'sabbatical suspension of works', rendering them inoperative, or *katargeō* – the word Paul chooses in this context to declare the messianic de-activation (and not 'destruction' as many translations would have it) of the law. In this space, Agamben observes how 'potentiality passes over into actuality and meets up with its *telos*, not in the form of force or *ergon*, but in the form of *astheneia*, weakness' (TR 97). These comments will further mirror Agamben's articulation of one's private life as it shadows one's public life in *The Use of Bodies*, the very relationship that makes possible the ability to embody form-of-life. That is, we can live out form-of-life only once the messianic suspension of suspension itself renders the anthropological machinery inoperative.

By demonstrating such a logic of what we might call a double division (akin, I would suggest, to certain readings of the 'negation of negation' as in Hegel, or the 'alienation of alienation' as in Jürgen Moltmann's theology),[3] Paul is credited with inverting the Aristotelean relationship of potentiality-actuality. Perhaps more importantly, Paul accomplishes this task 'not simply by negating or annihilating them, but by de-activating them, rendering them inoperative, no-longer-at-work' (TR 97). At risk of sounding repetitive, but needing to do so as it is so fundamental to Agamben's thought: the messianic force does not destroy law, but de-activates it as the form of its fulfilment. In this fashion, the messianic is what Agamben will call a moment of crisis in the separation between law and religion (TR 118–19; see also TR 135).

In political terms, this tension is itself likewise rendered inoperative, as Agamben makes clear:

> The caesura between constitutive and constituted power, a divide that becomes so apparent in our times, finds its theological origins in the Pauline split between the level of faith and that of *nomos*, between personal loyalty and the positive obligation that derives from it. In this light, messianism appears as a struggle, within the law, whereby the element of the pact and constituent power leans toward setting itself against and emancipating itself from the element of the *entolē*, the norm in the strict sense. The messianic is therefore the historical process whereby the archaic link between law and religion (which finds its magical paradigm in *horkos*, oath) reaches a crisis and the element of *pistis*, of faith in the pact,

tends paradoxically to emancipate itself from any obligatory conduct and from positive law (from works fulfilled in carrying out the pact). (TR 118–19)

This activity will place the one who believes in the possibilities of such a messianic force in a position that is apparently beyond all law, though it is not an antinomian negation of the law either. Recall, it is not a destruction that Paul was after, but a de-activation. From this site, one almost impossible to articulate in identifiable language, arises the suspicion that we are dealing with an antinomian impulse. However, what we actually witness is that such a position is removed from the dualistic opposition of *nomos* and anti-*nomos*, which merely replicates the categorical, dualistic tension and sustains the (Aristotelian) political machinery that gave rise to this tension in the first place (e.g. as with potentiality and actuality). This is what, recall from Chapter 4, Elliot Wolfson has termed a 'hypernomian' position – that which is in excess of the law and of representation, and which we have no name for because it strives for a space in excess of language itself.[4] In terms which will recall, but also differ significantly from, the separation and unity of sovereign power and governance, 'The messianic is the instance, in religion and equally in law, of an exigency of fulfillment which – in putting origin and end in a tension with each other – restores the two halves of prelaw in unison. At this same moment, it shows the impossibility of their ever coinciding' (TR 135).

As Agamben will subsequently and profoundly indicate, 'Grace is that excess which, while it always divides the two elements of prelaw and prevents them from coinciding, does not even allow them to completely break apart' (TR 120). This grace 'seems to even define a real "sovereignty" (*autarkeia*) of the messianic in relation to works of law', though this *other* form of sovereignty goes relatively unnoticed by many readers of Pauline literature who frequently assume that Paul's thought merely endorses whatever sovereign authority governs the land (cf. historical interpretations of Romans 13) (TR 120). The reality is actually much more complex as it appears to introduce *another* form of sovereignty into the world – a point that Agamben's work uncovers as latent within these Pauline formulations.

> The messianic instance, which takes place in historical time and renders Mosaic law inoperative, goes back genealogically before Mosaic law, toward the promise. The space that opens up between the two *diathēkai* [testament, law, covenant] is the space of grace. This is why the *kainē diathēkai* [the law of faith] cannot be something like a written text containing new and diverse precepts (which is how it ends up). As stated in the extraordinary passage right before the affirmation of the new covenant, it is not a letter written in ink on tables of stone; rather it is written with the breath of God on hearts of the flesh. In other words, it is not a text, but the very life of the messianic community, not a *writing*, but a *form of life*: *hē epistolē hemōn hymeis este*, 'You are our letter' (2 Cor. 3: 2)! (TR 122)

Elaborating upon the religious notion of the promise that, I would suggest, is analogous to his later formulation of a demand, Agamben brings us to a space for grace made available through the division of every identity and normative order that does not yet result in a new, utopian space. It is only the force of the messianic 'division of division itself' that makes possible the entrance of a messianic community existing only as a collective of various forms-of-life not subject to a normative (sovereign) order. As Agamben will develop briefly and incompletely in *The Use of Bodies*, it is a political notion of the multitude. Here the multitude represents the potential of thought and 'constitutes the multiple forms of life into form-of-life', rather than forming a political body of as 'the people' (UB 213/ OHS 1219).

However, according to Pauline thought, there is no escaping from the identities established in language and in the economies of the world, as 'Grace does not provide the foundation for exchange and social obligations; it makes for their interruption. The messianic gesture does not found, it fulfills' (TR 124). It is a permanently negative enterprise that only divides whatever social identity – already founded upon a previous division – already exists. As Agamben will continue, 'It is obvious that for Paul grace cannot constitute a separate realm that is alongside that of obligation and law. Rather, grace entails nothing more than the ability to *use* the sphere of social determinations and services in its totality' (TR 124).[5] Again, as with his study on Franciscan conceptualisations of use, there is not another identity we are searching for, but only a new use of an already existing one. This interpretation also explains why Paul, in his letter to Philemon, could encourage a runaway slave to return to his master while also reminding both individuals that their life in Christ means that they are beyond both identities (that of slave and that of master). Though such a position can obviously be co-opted in order to maintain the status quo, it can also be a principle striving for ever-greater social justice in terms of always moving toward the negation of a given identity within our world.

## DIALECTICS AT A STANDSTILL

Taking the Pauline division of division more fully into account will allow us at this point to understand why Agamben must resist any interpretation of the Hegelian *Aufhebung* as an attempt to suture together a tension that must remain forever unresolved. His critique of Hegelian dialectics as a secularisation of Christian messianism is therefore one that must be seen within this context. Though it is not clear if another reading of Hegel is possible – such as we find in the works of Theodor Adorno, Slavoj Žižek and Frederic Jameson, to name but a few who locate in Hegel something like a negative dialectic that might share with such Pauline formulations – Agamben finds the issue important enough that he returns to it at the end of *The Use of Bodies* where he comments on Luther's translation of Paul's term *katargein* as *aufheben*, which means both to abolish and preserve.[6] Agamben notes this was an 'intuition whose significance would not escape Hegel' (UB 273/OHS 1274).

For Agamben, Pauline thought engaged in its own version of a negative dialectics through its division of every pre-existing social division within our world. Whatever marker of social identity was taken as constitutive of a given social order – the Jew/Gentile divide, or the master/slave, male/female ones (as Paul, for example, spoke of in Galatians 3: 28) – could be further divided by making a 'second cut' to the first one. Introducing the division between flesh and spirit within any given identity, Paul was able to find a new freedom from social, legal, religious and political identities through the recognition that whatever identity was presented was 'not all' there is to the fullness of the person. Underneath every legal designation, underneath every law, we find a form-of-life attempting to find its way toward the surface. By enacting the second division – what Hegel, as well as a long history of Christian mystics, would have described as the 'negation of negation' – Paul is able to find a way beyond the law without actually nullifying any existing law (TR 47–58).

One of the simplest ways to comprehend the radical social justice import of Pauline thought enacted through just such a 'second division' is through its juxtaposition with the elaboration on history in the work of Benjamin, one of Agamben's greatest influences. At the conclusion to his study in *The Time that Remains*, Agamben quotes Benjamin's *Theses on the Philosophy of History* where Benjamin suggested a principle of historical recollection in line with the (weak) force of the messianic that Agamben also finds to be active in Pauline thought.[7] In Benjamin's description:

> The true image of the past *flees* by. The past can be seized only as an image which flashes up at the instant when it can be recognized and is never seen again. . . . For every image of the past that is not recognized by the present as one of its own concerns threatens to disappear irretrievably. (TR 141)

Capturing the essence of an image that cannot legitimate a sovereign fiction or myth because it is ephemeral and not foundational, we can perceive the flash of a messianic now-time that signals to us another way of allowing the past into the present – not as grounding or legitimating sovereign power, but as introducing *another* form of sovereignty that allows the past to move into the present, and to fleetingly move out of it again.

Quoting from Benjamin again, Agamben sees another perspective on time appear before him – one that seemingly matches step with Paul's depiction of kairological time:

> It is not that what is past casts its light on what is present, or what is present its light on what is past; rather, image is that wherein what has been comes together in a flash with the now to form a constellation. For while the relation of the present to the past is purely temporal (continuous), the relation of what-has-been to the now is dialectical, in leaps and bounds. (TR 141)

The past is fulfilled in the present moment through the act of citation, which gives meaning to the past image, yet *through* the present image. This forms a constellation of images that would bring the past and present together in a uniquely particular moment of liberation for the image that had been forgotten by history, but which nonetheless demanded to be seen (and so which recalls a promise made that becomes a demand, as we saw earlier). Of course, Agamben's radical conclusion is that Benjamin's dialectical constellations formed as 'weak messianic forces' stretching throughout history, from past to present in order to liberate the oppressed images of the past, are precisely in accord with Pauline notions of the time that remains – a kairological division of time itself. In Benjamin's words, which Agamben cites:

> image is dialectics at a standstill. For while the relation of the present to the past is purely temporal, the relation of what has been to the now is dialectical: not temporal in nature but imagistic. Only dialectical images are genuinely historical – that is, not archaic – images. The image that is read – which is to say, the image in the now of its recognizability – bears to the highest degree the imprint of the perilous critical moment on which all reading is founded. (TR 145)

Hence, here and elsewhere in Agamben's work, the photographic image becomes, again following Benjamin closely in this context, that which makes a demand upon us. It is that which asks something from us. There is an exigency that characterises our relationship to the image that stands before us, as if through the demand of a promise: 'Even if the person photographed is completely forgotten today, even if his or her name has been erased forever from human memory – or, indeed, precisely because of this – that person and that face demand their name; they demand not to be forgotten' (P 25). If resurrection is for theologians an issue of the form of the body, its *eidos*, then 'Photography is, in this sense, a prophecy of the glorious body' (P 27).

## THE MESSIANIC AND THE FUTURE OF DIALECTICS

It is at this point that we might take note of where Agamben joins this Pauline-Benjaminian dialectics at a standstill with a 'messianic modality' that, I will argue, stems directly from his elaboration of a modal ontology in *The Use of Bodies*. For Agamben, this union is the only way to perceive our relation to substance, office and identity that the messianic hollows out from within:

> This modality, which is rarely ever thematized as such in the history of philosophy, is exigency. So essential to philosophy, it could even be said to make it coincide with the possibility of philosophy itself. Let us attempt to inscribe this concept into the tale of modal categories alongside possibility, impossibility, necessity, and contingency. In the essay written in his youth on Dostoevsky's *Idiot*, Benjamin says that the life of Prince Mishkin must remain unforgettable, even if no one remembers it. This is exigency. Exigency does not forget, nor does it try to exorcise contingency. On the contrary, it says: even though this life has been completely forgotten, there is an exigency that it remain unforgettable. (TR 39)

As Agamben will frame the distinction, the ontology of demand, and so of exigency, is contrasted with the ontology of command that underlies every onto-theology and its many sovereign forms (for a refresher on the ontology of demand, see Chapter 1). At the same time, it is a regression into our pure potentiality, or potency, that resists ever becoming actual – and so not just by avoiding actual reality. Instead, we push through it and divide it from within by the potential that is latent within it (as the potentiality captured in the spirit, not the actuality of flesh, had once divided Jewish identity, in Paul's phrasing). Hence, 'each existent demands its proper possibility, it demands that it become possible. Exigency consists in a relation between what is or has been, and its possibility. It does not precede reality; rather, it follows it' (TR 39).

Ironically, however, it is in the nature of exigency and demand that we might be able to recover the use of anything like a substantial nature, which now lies open to each form-of-life that lives through it and which refuses to cast it as a particular, fixed identity. Whatever life we live has no teleological purpose, but only derives any sense of purpose through the intimacy it shares (beyond all pre-established relationships) through contact with another – the main reason, I would wager, that the concept of love begins to recur with some frequency in Agamben's later writings (cf. his essay on 'The Passion of Facticity' in P 185–204). It should also be noted this experience is in radical contrast to the 'natural laws' that frequently, and mythologically, govern humanity through the fiction of sovereignty which continues to dominate essentialist accounts of human nature while truly being devoid of any substance whatsoever.

However, in the context of historical forms, we must note that we obviously cannot recall everything and that one's conscious memory, even collective or cultural memories, cannot retain everything that has been forgotten.

> The alternatives as this juncture are therefore not to forget or remember, to be unaware or become conscious, but rather, the determining factor is the capacity to remain faithful to that which having perpetually been forgotten, must remain unforgettable. It

demands to remain with us and be possible for us in some manner. To respond to this exigency is the only historical responsibility I feel capable of assuming fully. (TR 40)

Ignoring the unforgettable subsequently triggers the Freudian return of the repressed, as it allows what has shadowed us to return in 'destructive and perverse' ways. The Pauline notion, on the other hand, is precisely 'the redemption of what has been' as 'the place of an exigency for the messianic' (TR 41). It is in this sense that this messianic force 'nullifies the subject' and offers the individual an opportunity to access forms-of-life beyond one's inscription within the law.

Lest we become complacent with the force of the messianic working within our lives, we are reminded that such a movement beyond all laws, identities, institutions and norms pushes a form-of-life toward the bankruptcy of all representations (as the realm of the Kantian 'as if'). It is therefore a deep dive into the presentation of a world that can only appear as beyond salvation, because it lies beyond what may appear as a utopian world always yet 'to come'. In many ways, to grasp the Pauline and Benjaminian sense of the messianic will mean to live beyond every ontotheological formulation and every metaphysical presumption. Hence, to live as if *without* the divine in order, paradoxically, is to dwell in the space of the messiah:

> He who upholds himself in the messianic vocation no longer knows the *as if*, he no longer has similitudes at his disposal. He knows that in messianic time the saved world coincides with the world that is irretrievably lost, and that, to use Bonhoeffer's words, he must now really live in a world without God. This means that he may not disguise this world's being-without-God in any way. The saving God is the God who abandons him, and the fact of representations (the fact of the *as if*) cannot pretend to save the appearance of salvation. The messianic subject does not contemplate the world as though it were saved. In Benjamin's words, he contemplates salvation only to the extent that he loses himself in what cannot be saved; this is how difficult it is to dwell in the calling. (TR 42)

Explicitly striking a contrast with Hegel's notion of dialectics in his short essay *The Unspeakable Girl*, Agamben returns to another reading of Hegelian dialectics that goes unexplored in other places in his writing where he appears only to critique Hegel. In this context, however, he imagines a 'third element' being produced between the polarised tensions that yet becomes 'another nature' from the initial, divided elements. It rather 'requires a different form of exposition, one in which the opposing elements are at once maintained and neutralized. It is the content but nothing contains it; it is form but it no longer forms anything – exposing, thereby, itself" (UG 38). What this third element becomes is an image breaking through time, one that captures the essence of Benjamin's dialectics at a standstill:

> The idea of an image philosophy that Walter Benjamin seemed at times to evoke is not a metaphor; on the contrary, it is to be taken literally. The 'image of thought,' like Renaissance allegory, is a mystery wherein that which cannot be discursively presented shines for a moment out of the ruins of language. (UG 39)[8]

It is this 'third element', a phrase he uses throughout both *The Use of Bodies* and *The Highest Poverty*, that gives rise in Agamben's thought to the form-of-life lived beyond the dualistic tensions that govern most of human existence and interaction.

# 7

# *Form-of-Life beyond the Law*

## THE TEMPORALITY OF FASHION AND ART

In Agamben's remarks on the notion of the contemporary, there is one example of its nature that I want to isolate as I believe it points us toward comprehending his eventual pronouncement of the significance of form-of-life: that of the realm of fashion, specifically in relation to the art of citation (and certainly understood here in line with the previous chapter's remarks on citationality in Benjamin's work). From Agamben's viewpoint, fashion becomes that which represents the experience of contemporariness as a division between something's 'relevance or irrelevance, its being-in-fashion or its no-longer-being-in-fashion'. In a way that recalls the messianic 'now-time' (*Jetztzeit*) in Benjamin's theses on history, Agamben discovers within the immediacy of fashion a similar dynamic that he wants to underscore in order to illustrate the dynamics of messianic time. In his words:

> This caesura, as subtle as it may be, is remarkable in the sense that those who need to make note of it do so infallibly, and in so doing they attest to their own being in fashion. But if we try to objectify and fix this caesura within chronological time, it reveals itself as ungraspable. In the first place the 'now' of fashion, the instant in which it comes into being, is not identifiable via any kind of chronometer. Is this 'now' perhaps the moment in which

the fashion designer conceives of the general concept, the nuance that will define the new style of the clothes? Or is it the moment when the fashion designer conveys the concept to his assistants and then to the tailor who will sew the prototype? Or, rather, is it the moment of the fashion show, when the clothes are worn by the only people who are always and only in fashion, the mannequins or models – those who nonetheless, precisely for this reason, are never truly in fashion? In this last instance, the being in fashion of the 'style' will depend on the fact that the people of flesh and blood, rather than the mannequins (those sacrificial victims of a faceless god), will recognize it as such and choose that style for their own wardrobe. (WA 15–16)

Fashion brings a moment of discontinuity into the continuous flow of time, breaking time into two parts, leaving everyone scrambling to be either 'in or out of fashion'. In this way, there is no possibility of establishing a fixed chronological sense of time wherein something is always 'in fashion'. And so, 'the "now," the kairos of fashion, is ungraspable: the phrase, "I am in this instant in fashion" is contradictory because the moment in which the subject pronounces it, he is already out of fashion' (WA 16).[1]

This is precisely the other temporal quality of fashion, one that is capable of creating a dialectical image through the citation of previous styles. Moreover, it is this citational quality that will enable Agamben to link the division introduced into time by fashion with Pauline notions of the messianic as a temporal phenomenon of the contemporary as well (WA 18). Through its citations of previous styles, fashion maintains a 'kairological saturation' that brings about an aura within a given iconography and wherein 'Every instant, every image virtually anticipates its future development and remembers its former gestures' (NY 4). In other words:

The signature of fashion tears the years (the 1920s, the 1960s, the 1980s) out of linear chronology, allowing them to have a special relation with the designer's gesture, who cites them to make them appear in the incalculable 'now' of the present. Yet this present is

> in itself ungraspable, since it lives only in kairological (not chronological!) relation to the signatures of the past. For this reason, being in fashion is a paradoxical condition that necessarily entails a certain ease or an imperceptible lag, in which up-to-dateness includes within itself a small part of its outside, a tinge of the démodé. Like a historian, the man of fashion is able to read the signatures of the time only if he instead of entirely placing himself in the past or coinciding wholly with the present, lingers in their 'constellation,' that is, in the very place of signatures. (ST 74)

Matters become more theological when we pause to consider how Paul conceives of the 'time of the now' which is not apocalyptic (TR 62), but rather is a time that does not coincide with representational time (TR 67).² For Agamben, it is a messianic time defined as the time that time takes to come to an end (TR 67). The moment or experience of *kairos* is something locatable within *chronos* and vice versa. *Kairos* could in fact be said to divide *chronos* from within (TR 68–9). Hence, messianic time is not that which is added on to normal time in order to divide it from within (TR 70). It is the time of the Sabbath and the suspension of the normal order that defines chronological time, as we have already seen. This experience of time as an intrusion of *kairos* within *chronos* interrupts secular time in the 'here and now' (TR 73).

Just as fashion introduces a break within the experience of chronological, linear time, so too is art able to disrupt the everyday sense of time through its positing of a dialectical image that suspends meaning. Such images, Agamben will claim, are capable of becoming a disruptive force that allows us to reimagine those images, and bodies, we use to construct meaning in our world. For example, in the context of discussing the outsider art of Chicago native Henry Darger, Agamben discusses how it is precisely the anonymous nature of Darger's art that should be elevated as a form of art capable of being an interrupting, messianic force. Darger's images, which were often of young, naked though de-sexualised girls, come from a place beyond the bodies we behold in the everyday world, and so seek out new forms of the body to approximate them. 'Like every true artist, he did not want to construct the image of a body but a body for the image' – what Agamben ends up calling the 'Dargerian nymph' (NY 19).

In Agamben's attempts to define exactly how such images break through ordinary conceptualisations of time, he has recourse to the permanent hermeneutical tension that seeks not to bring a dualistic opposition to coincidence (and so which would only maintain the presupposition of being), but to leave the tension forever embedded within the image that is presented.

> Where meaning is suspended, dialectical images appear. The dialectical image is, in other words, an unresolved oscillation between estrangement and a new event of meaning. Similar to the emblematic intention, the dialectical image holds its object suspended in a semantic void. Hence its ambiguity, criticized by Adorno ('the ambiguity must absolutely not be left as it is'). Adorno, who is ultimately attempting to bring the dialectic back to its Hegelian matrix, does not seem to understand that, for Benjamin, the crux is not a movement that by way of mediation leads to the *Aufhebung* of contradiction but the very moment of standstill – a stalling in which the middle point is exposed like a zone of indifference between the two opposite terms. As such it is necessarily ambiguous. The '*Dialektik im Stillstand*' of which Benjamin speaks implies a dialectic whose mechanism is not logical (as in Hegel) but analogical and paradigmatic (as in Plato). According to Enzo Melandri's acute intuition, its formulate is 'neither A nor B' and the opposition it implies is not dichotomous and substantial but bipolar and tensive – the two terms are neither removed from nor recomposed in unity but kept in an immobile coexistence charged with tensions. This means, in truth, that not only is dialectic not separable from the objects its negates but also that the objects lose their identity and transform into the two poles of a single dialectical tension that reaches its highest manifestation in the state of immobility, like dancing 'through phantasmata'. (NY 29–31)

Though I believe one might find more nuance within Adorno's negative dialectics than Agamben allows for – seeing as he charges Adorno's efforts as being a 'non-messianic' form of thought (TR 38) – Agamben nonetheless locates a possible way to break the logic of presupposition and its accompanying impasses of dualistic thought without resorting to a synthesis of the two polarities. Any feigned synthesis would only *appear* to overcome the scissions within being, while still holding them captive. In other words, Agamben attempts to think a 'third element' that is *not* a synthesis, but which is rather an ephemeral, dialectical image that contains and does not dispense with the tensions that are embedded in it.

It is through such an interruption that the image is able to provide humanity with a universal experience through the particularities of the tensions that cannot be effaced. 'In this instance, the universal is reached in the particular not inductively but analogically, by way of its arrest', and is thus 'capable of placing an instant from the past in relation to the present' (NY 31, 32). Moreover, as Agamben will go on to stress, it is the imagination that makes such a transition from the particular to the universal possible:

> The history of humanity is always a history of phantasms and images, because it is within the imagination that the fracture between individual and impersonal, the multiple and the unique, the sensible and the intelligible takes place. At the same time, imagination is the place of the dialectical recomposition of this fracture. The images are the remnant, the trace of what men who preceded us have wished and desired, feared and repressed. And because it is within the imagination that something like a (hi)story became possible, it is through imagination that, at every new juncture, history has to be decided. (NY 60–1)

We will see each of these dynamics return in Agamben's eventual elaboration upon the form-of-life, which gives us a new way to assess the significance of the imagination and of the role of ideas within every structure, tradition and identity.

## WHAT IS FORM-OF-LIFE?

To rethink politics, religion, economics and society today, Agamben suggests we will have to consider form-of-life as it is experienced beyond the impositions of law. This is perhaps the central concept toward which the entire *Homo Sacer* series has been aimed, and it is one that we must engage directly in order to comprehend why it is such an important notion to him. Early in the *Homo Sacer* series we discover the concept of 'form of life' (HS 52/OHS 46) juxtaposed with the possibility of a law without content becoming indistinguishable from life itself (HS 53/OHS 47). These considerations are provided through the illustration of a force of messianic nihilism in Benjamin that 'nullifies even the Nothing and lets no form of law remain in force beyond its own content' (HS 53/OHS 47). As such, law can become indistinguishable from life (HS 55/OHS 48). In this precise formulation, we discern the messianic as the limit concept of both law and of religious experience (HS 56/OHS 49). As Agamben will consistently argue, a form-of-life comes about through a messianic generic power that undoes every sovereign form, meaning that the only form of glory which would be available to humanity in an authentic way – *another* form of glory – would be an anonymous one, not one of celebrity or, as in the past, divine monarchy.

His contemplation of laws transforming themselves into lives toward the end of *Homo Sacer* (HS 187–8/OHS 153) eventually gives way to a 'form-of-life' which is defined as a 'being that is only its own bare existence and to this life that, being its own form, remains inseparable from it, we will witness the emergence of a field of research beyond the terrain defined by the intersection of politics and philosophy, medico-biological sciences and jurisprudence' (HS 188/OHS 153). Something new appears on the horizon of human possibility, and at times is something that can only be hinted at – a type of existence wherein form and content are truly indistinguishable from one another.

Form-of-life circulates around a number of very significant concepts in Agamben's work, including: the possibility for *another* form of glory to arise beyond the one that merely covers over our inoperativity (IP 128); the nudity of the human body that is not conscripted into a representational economy, such as with the glorious body of theological speculation (N 91–103); the almost Levinasian face that compels us to just ethical relations (MW 98–100); and the exposure of oneself before another's gaze but beyond the law's representations and an 'intimacy without relations' as will be taken up significantly in *The Use of Bodies* (UB 236/OHS 1242). Most prominently among these various concepts, certainly in terms of its explanatory potential, is the singularity of the 'whatever being' that Agamben takes up in *The Coming Community*; what I would argue is an early model of his later articulation of a form-of-life (CC 1–2). The 'whatever being', as he explained it there, has no prescribed form and no teleological aim; it is a generic sense of being that is truly 'whatever' in its appearance and nature.

Each of these models and concepts points toward the way in which form-of-life overcomes the divisions that characterise humanity, its languages and representations, each of which are beholden to historical theological, political and juridical forms. Each figure points toward a way beyond the exclusionary separations that characterise the boundaries and definitions of each singular domain. Each signals the rise of a paradigmatic example that moves beyond the caesuras, tensions, divisions, scissions and dualisms of human activity: 'The example, then, is the symmetrical opposite of the exception: whereas the exception is included through its exclusion, the example is excluded through the exhibition of its inclusion' (ST 24). As such, the exception is an 'inclusive exclusion', whereas the example, or paradigm, is an 'exclusive inclusion' (HS 21–2/OHS 22). This is a major logical distinction for Agamben – one that he had brought up prominently in the first volume of the series – though he also recognises that they are at times indistinguishable as well (HS 22/OHS 22–3).

However, the example is excluded in the sense of being unique, special or unlike anything else within our given symbolic realm of representations – existing as truly 'whatever' it might be, beyond all labels and classifications we might otherwise recognise, as he had earlier described it – though it is also included within a particular and shared social collectivity. The example is not included within society precisely through its exclusion, which is how one rightly imagines marginalised populations, oppressed or subjugated peoples, the poor, the destitute, and those indebted to the machinery of a given social, cultural, political, religious or even economic system (which always function, as Agamben makes abundantly clear, as economies in their own right). Form-of-life is more like the saintly figure who is removed from the normative order as exemplary, though they are also part of the order in some sense too.[3]

As we have seen throughout, the sovereign decides upon or dictates 'the normal structuring of life relations' (HS 26/OHS 25), granting the sovereign's subjects a sense of shared normativity while also immersing each one into the rule of law. In Agamben's words, 'The sovereign decision traces and from time to time renews this threshold of indistinction between outside and inside, exclusion and inclusion, *nomos* and *physis*, in which life is originally excepted in law' (HS 27/OHS 26). It is in this sense that Agamben refers to the exception as the 'originary form of law' (HS 26/OHS 26). Law entraps everyone who becomes subject to it, a bizarre and disorientating state wherein one becomes subject to the given laws of a land merely by being exposed to the power that flows from the claims made by the sovereign of that land. Therefore, 'Law is made of nothing but what it manages to capture inside itself through the inclusive exclusion of the *exceptio*' (HS 27/OHS 26). The fiction of sovereignty is reflected in the fiction of law, though we realise at the same time that law functions as a sort of necessary illusion that *does* have a reality and grounding within the historical contexts in which it is established and practised.[4] For this reason, law functions precisely as a concrete reminder of why such fictive sovereignties are indispensable for human communal existence, as touched on in Chapter 1.

Christianity, especially as read through a Pauline lens, becomes philosophically significant as it offers humanity the chance to rethink its relationship to law. It portrays Christ as the 'end and fulfilment of the law', and so as part of a 'radical messianic thesis' that can only appear as aporetic in its existence, but not as something to be formulated in juridical terms. The force of the messianic is such that the individual liberated by it begins to see how life is applied to the norm and not the norm to life (HP 61–2/OHS 937). As one of Jesus's central teachings about the law once put it: the sabbath, or law in this case, is made for humans, not humans for the sabbath.[5] In this sense, Christian life cannot be reduced to the law, but is only a rule, a general guide or line of advice that is provided based on the way in which one lives one's life (HP 46–7/OHS 926). This is the case, Agamben will repeatedly contend, despite the fact that the Church will slowly, but firmly and repeatedly, drift toward immersing itself in the realm of law, even in its establishment of canon law via the writings of Gratian.

In the history of Christianity and its various theological wagers, monasticism becomes available at almost the same time in history as Constantine steered the Church toward becoming a formal juridical institution, though monasticism comes to its form rather as a contestation of the Roman Empire's worldliness, of the latter's power and riches. Monasticism, analysed by Agamben in detail in *The Highest Poverty*, arose as an attempt 'to construct a form-of-life' or a life inseparable from its form through the link between rule and life as it is practised communally (HP xi–xii/OHS 887; and as was explored in Chapter 5). In the blending of rule and life, there was a concerted effort made to achieve a form-of-life lived beyond the law, but this was just as frequently also an opportunity missed due to the near impossibility of communicating such a form outside the realm of laws, communal politics and linguistic representations. Despite this reality, however, form-of-life became the 'third thing' sought after between the tensions and scissions that characterised the polarised dualisms that defined almost every interaction in this human life-together.

## Form-of-Life beyond the Law

In Agamben's narration of events, liturgy was a historical attempt made by priests to bridge the gap and find this ever-elusive third thing, or potentially 'suturing' element of the dualisms that criss-cross humanity due to the presupposition of its being. Monasticism, for its part, presents us with an almost complete merger between liturgy and life in order to more directly obtain access to this third thing (HP xii/OHS 888). Trying to think a form-of-life 'removed from the grasp of the law and a use of bodies and of the world that would never be substantiated into an appropriation' (HP xiii/OHS 889), means that any quest for such a third thing could never result in a substantial entity that could be defined or appropriated – again, thereby avoiding the problematics of searching after a new or utopian existence. It could never become one's property or identity, but only exist as that which was part of a 'common use' made possible through a messianic suspension of its identity, a 'whatever being' beyond all attempts to classify it.

This is where Agamben not only rereads the Pauline 'division of division itself' as that which is able to locate an ephemeral self beyond the dualistic identities that characterise our world (e.g. male/female, slave/free, Jew/Greek, among so many others), but also a complete re-examination of human being-together entirely: 'This dis-location of ethics and politics from the sphere of action to that of form of life represents the most demanding legacy of monasticism, which modernity has failed to recognize' (HP 61/OHS 937). However, what he also claims to have recognised is precisely the way in which monasticism, and Franciscanism more specifically, illuminates the political and ethical stakes of life as it has developed subsequently in the West. As explored in Chapter 6, Agamben continues to assert that we must try to re-envision political formations through the notion of a multitude as a type of being-together beyond what we have known thus far historically. The multitude, in this sense, is the generic term used for the gathering of the 'multiple forms of life' lived as forms-of-life (UB 213/OHS 1219).

If the monk's particular efforts to live a form of life in general 'creates the rules' by which they live, and which cannot be captured by a juridical or legal proscription, then a 'third thing' can only emerge through a form-of-life that is lived beyond all law and property (HP 71/OHS 946). This gives Agamben's 'Franciscan ontology' – as Alain Badiou has called it[6] – its particular emphasis through the Franciscan development of the concept of use, which was eventually blunted by turning its radical refusal to own anything into a symbiotic relation with the hierarchy of the Church and the papacy, which most certainly did attempt to possess material goods. In a pattern that has by now become quite common throughout history, the hierarchical Church frequently sought to co-opt each radical or messianic movement within its existing (monastic) orders, or else declare them heretical if need be (HP 93–4/OHS 963). What was eminently clear was that these cyclically occurring movements did not want to establish a new doctrine or exegesis, but only to 'reclaim a life and not a rule'. They wanted to identify *with* life, to live the Gospel and not simply interpret it – a proposition that somewhat recalls Marx's thesis that one should not simply interpret the world but should act to change it.[7]

It is in this context of the Franciscan challenge to the Church as an institution that Agamben rearticulates within the *Homo Sacer* series the notion of form as an example or paradigm (HP 95/OHS 964), and the *forma vitae*, or form-of-life, as a life that cannot be separated from its form. Once again, it is here that the general form of life is historically paired with rule in various religious orders so as to be reinscribed back into law on occasion (HP 96/OHS 965). But it is also where Saint Francis is shown not to be concerned with a rule 'in the proper sense' and to foster a movement that is not 'reducible to a normative code' (HP 98/OHS 966). In Agamben's analysis, Francis was trying to name something that was neither life nor law, but rather was searching within this tension between them in order to name something that cannot actually be named (HP 100/OHS 968). Hence Francis

## Form-of-Life beyond the Law

has recourse to the *formula vitae* and 'not a rule' (HP 103/OHS 970) in his search for a 'third thing between doctrine and law, between rule and dogma' (HP 104/OHS 971): 'The form is not a norm imposed on life, but a living that in following the life of Christ gives itself and makes itself a form' (HP 105/OHS 972). In the end, what becomes manifest is that normative rules cannot capture this third thing, and any attempt to do so ultimately captures every *thing*, or person, within the exclusive and even violent operations of politics, religion and law.

As would happen eventually too among the reform-minded Discalced Carmelites, among others, walking barefoot became for the Franciscans identifiable with the *forma vitae* and not with a rule (HP 107–8/OHS 974). The 'highest poverty' that Franciscanism sought to embody was stressed through the use of things rather than through their ownership, through their inappropriable nature and so though what Francis had ultimately been after was the 'abdication of every right' (HP 109/OHS 975). In other words, they were searching for 'the possibility of a human existence beyond the law' (HP 110/OHS 976). His efforts were aimed toward trying to 'realize a human life and practice absolutely outside the determinations of the law' (HP 110/OHS 976), defining not only its radical nature outside of the realms of law and possession, but also embracing the *forma vitae* as the only way to truly live beyond the law.

As Agamben makes clear in this context, even Francis' relationship to animals was more than symbolic of his radical nature. Taking us all the way back to the theoretical distinctions that anchored the first volume in the series, here he reflects upon how *zoē* and *bios* were distinguished as vegetative and animal life (*zoē*) as opposed to the 'virtuous behavior of the saints' (HP 106/OHS 972), wherein *bios* became 'equivalent to *sancta conversatio*, that is to the perfect form of life' (HP 106/OHS 973, emphasis in the original). Francis' proximity to animal life, however, takes the juxtaposition of *zoē* and *bios* and attempts, once again, to name the third thing that cannot be named as such directly between them.

The poverty of world that animals experience, as Heidegger had once put it, becomes further radicalised by Agamben in this regard as poverty is defined as a return to the state of nature, but not the general, fictitious one of political philosophy, through 'the separation of ownership from use' (HP 113/OHS 978). In this fashion, the state of necessity is inverted, suggesting that the Franciscans did not have rights to things, but did have a 'natural right' limited to extreme necessity (HP 114/OHS 979). As such, Agamben says, 'they have no right but only a license to use. In the state of extreme necessity, they recover a relationship with the law (natural, not positive)' (HP 115/OHS 979). As he continues to describe the context of this messianic radicality, 'Necessity, which gives the Friars Minor a dispensation from the rule, restores (natural) law to them; outside the state of necessity, they have no relationship to the law. What for others is normal thus becomes the exception for them; what for others is an exception becomes for them a form of life' (HP 115/OHS 979–80). No longer is a construct of nature declared to exist by necessity so that a particular 'natural' order might be extended as a means of governance over people. Rather, there is only the 'extreme' state of necessity discovered in the contingency of daily life that dictates a different experience of nature – the real nature that can only be viewed from this perspective of use and not circumscribed into a series of 'natural', positive laws.

There is a 'juridical paradox' present in this aporia that removes life from the sphere of law, a 'juridical void', as Agamben will phrase it (HP 115–16/OHS 980). This paradox is understood as the state of necessity 'that is the apparatus through which they seek to neutralize law and at the same time to assure themselves an extreme relationship with it (in the form of *ius naturale*)' (HP 116/OHS 980). His conclusion, one that contains significant political implications, is that 'Use and state of necessity are the two extremes that define the Franciscan form of life', though it is a state of necessity that does not ground or legitimate sovereign rule (HP 116/OHS 980). It is an exemplary state of necessity that speaks rather to the uniqueness of human existence lived beyond the law – *another* form of sovereignty, an *anonymous* form, that places Francis' efforts alongside Jesus's in that both seemed to have sought a way to live out the unique forms-of-life that they had recognised within themselves (and which many saints, among other exemplary persons, have carved out for themselves as well).

The hierarchical Church returns to our gaze at this point because of its defence of the office of the priest over and beyond whatever the (unworthy) priest might be up to time and again (HP 117/OHS 981). Monasticism, and later Protestantism in general, sought to counter this claim through its focus on acting over being (rather than the Church's prioritising of being, through the office, over acting):

> To a life that receives its sense and its standing from the Office, monasticism opposes the idea of an *officium* that has sense only if it becomes life. *To the liturgicization of life, there corresponds here a total vivification of liturgy*. Recall from Chapter Five that the monk is a being who is defined solely by his form of life, so that at the limit, the idea of an unworthy monk seems to imply a contradiction in terms. (HP 117/OHS 981, emphasis in the original)

Despite such distinctions, and as with most movements that are institutionalised to some degree or another, monasticism is eventually also incorporated into the Church. Monastic life is slowly taken over by a clericalisation of monks, as he will describe the historical development of the situation.

In Agamben's historical survey, these pre-Reformation tensions, as are found in Franciscanism in particular, reach a critical juncture in the religious movements that come to stress the 'apostolic life' seemingly over and against the hierarchical Church. Many such movements in fact focused on the lack of social or ecclesial title and position in order to approximate the form of life they believed Jesus had radically embodied beyond the religious institutional forms he had shied away from. What was 'stigmatized as heresy is not, in truth, a doctrinal principle, but only the necessary consequence of a spiritual attitude that makes form of life and not office the decisive question' (HP 118/ OHS 982). Hence life is defined by poverty, not by office. In a most significant move, Franciscanism can be said to reject identity as a type of property (HP 120/OHS 983). In another sense, Francis was *not* anticlerical because he simply did not focus on the holding of an office or particular identity. This form of life that he sought to embody became 'radically extraneous' to law and liturgy and so to 'civil and canon law' at the same time (HP 121–2/OHS 984). At least in theory, it did not conflict with the Catholic Church since this form of a highest poverty is extraneousness to the law as it is practised through use.

Since what had been common among the original apostles was use and not ownership, Agamben can designate an 'ontology of use' as that wherein 'being and becoming, existence and time seem to coincide' (HP 131–2/OHS 991–2). He depicts a form of life as 'unassimilable for the ecclesiastical order in juridical terms in this way, even if purely negative ones' (HP 137/OHS 996). Agamben estimates that Francis was being 'prescient' in giving an indeterminate sense of his order, with no juridical precepts, though he also acknowledges that this state of affairs, as with Jesus's life, had to change as the order grew more institutional in form over time, becoming in reality 'a large and powerful religious order'.

It is at this point, uniquely in his study *The Highest Poverty*, that Agamben expands on a discussion of what the Franciscans missed, noting Paul's considerations of 'using the world as not using it' in order to supplement the Franciscan theoretical structure (HP 139/OHS 997). However, this should come as no surprise at this point in our analysis, as the Pauline weak messianic force is precisely what allows for a division of division itself to emerge as the force of inoperativity that makes a new use of all things possible. Agamben takes Paul's notion of a messianic revocation of all vocations, or the sense of living 'as if not' in possession of what we had thought we possessed, in order to refocus the Franciscan refusal of the will, as well as in order to isolate that which remains 'inappropriable' within it (HP 140/OHS 998). It is through the inappropriable, which can only be used but never possessed, that the Franciscans had truly avoided ever becoming a habit or custom, as the monks do: 'Use, from this perspective, could have been configured as a *tertium* with respect to law and life, potential and act, and could have defined – not only negatively – the monk's vital practice itself, their form-of-life' (HP 141/OHS 998).

What we witness unfolding in his analysis of the Franciscan stress placed on use over possession is a deep thematic undercurrent in Agamben's work that has become more focused on exploring alternative notions of love, but also of happiness and joy – notions that exist only insofar as they are practised, or *used* and not possessed. Though he refrains from stating this directly, there seems to be within his formulation of a modal ontology a notion of love that is capable of admitting its lack of substance except insofar as it exists in relationship with another person – a point we almost intuitively understand to be true in our experiences of love. As such, we might suggest, one cannot possess love, or if one tries to, they have lost it. The nature of this state of love is only achieved through its being enacted, not merely as a (sovereign) declaration of its being (as with one's office, vocation, marriage, institutional standing and so forth), but as a recognition of one's incapacity to love what is proper. Love functions, if read in this light, as a suspension or interruption of one's capacities, as he once remarked in an essay devoted to Heidegger's work on facticity (P 204). Seeing love as the 'third thing' that is sought after has often traditionally been ascribed to the children of a couple said to be 'in love', though this has been utilised just as frequently in order to reinscribe love within an ecclesial-doctrinal presupposition of being to be sure. Love as the 'third thing', in this context, might go some ways as well toward comprehending what it is that Agamben is after in his explorations of a modal ontology that undoes any 'natural' relations in favour of an intimacy without, or *beyond*, established relations. What we observe in his formulation of this concept is what might more genuinely characterise the exchanges between forms-of-life that we encounter in something like a multitude (of various forms-of-life). This was what the Franciscans had ultimately sought after, and it is what Agamben seeks to unfold in ways that the Franciscans failed to consider.

## FORM-OF-LIFE AS END GOAL

The Situationist Guy Debord's recognition of something 'in his own existence or in that of his friends, something unique and exemplary, which demanded to be recorded and communicated' brings Agamben to the threshold of the private life lived as 'clandestine, our form-of-life' (UB xv/OHS 1021). Agamben claims it is that which is experienced as 'so intimate and close at hand' that 'if we attempt to grasp it, only impenetrable tedious everydayness is left in our hands' (UB xv/OHS 1021). It is in this form-of-life, however, that we can also locate what is preserved as 'the stowaway of the political [. . .] on which every biography and every revolution makes shipwreck' (UB xvi/OHS 1021). In Agamben's recounting of this individual life that he knew and appreciated, Debord peered 'into the flame of singular and private existence' (UB xviii/OHS 1023), bringing the clandestine to the foreground in the 'banality of its documents' (UB xviii/OHS 1024).

Again, we find in Agamben's attempts to bring the anthropological machinery to a halt – to render it inoperative through its messianic suspension – another representation of the mystery of the human being, though it is not one inherently declared to be sacred. Rather, it is one wherein the fractures so often made to coincide – in order to fabricate their union as the sacred legitimation of sovereign rule – are left apart, forcing the machinery to come to a fantastic halt. It is from this place that we are taken back to the primary fissures in the human being, as between *zoē* and *bios*, in order to witness these originary separations anew and so no longer attempt to bring them together into harmony; in fact, the aim is to no longer even witness the separation itself as an essential part of the constitution of the human being. The separation has only come about through the capture and control of our being. As Agamben will describe this situation, and in terms that parallel most of what I have been suggesting so far about his thought on the whole:

> If thought, the arts, poetry, and human practices generally have any interest, it is because they bring about an archeological idling of the machine and the works of life, language, economy, and society, in order to carry them back to the anthropogenetic event, in order that in them the becoming human of the human being will never be achieved once and for all, will never cease to happen. Politics names the place of this event, in whatever sphere it is produced. (UB 208/OHS 1215)

The political stakes of such a return to the origins of the creation of the human being, in its 'sacred mystery', are manifold and important to consider at this point in his analysis. For Agamben, the truly political life 'one oriented toward the idea of happiness and cohering in a form-of-life, is thinkable only starting from emancipation from this scission' (UB 210/OHS 1217). Returning to the scission or fracture within the human being that is actually constitutive *of* the human being and its many means of repeating such fractures, as exclusionary measures within the political world around us, means learning to respect the life that is lived before our eyes as yet removed from those scissions and fractures. Hence, it means learning to see the form-of-life lived beyond the dualisms and exclusionary mechanisms that bring most of life into clearly identifiable and representational terms. It is from this place that humanity is capable of ceasing its production of bare life in order to construct both a self and a community and discover whatever being that stands before it.

> Only if act is never totally separated from potential, only if, in my lived experiences and my acts of understanding, I always have to do with living and understanding in themselves – that is to say, if

there is, in this sense, thought – then a form of life can become, in its very facticity and thingliness, *form-of-life*, in which it is never possible to isolate something like a bare life. (UB 211/OHS 1217)

To genuinely observe an 'intimacy without relations' we must become attuned to the bodies that we all are, and the personal lives that are concealed within every philosophical expression. This is why Agamben asks, 'What does it mean that private life accompanies us as a secret or a stowaway?' (UB xx/OHS 1026). Firstly, it is that which 'shares existence with us', like our bodies, but which often goes unnoticed within the social identities we construct for ourselves. Secondly, it means that the forms-of-life we are searching for are not elsewhere than where we find ourselves at the present moment – they are hidden *within* the present, much as messianic time was hidden within chronological time if we recall our conversation from the previous chapter (UB 227/OHS 1234). They may not exist in their fullness, to be sure, but trying to define a form-of-life means searching for 'a paradigmatic fact – extravagant and significant', within the lives that we already live, as ancient biographers were wont to isolate and lift up above the factual details of their subjects' everyday lives (UB 229/OHS 1235). In his words, 'What we call form-of-life corresponds to this ontology of style; it names the mode in which a singularity bears witness to itself in being and being expresses itself in the singular body' (UB 233/OHS 1239).

Here, again, we witness something like a tautology present within form-of-life as *another* form of sovereignty that we must note as a significant counter-force to the sovereign powers that permeate political, religious and historical interactions in our world. It is what Agamben characterises as a 'double tendency' within form-of-life that somehow yet avoids being autonomous at the same moment as it develops its sense of being (though *not* an identity per se as we might otherwise think of it):

> On the one hand, it is a life inseparable from its form, an indissoluble unity in itself, and on the other, it is separable from every

thing and every context. This is evident in the classical conception of *theoria*, which is in itself united but separated and separable from every thing, in perpetual flight. This double tension is the risk inherent in form-of-life, which tends to separate itself ascetically into an autonomous sphere, theory. It is necessary instead to think form-of-life as a living of its own mode of being, as inseparable from its context, precisely because it is not in relation but in contact with it. (UB 232/OHS 1238)

The singularity of what takes place in a form-of-life is due to its implicit willingness not to claim to possess any normative posture or identity. It is perpetually given over to recreating itself – a permanent conversion of sorts that avoids becoming a wholly autonomous sovereign form in that it refuses (normative) relations in order to touch or be 'in contact' with another form-of-life. It is beyond all identities or descriptions, and so autonomous in *another* sense, though it is not simply, for this reason, able to rest contentedly or solely in itself. If we recall, the messianic revocation of all vocations is nearly impossible, or at least incredibly difficult, to dwell within. Nothing less than the constant re-examination of its being is at stake in its development: 'This means that what we call form-of-life is a life in which the event of anthropogenesis – the becoming human of the human being – is still happening' (UB 208/OHS 1215).

## MYSTERY AND DESIRE

Throughout a good portion of the *Homo Sacer* series, Agamben refers to the concept of mystery from a variety of angles, mostly critical of how mystery has been deployed within Western theological thought as a cover for economic activities. For instance, in *The Kingdom and the Glory* there is the sustained critique delivered of the reversal of the Pauline 'economy of the mystery' into 'the mystery of the economy' (KG 35/OHS 403). Whatever mystery Paul was pointing toward, and which had maintained its own economy, becomes obscured by its reversal so that divine praxis (or economy, activity) itself becomes the mystery operative within the world (KG 38–9/OHS 406). Christianity consequently presents a theology of history that is formed under an economic paradigm and which grants a sense of purpose or destiny that is sharply distinguished from pagan fate or stoic necessity (KG 44–6/OHS 411–12). Hence the issue of free will keeps returning in Christian thought as itself a mystery – the 'mystery of freedom' that is 'nothing but the other face of the "mystery of the economy"' (KG 46/OHS 413).

Agamben will go on to claim that the mystery of God and the mystery of government are forever divided and yet inseparable (KG 50/OHS 417).[8] *Mysterium* and *ministerium* are further merged when angelology gives rise to a particular conceptualisation of civil administration in governmental terms (KG 158/OHS 514). As he will go on to elaborate in subsequent volumes of the series, the 'ministry of the mystery' is made possible through the mystery of liturgy as the 'mystery of effectiveness', through which ontology, ethics, politics and economy are thought, as we have already seen (OD xii/OHS 649). What is illuminated through this study is a relationship between various pagan cults and Christian liturgy itself that simultaneously contains possibilities for a corruption of the notion of mystery (e.g. OD 33/OHS 678), but also an extension that Agamben will elsewhere trace under another heading, as we will now see.

In a short essay on *The Unspeakable Girl*, he offers us a commentary on the Eleusinian mystery cults and their initiation rites wherein one was expected not only to refrain from expressing what was ultimately inexpressible ('to ecstatically experience his or her own silencing'), but also 'to experience the power and potentiality offered to mankind of the "unspeakable girl" – the power and potentiality of a joyfully and intransigently *infantile* existence' (UG 13). This is the moment where form and content become indistinguishable and the 'third element' that made this experience possible can only appear as 'mysterious', 'because in it there is no longer anything to conceal' (UG 37). Just as Agamben would depict form-of-life at the conclusion to the series, he will here establish the coincidence of form and content in the absolutely singular being as a mystery beyond the bounds of representation. In his words, 'Form and content coincide not because the content now appears unveiled but because, as in the literal meaning of the Latin verb *concidere*, they "fall together," are reduced and reconciled. What we are then given to contemplate is pure appearance' (UG 37).[9]

Just as we saw in the previous chapter how Agamben's appropriation of Benjamin's dialectical image was itself 'a mystery wherein that which cannot be discursively presented shines for a moment out of the ruins of language', so too do we see mystery return in the context of myth at the end of *The Use of Bodies* (UG 39). What we witness in the concluding section on myth at the tail end to the entire *Homo Sacer* series is the possibility of using myth to describe what *logos* cannot, and so finding another way to portray the mysteries that lie beyond language (UB 255/OHS 1257). In this reading, myth seeks to explain the moral choice one makes, and the responsibility accrued, in order to embody a particular form of life. Form-of-life is revealed in this context as an entirely immanent description of the soul, positing itself as a mystery that we cannot locate within language, and so frequently have had recourse to the theological mysteries in order to try to cover over such a 'void of representation'.

> The soul, just like form-of-life, is what *in* my *zoè*, in my bodily life does not coincide with my *bios*, with my political and social existence, and yet has 'chosen' both, practices them both in this certain, unmistakable mode. It is itself, in this sense, the *mesos bios* that, in every *bios* and every *zoè*, adventurously severs, revokes, and realizes the choice that unites them by necessity in this certain life. Form-of-life, the soul, is the infinite complement between life and mode of life, what appears when they mutually neutralize one another and show the void that unites them. *Zoè* and *bios* – this is perhaps the lesson of the myth – are neither separate nor coincident: between them, as a void of representation of which it is not possible to say anything except that it is

'immortal' and 'ungenerated' (*Phaedrus*, 246a), stands the soul, which holds them indissolubly in contact and testifies for them. (UB 262/OHS 1263–4)

Here Agamben demonstrates the way in which access to form-of-life means going back to the fundamental scission within the human being – the one between *bios* and *zoē* – and recognising the void between them before exposing it as what we have taken the soul to be throughout the centuries. If Greek mythology separated the gods and animals, but refrained from experiencing humanity directly, and Christianity condemned us to humanity through its separation from the animals, Agamben seems to want to return to something like a recognition of the mystery of life itself, which is actually no mystery at all: 'We are to live life like an initiation. But to what? Not to a doctrine but to life itself and its absolute absence of mystery. There is no mystery' (UG 47).

If there is no mystery that theology has to seek incessantly to try to cover up, then what exactly is the role of mystery in our world? Turning to literature and the form of the novel in his short work *The Fire and the Tale*, published around the same time as *The Use of Bodies*, Agamben provides an answer as he tries to locate the space where imagination and the story speak to the place and function of mystery, that which began as a 'genetic link between pagan mysteries and the ancient novel' wherein both initiates and protagonists are constituted as a mystery in relation to the gods (FT 3). He posits: 'Just like the initiated [. . .] penetrated mystery and found in it the hopes of having his life saved, so the reader, following the series of situations and events that the novel weaves pitifully or ferociously around its character, somehow participates in his destiny and, at any rate, introduces his own existence to the sphere of mystery' (FT 3). Hence, the novel becomes 'that which initiates us and that into which we are initiated' while at the same time the sense of mystery that the novel and the mystery cult announce is lost in history, presenting us with a somewhat unique dilemma (FT 4; UG 34). As he continues, and in terms that entirely parallel the tensions addressed above regarding the existence of the Church, 'The fire and the tale, the mystery and the story are the two indispensable elements of literature. But in what way can one of the elements, whose presence is the irrefutable proof of the loss of the other, bear witness to this absence, exorcising its shadow and memory? Where there is the tale, the fire is out; where there is the mystery, there cannot be the story' (FT 8). At this point, humanity appears to be stuck within a tension that cannot be effaced and that cannot simply be reconciled through their coming together – a notion that drives Agamben's thoughts in more than one place, as we have repeatedly seen already.

> Something similar also happens in the lives of men. Without a doubt, in its inexorable course, existence – which initially seemed so available, so rich with possibilities – little by little loses its mystery, one by one puts out its fires. It is, in the end, only a story, insignificant and disenchanted like any other. Until one day – perhaps not the last, but the second to last – existence finds again for an instant its enchantment and all of a sudden atones for its disappointment. What has lost its mystery is now truly and irreparably mysterious, truly and absolutely unavailable. The fire, which can only be told, the mystery, which was integrally violated in a story, now leaves us speechless and shuts itself away forever in an image. (FT 10)

This is as much to say that, in form-of-life there is no mystery, even perhaps no saintliness, only the singularity of 'whatever being' left to itself outside the bounds of representation and identification. Form-of-life may appear to inhabit a space of mystery as it dwells outside the boundaries of what is classifiable as known, but it merely exists beyond the borders of intelligibility and communicability, offering the living being who inhabits such a space the chance to breathe freely and to contemplate existence without trying to possess it.

Resonant with this search for a form-of-life lived beyond the law is Agamben's description of the human being towards the conclusion of *Remnants of Auschwitz*, where the figure of the Muselmann is the 'complete witness' to the horrors of the camps, but who also instructs us to learn that 'The human being is the one who can survive the human being' (RA 133/OHS 850, de-emphasised from the original). Leaving behind whatever appeared to characterise the human being is one who recognises the 'inhuman' within them and so 'the one whose humanity is completely destroyed is the one who is truly human' (RA 133/OHS 850, de-emphasised from the original). The witness, we are told, is the one who is left over, the 'remnants of Auschwitz', who testifies to the humanity that remains once the human has been destroyed. It is because the human being lives in the space of a permanent and unhealable fracture – where the possibility of performing a division of an already existing social division takes place – that there is always something left over when one's humanity is destroyed (RA 134–5/OHS 851). This is the non-mysterious form-of-life lived beyond the laws that construct the human being. This is what is revealed when the presupposition of being has been rendered inoperative.

What is left of the human being at the end of this series dedicated to exploring the intimate relationship between the sovereign and the excluded figure of bare life, the *homo sacer*? Clearly, there is no new human being, something like Nietzsche's *Übermensch*, to clamour for. There is no premodern 'golden age' of humanity or utopian, even antinomian, existence to return to. There is only the failure of every human identity that yet somehow indicates to us, all of us, our truest being. There is only the suspension of every representation as the means to develop new uses for what has already been given to us. In the regression to our pure potentiality before every enacted human ('actual') identity, we are finally capable of repeating the epiphany of Damascius and his blank writing tablet, which Agamben had many years before he had even begun the *Homo Sacer* series contemplated in his *Idea of Prose*:

> The uttermost limit thought can reach is not a being, not a place or thing, no matter how free of any quality, but rather, its own

absolute potentiality, the pure potentiality of representation itself: the writing tablet! What he had until then been taking as the One, as the absolutely Other of thought, was instead only the material, only the potentiality of thought. And the entire, lengthy volume the hand of the scribe had crammed with characters was nothing other than the attempt to represent the perfectly bare writing tablet on which nothing had yet been written. This was why he was unable to carry his work through to completion: what could not cease from writing itself was the image of what never ceased from not writing itself. In the one was mirrored the ungraspable other. But everything was finally clear: now he could break the tablet, stop writing. Or rather, now he could truly begin. He now believed that he understood the sense of the maxim stating that by knowing the unknowable it is not something about it we know, but something about ourselves. That which can never be first let him glimpse, in its fading, the glimmer of a beginning. (IP 34)

# *Conclusions*

The defence given for a form-of-life lived beyond any inscription within the laws and normative boundaries that would otherwise seek to define it is Agamben's most significant and original contribution made through the *Homo Sacer* series, but it is not the only conclusion that he reaches regarding our modern configurations of politics, ethics, ontology and theology. His genealogical explorations and ontological reformulations of these fields probe deep and lay a solid foundation for the conclusions of this major philosophical series. There is also, for example, his unceasing commentary upon the fiction of sovereignty as what lies beneath every representation or linguistic system. To face the force of sovereignty means to face the potential dissolution of every identity and community, along with each of their political and social dynamics included. Moreover, the sheer prevalence of his remarks on sovereignty is what has caused his critical studies of sovereign power to appear to many as a call to do away with all forms of law, politics, theological or doctrinal claims and even languages (which are no more important 'than bird song', as he had put it). Yet if sovereignty is what underlies every existent identity and community, how are we to reimagine our relationship to these most commonly utilised associations?

In order to understand the creativity of Agamben's response, this is precisely where we must keep in mind that what repeatedly appears throughout the series alongside every critique of the structures and representations that do exist in our world is likewise a staunch defence of the *idea*, of critical, philosophical thought itself, as applicable to every paradigm or field of inquiry. It is the power of contemplation that Agamben has signalled as an essential suspension of activity at the heart of the political. The power of the suspension for any normative order, as with the worker's strike that Benjamin had once found so inspiring, is where we can locate the terrain of abstract thought – the only thing that is capable of remaking reality as we know it from within. The creativity of making a space available for thought itself is what we encounter in the suspension of all activity that otherwise characterises (political, social and economic) life in this world.

It is the preservation of ideas and critical thought within every activity, institution or structure that is embodied by a form-of-life that Agamben has sought hard to articulate. Living as a form-of-life beyond any representational system is a protest against the system, *any* system, order, institution or normative tradition, though it is also the most commonly practised human trait, at the source of all creative and imaginative acts. It is a physical embodiment of the pure thought that resides in a space beyond any ability to inscribe it within an already active and codified matrix of (legal) representations. Though we are by definition unable to 'identify' precisely how a form-of-life presents its existence, this inability is also the very means by which a form-of-life preserves its creativity, giving rise to new models for human existence that push beyond whatever forms we had previously known and upon which we had been reliant. In short, this is the primary recipe for the creation of those new ideas which ultimately reshape the landscape of whatever political, social, linguistic, religious, economic, anthropological or literary endeavour we, as human beings, undertake. It is simultaneously the very definition of the philosophical that grants humanity access to the tool that is merely thought itself. This is why, time and again, Agamben's work becomes a staunch defence of philosophy itself as the capacity to suspend the normal, everyday affairs of activity and to think ideas that are capable of suspending established, shared and so regulative thoughts.

As he steadily works toward in his summative considerations of just what exactly is at stake in the series, *demand*, he finds, is bound up with the tendency to defend persons whose lives are being lived in a particular way, even in ways humanity is unable to codify or represent. These are forms-of-life that demand to be seen and heard, even if they have nothing in particular to express. They do not choose to present themselves in a particular way or through a given representation. There is rather something within each that itself demands to be seen. They merely express, through their existence, what I have been calling throughout 'another form of sovereignty'. From this perspective we can see how another form of sovereignty exists at the heart of each individual, irreducibly singular existence, but only insofar as this form of sovereignty is not based on the exclusionary tactics of political actualities. It is rather a sovereignty that cannot be inscribed socially or politically as such (i.e. through the activities that constitute the dealings of actuality). In the suspension of actuality, which thought embodies in a form-of-life, we encounter our ownmost potentiality as the site of ideas, those creative and internal processes that become the source of all reformation and revolution in whatever external space we find ourselves.

*Command*, on the other hand, is the force that seeks to preserve the desire for autonomy and sovereignty itself as exclusionary activities, to create sovereign representational forms through imperative speech acts that bring sovereign forms into being. It is an almost inevitable result of being the social and linguistic animals that we are, but it is not the only thing that defines us, as Agamben will tirelessly stress again and again. The language of command may have dominated history as well as our sense of humanity, but it is not the only activity that defines our being.

In witnessing this tension between demand and command, there appears to be a conflict of sovereignties between these two opposing camps. Yet, the sovereignty of a form-of-life is, by definition, not inclined toward the construction of recognisable sovereign forms, ones that contain a particular political valence or power. Demand leans toward the singular individual alone, while command more often implies an intelligible communal form. By preserving a space for thought to arise, we encounter through demand *another* form of sovereignty possible for our being, but one that is not immersed in the ceaseless activity that characterises politically sovereign forms. We witness instead a form of sovereignty that is developed only as a suspension of common political action, what takes place interiorly beyond all law and identity. It is this form-of-life lived beyond the law that becomes the primary location of *another* form of sovereignty made possible through the creativity of ideas themselves.

Though his comments on the multitude as an attempt to rethink the political implications of forms-of-life beyond typical political forms of association is somewhat underdeveloped in *The Use of Bodies*, it still holds forth the possibility of introducing new ideas into politics 'as we know it', through the critical space of thought itself. Locating more just social and political structures depends on our ability to recognise the undefined forms-of-life around us without subsuming them into a general representational matrix. Making space at the heart of political activity for its very suspension – for reflective, 'unproductive' and contemplative time to take place and so for thought itself to appear – is the crucial dimension that is often overlooked amidst the ceaseless activity that otherwise frequently characterises the 'productivity' of our worldly economies.

What Agamben is after is not the eventual dissolution of, for example, every political structure and institution in our world – the antinomian temptation I had earlier referred to. What he wants to provide us with is a way to find new uses for these identities and communities that we cannot simply discard once and for all. Finding new uses for some of the most cherished concepts that humanity has to offer is something of a recurring motif for Agamben, who has sought to deploy a variety of new perspectives on age-old questions throughout his oeuvre. Rendering the anthropological machinery of our world inoperative consequently means, for Agamben, maintaining the possibility of creating new uses for old things, including the form of the human being. If we take seriously the activities of play and parody, as he frequently suggests, in order to establish new forms in our world – such as the image of humanity playing with law as children play with a cancelled passport (SE 64/OHS 221) – then perhaps we will also one day be able to move beyond the implicit dominance of the (sovereign) form of the human being, learning to (co)exist alongside other forms-of-life within our world and environment that cry out daily not to be the excluded figures upon which our society is built.

This is not to suggest that we will ever abandon the human being altogether; rather we might learn to exercise our capacity for self-reflexive thought and the creative ideas that are generated through it, in order to re-envision our relationship to every other living thing, every other form-of-life, that moves around us. At a time of great ecological degradation brought about through the severance of an intimacy with those forms-of-life that comprise what we have typically called 'nature', there is perhaps no greater summons than this for all of us to take note of.

At its core, the *Homo Sacer* series provides us with a philosophical defence for 'thinking otherwise' than those models of thought that have brought humanity to this point, at the same time that it also provides us with a defence of philosophy itself. If humanity is to embrace its unique vocation as that animal which is capable of suspending its own animality, then we need look no further than our potential to render things, even ourselves, inoperative in order to find new uses of things, including the very bodies we inhabit. Agamben's refocusing of philosophy upon the imaginative potentiality of thought, rather than the necessities of actuality that have historically dominated our reflections, gives humanity another pathway by which to embrace the contingency of life as a creative force for the radical reformations of life itself. Though the traditional political-theological signatures that had governed things historically have begun to fade into the twilight, there is a blueprint in Agamben's thought that points the way toward another horizon, one that humanity is only just beginning to comprehend as possible.

# Notes

## INTRODUCTION

1. A work that makes such gesture transparent, while also serving as a fantastic introduction to Agamben's thought on the whole, is Leland de la Durantaye's *Giorgio Agamben: A Critical Introduction* (Stanford: Stanford University Press, 2009).
2. See my prior engagement with these early topics in *Agamben and Theology* (London: T&T Clark, 2011). See also the analysis of Agamben's early work in relation to his more recent writings in William Watkin, *Agamben and Indifference: A Critical Overview* (London: Rowman & Littlefield, 2014).
3. Though Agamben does repeatedly dwell on particular philosophical issues, an argument can also be made that there have been some significant shifts in his thinking over time as well. See, in this regard, Adam Kotsko, *Agamben's Philosophical Trajectory* (Edinburgh: Edinburgh University Press, 2020).
4. Agamben's thought, in particular, has been utilised to critique such institutional knowledges, such as those found in legal codes and linguistic structures. See, in this regard, Kalpana Rahita Seshadri, *HumAnimal: Race, Law, Language* (Minneapolis: University of Minnesota Press, 2012).
5. Agamben's genealogical methods are significantly indebted to the work of Michel Foucault and are, for that reason, subject to the same criticisms. On Foucault's genealogical-archaeological methods, see Michel Foucault, *The Archaeology of Knowledge*, trans. A. M. Sheridan Smith (London: Routledge, 1972). For a sustained

critique of these methods, see Jacques Derrida, *Archive Fever: A Freudian Impression*, trans. Eric Prenowitz (Chicago: University of Chicago Press, 1996). In this vein of critique, Derrida was particularly harsh in his remarks on Agamben's methods, such as those offered throughout his lectures on sovereignty. See Jacques Derrida, *The Beast & the Sovereign, Volume 1*, ed. Michel Lisse, Marie-Louise Mallet and Ginette Michaud, trans. Geoffrey Bennington (Chicago: University of Chicago Press, 2009).

6. In this way, my aim here is to deliver something that Agamben scholarship has not yet witnessed through a sustained focus on the main themes of the completed *Homo Sacer* series. For general guides to the thought of Agamben and the philosophical context in which his work has developed, see Alex Murray and Jessica Whyte (eds), *The Agamben Dictionary* (Edinburgh: Edinburgh University Press, 2011) as well as Adam Kotsko and Carlo Salzani (eds), *Agamben's Philosophical Lineage* (Edinburgh: Edinburgh University Press, 2017).

7. My suggestion shares an obvious affinity with the insightful work on the concept of sovereignty given by Arne De Boever in *Plastic Sovereignties: Agamben and the Politics of Aesthetics* (Edinburgh: Edinburgh University Press, 2016).

8. Giorgio Agamben, *The Omnibus Homo Sacer* (Stanford: Stanford University Press, 2017).

9. See Michel Foucault, *'Society Must be Defended': Lectures at the Collège de France, 1975–1976*, ed. Mauro Bertani and Alessandro Fontana, trans. David Macey (New York: Picador, 2003), *Security, Territory, Population: Lectures at the Collège de France, 1977–1978*, ed. Michel Senellart, trans. Graham Burchell (New York: Picador / Palgrave Macmillan, 2007) and *The Birth of Biopolitics: Lectures at the Collège de France, 1978–1979*, ed. Michel Senellart, trans. Graham Burchell (New York: Picador, 2008) for perhaps more speculative and tangential accounts as Foucault was still working through the implications of this theory.

10. See Carl Schmitt, *The Concept of the Political*, trans. George Schwab (Chicago: University of Chicago Press, 1995).

11. Jean-François Lyotard, *The Differend: Phrases in Dispute*, trans. Georges Van Den Abbeele (Minneapolis: University of Minnesota Press, 1988).

# Notes

## CHAPTER 1

1. Thanos Zartaloudis has referred to Agamben's efforts in this regard as a form of 'pure antinomianism'. See Thanos Zartaloudis, *Giorgio Agamben: Power, Law and the Uses of Criticism* (London: Routledge, 2010).
2. Early discussions on these themes can be found in Catherine Mills, 'Playing with Law: Agamben and Derrida on Postjuridical Justice' and Thanos Zartaloudis, 'On Justice', in *Agamben and Law*, ed. Thanos Zartaloudis (London: Routledge, 2015).
3. See Schmitt, *The Concept of the Political.*
4. For a lucid exposition of Agamben's understanding of liturgy from a theological point of view, see Nicholas Heron, *Liturgical Power: Between Economic and Political Theology* (New York: Fordham University Press, 2017).
5. See the summary of the tensions between Jesuits and Jansenists in John W. O'Malley, SJ, *The Jesuits: A History from Ignatius to the Present* (London: Rowman & Littlefield, 2017), pp. 67–77.
6. As with a good many philosophical-genealogical studies of Christian theological sources, Agamben's analyses adhere only to brief surveys of primary sources (e.g. Augustine, Origen, Clement of Alexandria, Cyril of Jerusalem, Ignatius of Antioch, Thomas Aquinas and so forth) rather than directly engage or cite centuries of scholarship on these sources. This procedure enables him to jump quickly to profound conclusions, though it does not ensure critical depth in terms of working with these sources. Much the same can be said of the work of Foucault, whom Agamben imitates on this score.
7. The influence of Spinoza upon Agamben's thought runs deep, most notably beginning with his remarks on pantheism in the Appendix to *The Coming Community*. Even when mostly unmentioned throughout the *Homo Sacer* series, Spinoza maintains a significant influence upon Agamben's own original, philosophical contributions, and so he returns prominently at the end of the series – after the genealogical studies have been left behind – in order to postulate a modal ontology. Agamben's modal ontology, in this sense, must be read beside Spinoza's thought.

*Notes*

8. Though Agamben mostly refrains from citing the work of Nietzsche directly or even explicitly referring to his pronouncements on the 'death of God', there is a steady resonance with Niezsche's thought, and certainly regarding the use of the genealogical method, that occasionally comes to the surface, such as in this particular passage. At the same time as he attempts to build upon Nietzsche's thought, Agamben clearly seeks also to enter new territory and advance new genealogical insights of a more linguistic-existential nature.

9. He goes on to make a series of connections between the decline in the political function of acclamations and liturgies (KG 253–4/OHS 602), as the rituals disappear and people lose sight of their original meanings, yet the fascist insignias of power return; how popular acclamations survive in democracies through public opinion (KG 254–5/OHS 603); relations between the media and authoritarianism (KG 155–256/OHS 604), and the society of the spectacle in the work of Guy Debord. As he suggestively frames the conversation: 'Contemporary democracy is a democracy that is entirely founded upon glory, that is, on the efficacy of acclamation, multiplied and disseminated by the media beyond all imagination' (KG 256/OHS 604).

10. In terms that will very directly link the claims made here to the figure of the *homo sacer*, Agamben will claim moreover that, 'In other words, the acclamation points toward a more archaic sphere that brings to mind the one the Gernet used to call, using an infelicitous term, prelaw, in which terms that we customarily consider juridical appear to act in a magic-religious manner. More than a chronologically earlier stage, we must here think of something like a threshold of indistinction that is always operative, where the juridical and the religious become truly indistinguishable. A threshold of this type is that which elsewhere we have called *sacertas*, in which a double exception, from both human and divine law, allows a figure to emerge, *homo sacer*, whose relevance for Occidental law and politics we have attempted to reconstruct. If we now call "glory" the uncertain zone in which acclamations, ceremonies, liturgies, and insignia operate, we will see a field of research open before us that is equally relevant and, at least in part, as yet unexplored' (KG 188/OHS 542).

11. Though it may be argued that dualistic thought in Western monotheism certainly predates any Gnostic influence on Christianity, Agamben is attempting to provide a connection between the heretical deviations of Gnosticism and Christian orthodoxy, hence his stress upon the so-called Gnostic dualistic elements within Christianity.
12. On Agamben's theory of citationality which is borrowed from that of Walter Benjamin, see my chapter 'Citing "Whatever" Authority' in Colby Dickinson and Adam Kotsko, *Agamben's Coming Philosophy: Finding a New Use for Theology* (London: Rowman & Littlefield, 2015), pp. 67–82. See also the critique of Agamben's genealogical methods in this context explicitly in Alberto Toscano, *Fanaticism: On the Uses of an Idea* (London: Verso, 2017), pp. 227–32.
13. Lucretius, *On the Nature of the Universe*, trans. Ronald Melville (Oxford: Oxford University Press, 2009). See also the popular historical narrative provided on the modern reception of this work in Stephen Greenblatt, *The Swerve: How the World Became Modern* (New York: W. W. Norton, 2011).
14. 'The attempt to reconcile the idle god who is foreign to the world with the *actuosus* god who creates and governs it is certainly one of the crucial stakes of the Trinitarian economy: both the very concept of *oikonomia* and the aporias that make its definition so arduous depend on it' (KG 55/OHS 421).
15. Baruch Spinoza, *Ethics: Treatise on The Emendation of the Intellect and Selected Letters*, ed. Seymour Feldman, trans. Samuel Shirley (Indianapolis: Hackett, 1992), p. 108.
16. These suggestions can be compared to those offered in Pierre Bourdieu, *Distinction: A Social Critique on the Judgement of Taste*, trans. Richard Nice (London: Routledge, 1984).
17. See, in particular, Walter Benjamin, 'On the Concept of History' in *Selected Writings*, vol. 4, ed. Howard Eiland and Michael W. Jennings, trans. Edmund Jephcott et al. (Cambridge, MA: Belknap, 2003).

## CHAPTER 2

1. On this Heideggerian inheritance vis-à-vis Foucault, see Robert Nichols, *The World of Freedom: Heidegger, Foucault, and the*

*Politics of Historical Ontology* (Stanford: Stanford University Press, 2014).
2. This is a recurring theme throughout Fernando Pessoa, *The Book of Disquiet*, trans. Richard Zenith (London: Penguin, 2002).
3. Jacques Derrida, *The Gift of Death*, trans. David Wills (Chicago: University of Chicago Press, 1995), p. 51.
4. See Walter Benjamin, 'Notes toward a Work on the Category of Justice', trans. Peter Fenves in Peter Fenves, *The Messianic Reduction: Walter Benjamin and the Shape of Time* (Stanford: Stanford University Press, 2011).
5. As he will go on to suggest concerning the politics of intimacy: 'Against this attempt to appropriate the inappropriable to oneself, by means of right or force, in order to constitute it as an *arcanum* of sovereignty, it is necessary to remember that intimacy can preserve its political meaning only on condition that it remains inappropriable. *What is common is never a property but only the inappropriable.* The sharing of this inappropriable is love, that "use of the loved object" of which the Sadean universe constitutes the most serious and instructive parody' (UB 93/OHS 1111–12, emphasis in the original).
6. As he will go on to state, 'In the mind of God – that is, in the state of the mind that corresponds to demand as the state of being – demands have already been fulfilled since all eternity. Insofar as it is projected onto time, the messianic presents itself as another world that demands to exist in this world, but cannot do so except in a parodic and approximate way, as if it were a – not always edifying – distortion of the world. In this sense, parody is the only possible expression of demand' (WP 33).
7. The notion of the idea, and of thought itself, will eventually be linked to the form-of-life lived beyond the law as well. For example, as he will suggest in *The Use of Bodies*, 'We call *thought* the connection that constitutes forms of life into an inseparable context, into form-of-life. By this we do not understand the individual exercise of an organ or psychic faculty but an experience, an *experimentum* that has as its object the potential character of life and human intelligence. Thinking does not mean simply being affected by this or that thing but this or that content of thought in act, but being at the same time affected by one's own receptivity, gaining experience, in every thought, of a pure

potential of thought. Thought is, in this sense, always use of oneself, always entails the affection that one receives insofar as one is in contact with a determinate body [. . .]' (UB 210/OHS 1217, emphasis in the original).

## CHAPTER 3

1. Beyond Agamben's comments, Roberto Esposito has elaborated on this movement in his study *Two: The Machine of Political Theology and the Place of Thought*, trans. Zakiya Hanafi (New York: Fordham University Press, 2015), p. 51. This prevalence and subsequent insistence of 'the Two' within Western political history – and as Ernst Kantorowicz's famous study of the king's two bodies further illustrates – is, I would add, what will allow for relations of domination and subordination to usurp a perhaps more primordial undoing of binary systems of oppression which early (non)conceptualisations of the Trinity may have originally sought to promote.
2. As one might observe at play as well in the work of Michel Foucault, such a relationship was what had once guaranteed that the governance of pastoral power within a Western theological context would effectively permeate the subjects of a given sovereign power. Foucault, *Security, Territory, Population*.
3. Carl Schmitt, *Political Theology: Four Chapters on the Concept of Sovereignty*, trans. George Schwab (Chicago: University of Chicago Press, 2005). See too the more recent defence of sovereignty in Paul W. Kahn, *Political Theology: Four New Chapters on the Concept of Sovereignty* (New York: Columbia University Press, 2011).
4. See the analysis of governmentality offered in Foucault, *Security, Territory, Population*.
5. Cf. the historical commentary on these impulses in Benjamin Lazier, *God Interrupted: Heresy and the European Imagination Between the World Wars* (Princeton: Princeton University Press, 2008).
6. The conclusion that Agamben underscores is therefore that 'Modernity, removing God from the world, has not only failed to leave theology behind, but in some ways has done nothing other

than to lead the project of the providential *oikonomia* to completion' (KG 287/OHS 632).
7. See the conclusions offered in Ludwig Feuerbach, *The Essence of Christianity*, trans. George Elliot (Amherst, NY: Prometheus, 1989).
8. 'Trinitarian *oikonomia*, *ordo*, and *gubernatio* constitute an inseparable triad, whose terms interpenetrate, insofar as they name the new figure of ontology that Christian theology bequeaths to modernity' (KG 91/OHS 452).
9. James Alison, *Faith Beyond Resentment: Fragments Catholic and Gay* (New York: Crossroad, 2001). See also, for a concise Girardian framing of the scapegoat mechanism, René Girard, *The Scapegoat*, trans. Yvonne Freccero (Baltimore: Johns Hopkins University Press, 1986).
10. See, for foundational Girardian analysis around violence and sacrality, René Girard, *The Violence and the Sacred*, trans. Patrick Gregory (Baltimore: Johns Hopkins University Press, 1977).
11. In a very precise manner, this political tension mirrors the theological one, taken up by so many theologians in the modern period, between natural revelation and what it must always and only refer to, the revealed scripture. What Agamben essentially helps us to see, though he does not venture this deeply into the historical argument, is that the natural must point toward the revealed just as the revealed could only point toward nature – though the tension between them is really a reflection of both positions already being compromised by a larger political-theological machinery. It is no mistake that theology has often been politicised through its division between those who stress the pluralistic essence of natural revelation (its 'liberal' temptation, embodied in someone like Friedrich Schleiermacher, for instance) and those who emphasise the sovereignty of revealed truth (its 'conservative' leaning, as with Karl Barth, for example).
12. Immanuel Kant, 'An Answer to the Question: What Is Enlightenment?', in *Practical Philosophy*, ed. Mary J. Gregor (Cambridge: Cambridge University Press, 1996), p. 17.
13. These claims are reiterated in a slightly different context in Esposito, *Two*.

14. Jacques Derrida, *Rogues: Two Essays on Reason*, trans. Pascale-Anne Brault and Michael Naas (Stanford: Stanford University Press, 2004).
15. Agamben's suggestion has an interesting resonance here with Theodor Adorno's critique of bureaucracy as that which 'rests on nothing except the fact of bureaucracy itself' and which is deeply resonate with Foucault's analysis of governmentality. Theodor W. Adorno, *Against Epistemology: A Metacritique*, trans. Willis Domingo (Malden, MA: Polity, 2013), p. 34.
16. Parallel to this suggestion, and to complete the parallel references earlier, is the Girardian conclusion that after the false sacred has been eliminated, there is only the empty tomb of Christ upon which no violent or exclusionary community can be constructed. See the conclusions reached in René Girard, *I See Satan Fall Like Lightning*, trans. James G. Williams (Maryknoll, NY: Orbis, 2004).
17. See 'The Celestial Hierarchy' and 'The Ecclesiastical Hierarchy' in Pseudo-Dionysius, *Pseudo-Dionysius: The Complete Works*, trans. Paul Rorem (Mahwah, NJ: Paulist, 1987).
18. On the concept of inoperativity in Agamben's thought, see his lucid exposition of the concept in UB 93–4/OHS 1112.
19. Martin Heidegger, *The Metaphysical Foundations of Logic*, trans. Michael Heim (Bloomington: Indiana University Press, 1984).

## CHAPTER 4

1. Hans Urs von Balthasar, *The Glory of the Lord: A Theological Aesthetics*, vol. 1 (San Francisco: Ignatius Press, 2009). See also Hans Urs von Balthasar, *The Theology of Karl Barth* (San Francisco: Ignatius Press, 1992).
2. Ernst H. Kantorowicz, *The King's Two Bodies: A Study in Medieval Political Theology* (Princeton: Princeton University Press, 1957).
3. On this topic, see the overlap between Agamben's account offered here and the historian Larry Siedentop, *Inventing the Individual: The Origins of Western Liberalism* (Cambridge, MA: Belknap, 2017).
4. See the commentary offered in Esposito, *Two*, 51–2.

5. An example of a resonance with Agamben's work from a theological perspective that goes unexplored by him is potentially found in Jürgen Moltmann, *The Trinity and the Kingdom*, trans. Margaret Kohl (Minneapolis: Fortress Press, 1993).
6. Barth's theological point of view was itself critical of religious identifications as they offered themselves as potential political ploys for power. This does not remove the possibility, however, that a Barthian theology might yet conceal its own sovereign claims. See, among other places, Karl Barth, *On Religion*, trans. Garrett Green (London: Bloomsbury, 2013).
7. Marcella Althaus-Reid, *The Queer God* (London: Routledge, 2003). She takes up these issues most prominently in the 'Demonology' chapter.
8. 'Contemplation, the zone of non-consciousness, is the nucleus – unforgettable and at the same time immemorial – inscribed in every tradition and in every memory, which signs it with a mark of infamy or glory. The user, always unauthorised, is only the *auctor* – in the Latin sense of witness – who bears testimony of the work in the very gesture in which, in contemplation, he revokes it and constantly puts it back in use' (UB 64/OHS 1086).
9. Žižek himself cites Agamben as justification on this point – 'thought is the courage of hopelessness' – in Slavoj Žižek, *Against the Double Blackmail* (London: Penguin, 2016), p. 107.
10. Theodor W. Adorno, 'Resignation', in *Critical Models: Interventions and Catchwords*, trans. Henry W. Pickford (New York: Columbia University Press, 1998), p. 292.
11. Geoffrey Bennington, *Scatter 1: The Politics of Politics in Foucault, Heidegger, and Derrida* (New York: Fordham University Press, 2016). See also my discussion of the debates between Agamben and Derrida in *Between the Canon and the Messiah: The Structure of Faith in Contemporary Continental Thought* (London: Bloomsbury, 2013).
12. I pursue this line of inquiry, and those that follow regarding Derrida's relationship to Agamben in the second chapter of my *Between the Canon and the Messiah*.
13. Elliot R. Wolfson, *Open Secret: Postmessianic Messianism and the Mystical Revision of Menahem Mendel Schneerson* (New York: Columbia University Press, 2009).

14. This is a movement parallel, at least at one brief point in Agamben's analysis, to Jesus's possible subversion of the doxologial use of the Amen (KG 232/OHS 582).
15. See Derrida, *Archive Fever*. Derrida had critiqued the genealogist's method as an 'archive fever', where there is an intent to let objects speak for themselves, and so as a form of encounter that is somehow supposed to elicit an almost magical knowing.
16. There is no doubt that Agamben's project shares with Esposito's a certain critique of humanism as bound up with modern conceptualisations of personhood and 'human rights' that are posited only at the expense of the rest of life (animal, plant and mineral) that is either blatantly ignored or unconsciously sidestepped in an effort to construct the human person as sovereign over its environment. As Bruno Latour has already indicated, and as I believe Agamben's work compliments to a high degree, our movement beyond such a position of dominance and oppression over the other members of a very complex eco-sphere is a necessary next step in the evolution of our species, but it is one that will also come at a very high cost for those more vested in traditional defences of the political-theological nexus that sustains certain mechanisms of exclusion and violence in order to maintain a 'reasonable' and 'natural' hegemonic order. See, among others, Bruno Latour, *An Inquiry into Modes of Existence: An Anthropology of the Moderns*, trans. Catherine Porter (Cambridge, MA: Harvard University Press, 2018).

## CHAPTER 5

1. See too the argument laid out in Martin Heidegger, *Being and Time*, trans. Joan Stambaugh (Albany: State University of New York, 1996).
2. We can recall from Chapter 4 that bare life is produced through an inclusive exclusion.
3. See, among many other writings and lectures, the descriptions given of this situation in Michel Foucault, *Discipline and Punish: The Birth of the Prison*, trans. Alan Sheridan (New York: Vintage, 1977).
4. On the notion of 'bloodless violence', see Jacques Derrida, 'Before the Law', in Gil Anidjar (ed.), *Acts of Religion*, trans. Mary Quaintance (London: Routledge, 2002).

*Notes*

5. Theodor W. Adorno, *The Psychological Technique of Martin Luther Thomas' Radio Addresses* (Stanford: Stanford University Press, 2000), 1ff.
6. Martin Heidegger, *Parmenides*, trans. André Schuwer and Richard Rojcewicz (Bloomington: Indiana University Press, 1992), p. 150.
7. Schmitt, *The Concept of the Political*.

## CHAPTER 6

1. Related to this tension, and as he had mentioned earlier in the same essay, 'Benedict XVI's decision has again brought to light the eschatological mystery in all its disruptive force; but only in this way will the Church, which has gone astray in time, be able to find the right relationship with the end of time. In the Church, there are two irreconcilable and yet closely intertwined elements: economy and eschatology, the worldly-temporal element and that which keeps itself connected with the end of time and of the world. When the eschatological element disappears into the shadows, the worldly economy becomes properly infinite, which is to say, interminable and aimless. The paradox of the Church is that, from the eschatological point of view, it must renounce the world, which it cannot renounce without renouncing itself. But this is exactly where the decisive crisis is situated: because courage – and this seems to us to be the ultimate sense of Benedict XVI's message – is nothing but the capacity to keep oneself connected with one's own end' (ME 16).
2. What he is looking to avoid is abundantly clear in the failed politics of Western history. For example, as he suggests, 'Whenever the distinction between legitimacy and legality is evoked, it is necessary to specify that one does not mean by this, according to a tradition that defines so-called reactionary thought, that legitimacy is a hierarchically superior substantial principle, of which juridico-political legality would be only an epiphenomenon or effect. We mean rather that legitimacy and legality are the two parts of one single political machine, which not only must never be flattened out into one another, but must also remain in some way operative so that the machine can function. If the Church lays claim to a spiritual power to which the temporal power of the Empire or the State must remain subordinate, as happened

in medieval Europe, or if, as happened in the twentieth-century totalitarian State, legitimacy insists on doing without legality, then the political machine spins in circles with often lethal results; if, on the other hand, as has happened in modern democracies, the legitimating principle of popular sovereignty is reduced to the electoral moment and is dissolved into procedural rules that are juridically fixed in advance, legitimacy runs the risk of disappearing into legality and the political machine is equally paralyzed' (ME 3–4).
3. See Jürgen Moltmann, *The Crucified God: The Cross of Christ as the Foundation and Criticism of Christian Theology*, trans. R. A. Wilson and John Bowden (Minneapolis: Fortress Press, 1993). I elaborate much more in-depth on the dynamics of the negative dialectic in *Theology and Contemporary Continental Philosophy: The Centrality of a Negative Dialectics* (London: Rowman & Littlefield, 2019).
4. Wolfson, *Open Secret*.
5. He goes on to issue a stern warning of how such a grace might be corrupted within the Church, stating that 'The Church would, however, advocate the *amissible*, perishable, quality of grace as well as the necessity of further intervention so as to counter the loss of grace through sin. This amounts to reintroducing an openly juridical theme with regard to grace, a kind of compromise between *charis* and *nomos*. Through transgression and guilt, man constantly loses that grace which once figured as the only counterservice of loyalty to the pact. In a more general way, with the reintroduction of *nomos* into Christian theology, grace will end up occupying just as aporetic a place as does law in Judaism' (TR 123).
6. See, among others, Frederic Jameson, *Valences of the Dialectic* (London: Verso, 2010).
7. See also Walter Benjamin, 'On the Concept of History' in *Selected Writings*, vol. 4, ed. Howard Eiland and Michael W. Jennings, trans. Edmund Jephcott et al. (Cambridge, MA: Belknap, 2003).

## CHAPTER 7

1. As he continues the thought, 'The time of fashion, therefore, constitutively anticipates itself and consequently is also always

too late. It always takes the form of an ungraspable threshold between a "not yet" and a "no more." It is quite probable that, as the theologians suggest, this constellation depends on the fact that fashion, at least in our culture, is a theological signature of clothing, which derives from the first piece of clothing that was sewn by Adam and Eve after the Original Sin, in the form of loincloth woven from fig leaves' (WA 16).
2. It is what Jean-Yves Lacoste will call 'liturgical time', or what produces a division considered as a liturgical reduction. Jean-Yves Lacoste, *Experience and the Absolute: Disputed Questions on the Humanity of Man*, trans. Mark Raftery-Skehan (New York: Fordham University Press, 2004).
3. As an onlooker today might have trouble making clear, it is often difficult to distinguish the saint from the refugee. Wherein the former is generally taken as an example and the latter as a *homo sacer*, it is precisely when championing the rights of the latter that common perception frequently uplifts the marginalised as saint-like. Refugees, or other marginalised persons, are those who dwell literally in a zone of indistinction, and this is why people in more privileged circumstances have such trouble seeing them as anything other than a fiction. Their stories then, perhaps are, even if true, unbelievable. Humanity commonly (mis)perceives these figures one way or another (as saint or as refugee, as believable, or something we want to believe in, and as unbelievable, or something we have great difficulty believing even if historically accurate), depending on the position where one stands.
4. As Agamben will also point out, guilt, accompanying law the entire time, and as Saint Paul himself once saw, refers purely to one's subjection in light of the law's existence, not to an infraction of the law, or the division between the licit and the illicit. This was something, he notes, that Kafka understood as well as Paul, and which demonstrates that one best stands up to the law through not feeling guilty before it.
5. Mark 2: 27–8.
6. Alain Badiou, *Logiques des Mondes: L'Être et l'événement, 2* (Paris: Seuil, 2006), p. 584.
7. Karl Marx, with Friedrich Engels, *The German Ideology, including Theses on Feuerbach and the Introduction to the Critique of Political Economy* (Amherst, NY: Prometheus, 1998), p. 574.

8. 'Between the inarticulate unitarism of the Monarchians and Judaism and the Gnostic proliferation of divine hypostases, between the noninvolvement in the world of the Gnostic and Epicurean God and the Stoic idea of a *deus actuosus* that provides for the world, the *oikonomia* makes possible a reconciliation in which a transcendent God, who is both one and triune at the same time, can – while remaining transcendent – take charge of the world and found an immanent praxis of government whose supermundane mystery coincides with the history of humanity' (KG 50–1/OHS 417).

9. Hegel, he notes as well, had been influenced by the 'Osirean mysteries' that sought to produce a third term from the *coincidentia oppositorum* that confronted them: 'The third element, in which opposites meet, cannot be of the same nature as them [the opposed elements] and requires a different form of exposition, one in which the opposing elements are at once maintained and neutralized. It is the content but nothing contains it; it is form but it no longer forms anything – exposing, thereby, itself' (UG 38).

# *Bibliography*

Adorno, Theodor W. *Against Epistemology: A Metacritique*, trans. Willis Domingo. Malden, MA: Polity, 2013.

Adorno, Theodor W. *The Psychological Technique of Martin Luther Thomas' Radio Addresses*. Stanford: Stanford University Press, 2000.

Adorno, Theodor W. 'Resignation', in *Critical Models: Interventions and Catchwords*, trans. Henry W. Pickford. New York: Columbia University Press, 1998.

Alison, James. *Faith Beyond Resentment: Fragments Catholic and Gay*. New York: Crossroad, 2001.

Althaus-Reid, Marcella. *The Queer God*. London: Routledge, 2003.

Badiou, Alain. *Logiques des Mondes: L'Être et l'événement, 2*. Paris: Seuil, 2006.

Balthasar, Hans Urs von. *The Glory of the Lord: A Theological Aesthetics*, vol. 1. San Francisco: Ignatius Press, 2009.

Balthasar, Hans Urs von. *The Theology of Karl Barth*. San Francisco: Ignatius Press, 1992.

Barth, Karl. *On Religion*, trans. Garrett Green. London: Bloomsbury, 2013.

Benjamin, Walter. 'On the Concept of History', in *Selected Writings*, vol. 4, ed. Howard Eiland and Michael W. Jennings, trans. Edmund Jephcott et al. Cambridge, MA: Belknap, 2003.

Bennington, Geoffrey. *Scatter 1: The Politics of Politics in Foucault, Heidegger, and Derrida*. New York: Fordham University Press, 2016.

# Bibliography

Bourdieu, Pierre. *Distinction: A Social Critique on the Judgement of Taste*, trans. Richard Nice. London: Routledge, 1984.

De Boever, Arne. *Plastic Sovereignties: Agamben and the Politics of Aesthetics*. Edinburgh: Edinburgh University Press, 2016.

Derrida, Jacques. *Archive Fever: A Freudian Impression*, trans. Eric Prenowitz. Chicago: University of Chicago Press, 1996.

Derrida, Jacques. *The Beast & the Sovereign, Volume 1*, ed. Michel Lisse, Marie-Louise Mallet and Ginette Michaud, trans. Geoffrey Bennington. Chicago: University of Chicago Press, 2009.

Derrida, Jacques. 'Before the Law', in *Acts of Religion*, ed. Gil Anidjar, trans. Mary Quaintance. London: Routledge, 2002.

Derrida, Jacques. *The Gift of Death*, trans. David Wills. Chicago: University of Chicago Press, 1995.

Derrida, Jacques. *Rogues: Two Essays on Reason*, trans. Pascale-Anne Brault and Michael Naas. Stanford: Stanford University Press, 2004.

Dickinson, Colby. *Agamben and Theology*. London: T & T Clark, 2011.

Dickinson, Colby. *Between the Canon and the Messiah: The Structure of Faith in Contemporary Continental Thought*. London: Bloomsbury, 2013.

Dickinson, Colby. *Theology and Contemporary Continental Philosophy: The Centrality of a Negative Dialectics*. London: Rowman & Littlefield, 2019.

Dickinson, Colby and Adam Kotsko. *Agamben's Coming Philosophy: Finding a New Use for Theology*. London: Rowman & Littlefield, 2015.

Durantaye, Leland de la. *Giorgio Agamben: A Critical Introduction*. Stanford: Stanford University Press, 2009.

Esposito, Roberto. *Two: The Machine of Political Theology and the Place of Thought*, trans. Zakiya Hanafi. New York: Fordham University Press, 2015.

Fenves, Peter. *The Messianic Reduction: Walter Benjamin and the Shape of Time*. Stanford: Stanford University Press, 2011.

Feuerbach, Ludwig. *The Essence of Christianity*, trans. George Elliot. Amherst, NY: Prometheus, 1989.

Foucault, Michel. *The Archaeology of Knowledge*, trans. A. M. Sheridan Smith. London: Routledge, 1972.

Foucault, Michel. *The Birth of Biopolitics: Lectures at the Collège de France, 1978–1979*, ed. Michel Senellart, trans. Graham Burchell. New York: Picador, 2008.

Foucault, Michel. *Discipline and Punish: The Birth of the Prison*, trans. Alan Sheridan. New York: Vintage, 1977.

Foucault, Michel. *Security, Territory, Population: Lectures at the Collège de France, 1977–1978*, ed. Michel Senellart, trans. Graham Burchell. New York: Picador / Palgrave Macmillan, 2007.

Foucault, Michel. *'Society Must be Defended': Lectures at the Collège de France, 1975–1976*, ed. Mauro Bertani and Alessandro Fontana, trans. David Macey. New York: Picador, 2003.

Girard, René. *I See Satan Fall Like Lightning*, trans. James G. Williams. Maryknoll, NY: Orbis, 2004.

Girard, René. *The Scapegoat*, trans. Yvonne Freccero. Baltimore: Johns Hopkins University Press, 1986.

Girard, René. *The Violence and the Sacred*, trans. Patrick Gregory. Baltimore: Johns Hopkins University Press, 1977.

Greenblatt, Stephen. *The Swerve: How the World Became Modern*. New York: W. W. Norton, 2011.

Heidegger, Martin. *Being and Time*, trans. Joan Stambaugh. Albany: State University of New York, 1996.

Heidegger, Martin. *The Metaphysical Foundations of Logic*, trans. Michael Heim. Bloomington: Indiana University Press, 1984.

Heidegger, Martin. *Parmenides*, trans. André Schuwer and Richard Rojcewicz. Bloomington: Indiana University Press, 1992.

Heron, Nicholas. *Liturgical Power: Between Economic and Political Theology*. New York: Fordham University Press, 2017.

Jameson, Frederic. *Valences of the Dialectic*. London: Verso, 2010.

Kahn, Paul W. *Political Theology: Four New Chapters on the Concept of Sovereignty*. New York: Columbia University Press, 2011.

Kant, Immanuel. 'An Answer to the Question: What Is Enlightenment?', in *Practical Philosophy*, ed. Mary J. Gregor. Cambridge: Cambridge University Press, 1996.

Kantorowicz, Ernst H. *The King's Two Bodies: A Study in Medieval Political Theology*. Princeton: Princeton University Press, 1957.

Kotsko, Adam. *Agamben's Philosophical Trajectory*. Edinburgh: Edinburgh University Press, 2020.

Kotsko, Adam and Carlo Salzani (eds). *Agamben's Philosophical Lineage*. Edinburgh: Edinburgh University Press, 2017.

Lacoste, Jean-Yves. *Experience and the Absolute: Disputed Questions on the Humanity of Man*, trans. Mark Raftery-Skehan. New York: Fordham University Press, 2004.

Latour, Bruno. *An Inquiry into Modes of Existence: An Anthropology of the Moderns*, trans. Catherine Porter. Cambridge, MA: Harvard University Press, 2018.

Lazier, Benjamin. *God Interrupted: Heresy and the European Imagination Between the World Wars*. Princeton: Princeton University Press, 2008.

Lucretius. *On the Nature of the Universe*, trans. Ronald Melville. Oxford: Oxford University Press, 2009.

Lyotard, Jean-François. *The Differend: Phrases in Dispute*, trans. Georges Van Den Abbeele. Minneapolis: University of Minnesota Press, 1988.

Marx, Karl, with Friedrich Engels. *The German Ideology, including Theses on Feuerbach and the Introduction to the Critique of Political Economy*. Amherst, NY: Prometheus, 1998.

Mills, Catherine. 'Playing with Law: Agamben and Derrida on Postjuridical Justice', in *Agamben and Law*, ed. Thanos Zartaloudis, pp. 239–60. London: Routledge, 2015.

Moltmann, Jürgen. *The Crucified God: The Cross of Christ as the Foundation and Criticism of Christian Theology*, trans. R. A. Wilson and John Bowden. Minneapolis: Fortress, 1993.

Moltmann, Jürgen. *The Trinity and the Kingdom*, trans. Margaret Kohl. Minneapolis: Fortress, 1993.

Murray, Alex and Jessica Whyte (eds). *The Agamben Dictionary*. Edinburgh: Edinburgh University Press, 2011.

Nichols, Robert. *The World of Freedom: Heidegger, Foucault, and the Politics of Historical Ontology*. Stanford: Stanford University Press, 2014.

O'Malley, John W., SJ. *The Jesuits: A History from Ignatius to the Present*. London: Rowman & Littlefield, 2017.

Pessoa, Fernando. *The Book of Disquiet*, trans. Richard Zenith. London: Penguin, 2002.

Pseudo-Dionysius. *Pseudo-Dionysius: The Complete Works*, trans. Paul Rorem. Mahwah, NJ: Paulist, 1987.

# Bibliography

Schmitt, Carl. *The Concept of the Political*, trans. George Schwab. Chicago: University of Chicago Press, 1995.

Schmitt, Carl. *Political Theology: Four Chapters on the Concept of Sovereignty*, trans. George Schwab. Chicago: University of Chicago Press, 2005.

Seshadri, Kalpana Rahita. *HumAnimal: Race, Law, Language*. Minneapolis: University of Minnesota Press, 2012.

Siedentop, Larry. *Inventing the Individual: The Origins of Western Liberalism*. Cambridge, MA: Belknap, 2017.

Spinoza, Baruch. *Ethics: Treatise on The Emendation of the Intellect and Selected Letters*, ed. Seymour Feldman, trans. Samuel Shirley. Indianapolis: Hackett, 1992.

Toscano, Alberto. *Fanaticism: On the Uses of an Idea*. London: Verso, 2017.

Watkin, William. *Agamben and Indifference: A Critical Overview*. London: Rowman & Littlefield, 2014.

Wolfson, Elliot R. *Open Secret: Postmessianic Messianism and the Mystical Revision of Menahem Mendel Schneerson*. New York: Columbia University Press, 2009.

Zartaloudis, Thanos. *Giorgio Agamben: Power, Law and the Uses of Criticism*. London: Routledge, 2010.

Zartaloudis, Thanos. 'On Justice', in *Agamben and Law*, ed. Thanos Zartaloudis, pp. 201–20. London: Routledge, 2015.

Žižek, Slavoj. *Against the Double Blackmail*. London: Penguin, 2016.

# *Index*

abandonment, pure, 150–1
actuality/*auctoritas,* 6–7, 16, 19, 23, 27, 40–1, 51, 59, 66, 68–70, 72–6, 81, 83, 87, 90, 95, 102, 136, 138–9, 145, 165, 170–1, 177, 208, 210
Adorno, Theodor, 124–5, 142, 173, 183–4, 220n, 221n, 223n
Alison, James, 103, 219n
animality, 8–9, 33, 71, 110, 112, 132–4, 136, 138–40, 142, 147–8, 150, 210
*anomie,* 18, 77, 127, 130, 136
*anomos,* 163–4, 169
anthropogenesis, 9, 83, 90, 92, 110, 124, 139–40, 145–9, 156
anthropogenic operator, 48
antinomian, -ism, 5, 32, 35–6, 49, 77, 117, 130, 154, 163, 169, 171, 204, 209, 214n
apparatus, 3, 14, 22, 29, 40, 42, 46, 49, 59, 62, 66–8, 74, 85, 92, 98, 102, 106–9, 111–12, 120, 127–8, 133, 136, 140–3, 149, 151, 153, 155–7, 192
Aristotle, 16, 24, 43, 55, 57, 59–60, 66–70, 73–4, 84, 90, 95, 139, 143, 156
as if (Kant), 32, 46, 61, 97–100, 129, 134, 176, 178, 194, 217n
atheism, 60–1, 100
authoritarian, -ism, 115, 142, 215n

ban, 73, 145
banquet, messianic, 155
bare life, 9, 15–16, 81, 113, 130, 136, 139–40, 142, 145, 153, 155, 197–8, 204, 222n
Barth, Karl, 105, 115–7, 219n, 220n, 221n
Bartleby, 6, 17, 72, 75–6, 78
Being, 2, 73, 96, 108, 111, 118, 132, 138–40, 147, 222n
being of distance, 138
being of possibility, 138
Benjamin, Walter, 11, 17–18, 32–3, 45, 64, 78, 85, 87–8, 91, 107, 119, 138, 151–2, 156, 166–8, 174–6, 178–80, 183, 185, 201, 207, 216n, 217n, 225n
Bennington, Geoffrey, 125, 213n, 221n
binity, 96, 116–17
*bios,* 15, 20, 30, 33, 102, 130, 143, 156, 191, 196, 201–2
boredom, 118, 142
boundary, 10, 134, 136, 146, 149

camp, 16, 26–7, 145, 153, 204, 209
Christianity, 21, 24, 32, 44, 55, 65, 96, 114–15, 120, 141, 163, 167, 188, 200, 202, 216n, 219n
Christomonism, 116
civil war, 1720, 38, 135
*clinamen,* 62–3

232

*Index*

*conatus*, 52, 61–2, 84, 91
contemplation, 6, 10, 30–1, 80–1, 83–6, 118, 121, 123–4, 130, 142, 156, 185, 207, 221n
culture, 30, 40–1, 109, 122, 135, 145, 147–8, 154, 161, 225n

Dasein, 132, 134
demand, 6, 52, 61–2, 64–5, 84, 90–4, 125, 172, 175–8, 189, 196, 208–9, 217n
Derrida, Jacques, 105, 125–6, 141, 213n, 214n, 217n, 220n, 221n, 222n, 223n
dialectics at a standstill, 151, 156, 173, 175–6, 179
disenchantment, 136, 152–3, 155
disinhibitors, 142, 147
division of division, 10, 31–2, 34, 84, 111, 127, 151, 155, 157, 159, 168–9, 172–3, 189, 194
duty, 14, 25–6, 28, 43, 52, 60, 75, 77, 136, 143

enchantment, 153, 203
Epicurus, 56, 62
Esposito, Roberto, 118, 218n, 219n, 220n, 222n
ethics, 2, 25, 43, 51–2, 60–1, 63, 67, 76, 83–4, 87, 102, 136–7, 189, 200, 206, 216n
exclusion, -ary, 5, 8, 15–17, 30, 33, 36, 44, 101, 110, 114, 122, 130, 145–6, 186–7, 197, 208, 220n, 222n
exclusive inclusion, 16, 103–4, 145, 185
exigency, 64, 171, 176–8

form, substantial, 134
form of life/*forma vitae*, 3–4, 6–7, 10–12, 14, 16–17, 27–30, 32, 49, 54, 62–4, 68–70, 73, 80–2, 85–7, 89, 102, 107, 109, 123–4, 127–8, 130–1, 144–5, 149, 153, 155, 157, 165–6, 170, 172, 174, 177–81, 184–6, 188–204, 206–10, 217n

Foucault, Michel, 15, 30, 38–9, 68–9, 97, 99–100, 141, 148, 166, 212n, 213n, 214n, 216n, 218n, 220n, 221n, 222n

genealogical method, 56, 117, 137, 212, 215n, 216n
Girard, René, 103, 219n, 220n
G/gnostic, -ism, 24, 53, 55, 58, 60, 96, 100, 216n, 226n
grace, 7, 32, 58, 67, 69, 77, 81, 83–5, 90, 93, 97, 107, 131, 148, 153, 166, 171–3, 224n

habit, 6, 29, 69–70, 82, 85–7, 103, 138, 161, 195, 203, 210
Heidegger, Martin, 2, 8–9, 30–1, 33, 68–9, 71, 75, 111, 132–3, 138–9, 142, 147, 150–1, 192, 195, 216n, 220n, 221n, 222n, 223n
*homo sacer*, 3–4, 15–17, 26–7, 35, 38, 110, 114, 142, 145, 149, 204, 215n, 225n
hope, 3, 7, 13, 93, 102, 106, 121, 128, 131, 202
human being, 2, 8–10, 21–3, 26–7, 31, 33–4, 36–7, 40, 42, 45, 47–9, 71, 77, 83, 89–90, 108–13, 116, 120, 124, 128–30, 132–5, 138–40, 143–50, 153–6, 189, 196–7, 199, 202–4, 207, 210
human-as-sovereign, 138
hypernomian, -ism, 8, 126–7, 129–30, 171

identity, 9–12, 31–4, 37, 49, 56, 64, 76, 78, 80–1, 98, 109, 111, 114, 117, 121–2, 126–7, 129, 146, 148, 151, 159, 162, 164, 168–169, 172–4, 176–7, 183–4, 189, 194, 198–9, 204, 206, 209
illegitimacy, 162–3
imago dei, 105, 136
impotentiality, 71–2, 74, 76, 86
inappropriable, the, 85, 88–9, 91–2, 130, 195, 217n
inclusion, 8, 16, 101, 103–4, 110, 114, 145–6, 187

233

inclusive exclusion, 16, 145, 186–7, 222n
inoperativity, 7, 9–10, 23–4, 30–1, 38, 81, 83–4, 86, 89, 91, 117–18, 121, 124, 128–30, 133, 150, 156, 160, 163, 186, 194, 220n
intimacy, 78, 90, 93, 151, 177, 210, 217n
intimacy without relations, 12, 31, 42, 63–4, 130, 139, 186, 195, 198

juridical apparatuses, 136
justice, 84, 88–9, 91, 106, 166–8, 173–4, 214n, 217n

Kant, Immanuel, 43, 50–1, 104, 178, 219n
Kantorowicz, Ernst, 115, 218n, 220n
*katechon*, 20, 163

language, 3, 5, 8, 10–11, 14, 19–22, 26–7, 31, 33, 36, 40, 42–50, 53, 59, 65, 79–81, 88–9, 92, 101, 108–13, 125, 127, 134, 137–8, 140–1, 144, 148, 151, 162, 171–2, 179, 186, 197, 201, 206, 208, 212n
law, 4, 6, 10–12, 15–21, 25, 28–9, 31–2, 35–6, 39–40, 47–9, 51, 53, 62, 76–81, 93, 97–9, 102, 106, 126–7, 129–30, 136–8, 151, 160, 162–74, 177–8, 180–1, 183, 185–94, 203–4, 206, 209–10, 212n, 214n, 215n, 217n, 223n, 224n, 225n, 226n
liberalism, 39, 49, 61, 98, 104, 125, 128, 220n
limit-experiences, 76
liturgy, 23, 25–6, 28, 38, 53–4, 66–8, 115, 118, 144–5, 189, 193–4, 200, 214n
*logos*, 21, 44–5, 48–9, 141, 201

machine, biopolitical, 136
machine, providential, 58, 101
machine, sacrificial, 8, 102, 130
machinery, anthropological, 9–10, 30–1, 34, 40, 74, 81, 103, 108, 112, 122, 124, 127, 129, 131, 134–5, 139, 146, 149, 151–2, 155, 165, 168, 170, 196, 210
machinery, bipolar, 22, 165
messianic force, weak, 6, 10, 18, 64, 94, 119, 121, 129, 159, 161–162, 170–1, 175, 178, 182, 194
messianic task, 119, 137
messianic vocation, 10, 32, 78, 106, 121, 143, 158, 161–2, 178
messianism, 8, 17, 71, 78, 126, 170, 173, 221n, 224n
metaphysics, 6, 21, 24, 43, 46–7, 51, 57, 59, 62, 68–70, 75, 140, 145–7, 149–51
modal category, 138
monasticism, 28, 130, 144–5, 188–9, 193
morality, 136
multitude, the, 11, 20, 31, 37, 172, 189, 196, 209
*mysterium burocraticum*, 112
mystery, 20, 23, 25, 45, 66–8, 112, 152–3, 163, 165, 179, 196–7, 199–203, 223n, 226n

natural law, 165, 177, 192
nature, 2–3, 5–6, 8, 18, 21, 23–7, 29, 31, 35, 38–41, 43, 56, 58–9, 62, 64–5, 73, 76–7, 80, 87–8, 90, 93, 97, 107, 109–11, 115–16, 125, 128, 134–6, 140, 145, 147, 151–3, 155, 157–8, 162, 175, 177, 179–80, 182, 186, 191–192, 195, 210, 215n, 216n, 219n, 226n
Nietzsche, Friedrich, 62, 151, 204, 215n
nihilism, 7, 17, 131, 151, 185
*nomos*, 49, 127, 136, 163–4, 169–71, 187, 224n
non-being, 139
normative relations, 12, 145, 199
nothing, 17, 39, 89, 107, 139, 148, 185
nothingness, 139
nudity, 89, 107–8, 129, 147, 153–4, 186

234

# Index

oath, 5, 14, 20–22, 38, 42–50, 53, 112, 170
office/*officium*, 25–6, 28–9, 33, 51, 55, 60, 136–7, 139, 143–4, 150, 176, 193–5
*oikonomia*, 22–5, 40, 55, 57–8, 64, 68, 96, 98, 108, 113, 120, 140, 142, 156, 164–6, 216n, 219n, 226n
ontology, 2, 23–6, 29–30, 42, 50–2, 55, 57, 59–60, 62–3, 65–6, 75, 92, 102, 111, 139–40, 146, 149, 194, 198, 200, 206, 217n, 219n
ontology, modal, 9, 27, 42, 52, 54, 61–3, 65, 75, 86, 93, 134, 176, 195, 214n
ontology, Franciscan, 12, 190
ontology of command, 43, 46, 50–2
ontology of demand, 6, 52, 62, 64, 84
ontology of performance, 50
onto-theology/ontotheology, 21, 46–7, 149, 151, 177
Open, the, 8, 13, 26–7, 31, 33, 71, 110, 132, 142, 146–8
original sin, 111, 225n
othering, 9, 140

pantheism, 60–61, 100
Plato, 49, 183
pornography, -ic, 123, 153–6
possibility, 4–5, 8, 10–11, 16, 18, 27, 36, 51, 70, 72, 74, 76–7, 81, 84, 86, 91–2, 106–7, 115–16, 121, 124–5, 129–30, 132–4, 136, 138–9, 142, 151, 154, 156, 167, 176–7, 181, 185, 191, 201, 204, 209–10, 221n
potential, *destituent*, 30, 102, 121, 130
potentiality, 6–7, 16, 27, 31, 40, 41, 44, 51, 59, 66, 68, 70–6, 78–9, 81–4, 87, 90–5, 102, 118, 123, 127, 130, 138–9, 145, 150, 170–1, 177, 200, 204–5, 208, 210
potentiality, pure, 70, 73–5, 78, 81, 83, 93, 102, 127, 150, 177, 204–5

*potestas*, 19, 23, 40, 102, 136, 165
power, sovereign, 5–7, 10, 14–17, 23, 35–6, 38, 44, 47–50, 52–53, 55, 62, 64, 67, 72–3, 75–6, 79–82, 88, 90, 93–5, 97, 99–100, 105–6, 114–17, 121, 127–8, 131–2, 134, 139–40, 144–6, 148–9, 151, 158, 161–2, 166–7, 171, 175, 198, 206, 218n
presupposition of being, 4, 14, 33, 40, 44, 70, 84, 98, 111, 135, 140, 160, 165, 183, 195, 204
presupposition, logic of, 40, 59, 66, 69, 101, 139, 146, 157, 184
profanation, 109, 122, 150, 152–3, 160
profanation, absolute, 55

receptors, 142
righteous, the, 155

S/sabbath, 24, 31, 117, 119, 120–1, 128, 182, 188
salvation, 11, 55, 82, 118, 151, 155, 160, 178
saved night, 152, 155
Scholem, Gershom, 45, 166
Schmitt, Carl, 16, 18, 22, 37, 40, 42, 54, 69, 96–8, 112, 124–5, 128, 149, 213n, 214n, 218n, 223n
secularism, 24, 61, 161
secularisation, 100, 152, 173
signature, 53, 57, 101, 103, 122, 124, 155, 181–2
signature, theological, 8, 63, 122–4, 148, 153, 155, 211, 225n
sociality, 26, 144
sovereign, -ty, 4–7, 9–12, 14–18, 20, 23–4, 35–44, 46–55, 59, 61–4, 66–9, 72–83, 86, 88–90, 93–101, 107, 110, 112, 114–18, 120–21, 125–28, 132–35, 137–40, 142, 144–49, 151, 154, 158, 161–62, 165–67, 171–72, 174–75, 185, 187, 192–93, 195–96, 198–99, 204, 206, 208–10, 213n, 217n, 218n, 219n, 221n, 222n, 224n
Spinoza, Baruch, 42, 52, 60, 84, 214n, 216n

235

state of exception, 4, 9, 14–15, 17–19, 23–4, 36, 40, 77–8, 99, 112, 120, 134–6, 138, 148, 166–8
substance, 6, 9, 23, 30, 37, 39, 42–3, 46, 50–1, 54, 57, 60–2, 64–6, 68, 75, 86, 91–3, 106, 121, 134–5, 144–5, 153, 156, 176–7, 195

third element, 179, 184, 200, 226n
time, chronological, 158–9, 180
time, contemplative, 209
time, eschatological, 163
time, kairological, 175
time, liturgical, 225
time, messianic, 31, 158–9, 163–4, 178, 180, 198
time, normal, 31
time, utopian, 159
T/trinity, 23, 96, 108, 110, 116–17, 120, 218n, 221n

vocation, 10, 28, 32, 71, 78, 106, 121, 126, 136–7, 143–4, 158, 161–2, 178, 195, 210
Von Balthasar, Hans Urs, 115–17, 220n
von Uexküll, Jakob, 142

Wolfson, Elliot R., 8, 126, 171, 221n, 224 (n. 4)

Žižek, Slavoj, 124, 173, 221n
zoē, 15, 20, 30, 33, 102, 130–1, 143, 156, 191, 196, 201–2
zone, 6, 17–18, 26, 32, 73–4, 86, 110, 134, 136, 147, 163, 183, 215n, 221n, 225n
zone of fiction, 134
zone of indistinction, 18, 73–74, 134, 136, 225n
zone of non-consciousness, 6, 86, 221n

CPSIA information can be obtained
at www.ICGtesting.com
Printed in the USA
JSHW050509300422
25374JS00001B/2